FROM COALITION TO CONFRONTATION:

Readings on Cold War Origins

FROM COALITION TO CONFRONTATION:

Readings on Cold War Origins

Edited by

John Gimbel
Humboldt State College

John C. Hennessy
Humboldt State College

Wadsworth Publishing Company, Inc.

Belmont, California

ISBN-0-534-00190-4

L. C. Cat. Card No.-72-86259

Printed in the United States of America

1 2 3 4 5 6 7 8 9 10---76 75 74 73 72

CONTENTS

INTRODUCTION

John C. Hennessy

In the years since the defeat of Germany and Japan in World
War II, a variety of explanations have been offered for the rapid
disintegration of the Allied coalition at the war's end. Although
many of the arguments currently in vogue were explicitly stated or
suggested in works dating back to 1945, recent investigations have
sharpened and enlarged the debate considerably. The reassessment
of current American foreign policy objectives occasioned by the
war in Vietnam, the increased availability of private papers and
documents, and the new perspectives permitted by the passage of
time and events are, perhaps, the main factors that explain the
intensified interest in cold war origins.
British, Russian, and American relations in the two decades
preceding World War II are basic to the postwar disharmonies between them. For if systemic and experiential differences between
Russia and her Western Allies did not preclude the possibility of
postwar cooperation, they nevertheless formed a barrier of mistrust and suspicion through which efforts to sustain the cooperation of wartime could not penetrate.
The history of Anglo-Russian relations is marked by clashes
in Central Asia and the Balkans, and Russians and Americans had
collided in the Far East long before 1914. But the Bolshevik
Revolution of 1917 introduced a new element. The Soviet socio-
economic structure and government presented a challenge to Anglo-
American political, economic, and social institutions. Americans
had long touted their system as the wave of the future, and they
generally took comfort in the view that monarchical Britain was
emulating their example. Bolsheviks claimed and, beginning in
1917 in Russia, acted as though the laws of social change dictated
the collapse of capitalism. As if underscoring the cleavage between East and West, the Bolsheviks repudiated the international
financial obligations of the Czarist government and negotiated the
treaty of Brest-Litovsk with Germany in March 1918, thereby withdrawing Russia from World War I.
Had Winston Churchill's desires prevailed in 1918, the Allies
would have committed sufficient military force in Russia to topple
the Bolshevik regime in its infancy. As it developed, British,
American, and Japanese troops dispatched to northern Russia and
eastern Siberia in the summer of 1918 neither returned Russia to
the war against Germany nor prevented Leon Trotsky's Red Army from
suppressing counter-revolutionary elements. But the foreign intervention, which lasted into 1920 for Britain and the United

1

States, and until 1922 for Japan, did implant an enduring suspicion of the Western powers in the minds of Russian revolutionists, to include Josef Stalin.

In the 1920s and 1930s Russian leaders labored to consolidate their power at home, strengthen an economy devastated by national and civil war, and ensure Soviet security by resuming normal relations with other states in the international community. Britain and Russia established diplomatic ties in 1924, but the United States deferred until 1933, at which time economic depression at home, the resurgence of Germany, Japanese aggression in Manchuria, and a new administration in Washington conjoined to urge the wisdom of recognition. Nevertheless, throughout the interwar years Americans and Britons resented the revolutionary propaganda coming out of Russia. They were also uneasy about the activities of the Communist International and Communist functionaries, especially in Germany, France, Italy, and Spain. If the hysterical anti-Communism apparent in the Red Scare in America and Britain following World War I subsided during these years, at no time could relations between Russia and her erstwhile Western partners be described as cordial or mutually respectful. To the contrary, as the 1930s wore on the chasm widened.

The Russian purges that began in 1934, following the assassination of Sergei Kirov, a prominent official and friend of Stalin, and the failure of Russian trade to reach the levels expected by those who had advocated diplomatic recognition, combined to revive American disenchantment with developments in the Soviet Union. When the purges were intensified in 1936, spreading through trade unions, the army, and into the general public, even liberal and leftist supporters of the socialist experiment reexamined the motives of Russian leaders. But the rise of Hitler and Mussolini, German and Italian truculence in Europe and Africa, the Spanish Civil War, and renewal of Japan's assault on China diverted public attention from Russian affairs. As a result, announcement of the Nazi-Soviet Non-aggression Pact of August 1939 shocked not only the American and British Left but the general public in both countries as well. From the Anglo-American viewpoint the pact verified and testified to Russian duplicity, vindicating those who for twenty years had decried the cancerous growth of Communism in Eurasia.

It was a different story from the Russian perspective. Remembering the anti-Bolshevik interference by the West in World War I, Soviet leaders justified the Nazi-Soviet pact on the basis of British and American reluctance to support anti-Franco forces in the Spanish Civil War, British and French appeasement of Hitler at the Munich Conference in September 1938, and the breakdown of British, French, and Russian negotiations in 1939 for a united stand against Hitler. Russians saw the agreement as necessary to gain time and space for defense of the nation's western frontiers.

Thus, secret clauses in the pact prepared the way for a Russian invasion of eastern Poland in the middle of September 1939 and the establishment of Soviet military bases in the Baltic states, followed in turn by a Russian attack on Finland in late November. The last action, carried out against the country so often applauded for meeting payments on its World War I debts to the United States, provoked outrage in the American press and spurred the British and French to promote Russia's expulsion from the League of Nations. Not surprisingly, a public opinion poll taken by *Fortune* magazine early in 1940 indicated that a large majority of Americans regarded Germany and Russia as the worst influences in Europe.

Having come full circle back to the intense anti-Communism of 1917-1920, why then did Britain and the United States come to the aid of Russia when that country was invaded in June 1941 by Hitler's Reich? The answer, in a word, was expediency. England, being lashed from the air and on the seas by Germany, understandably grasped for any ally. Upon receiving news of the German strike into Russia, Churchill delivered an address on radio in which he said, "No one has been a more consistent opponent of Communism than I have for the last twenty-five years. I will unsay no word I have spoken about it. But all this fades away before the spectacle which is now unfolding. . . . We are resolved to destroy Hitler and every vestige of the Nazi regime. From this nothing will turn us—nothing."

The German attack on Russia promised no direct and immediate relief to England, but it did engage a massive portion of Germany's air and land forces, all of which would abound to Britain's advantage if Russia could withstand the onslaught. As for the United States, its stake in the survival of Great Britain, if not broadly recognized by the general public, was accepted by government and military leaders and dramatized in the destroyers-for-bases agreement of September 1940, Lend-Lease in March 1941, and the Atlantic Charter in August of the latter year. In other words, by 1940-1941 German ambitions posed a threat to the security of all three powers—Great Britain, the Soviet Union, and the United States. After Germany declared war on the United States in December 1941, Allied cooperation was based on the imperatives of first stemming and subsequently crushing a mutual enemy. This did not mean that fundamental ideological differences were resolved and that mutual suspicions evaporated, or that traditional geopolitical factors vanished in the calculation of war aims. As a former State Department official recalls: "I can testify . . . that there was no time when the danger from the Soviet Union was not a topic of anxious conversation among officers of the State Department; and by the winter of 1944-45, as the day of victory approached, it became the predominant theme in Washington."[1]

[1] Louis J. Halle, *The Cold War as History* (New York, 1967), p. 38.

The prospects of turning the tide against Germany had not yet
brightened when it became clear that differences characterizing
the interwar period would intrude themselves into Allied relations
during and after the war. For example, negotiations among Britain,
France, and Russia in 1939 for a common policy against Hitler had
broken down over Russian demands for the right to occupy territory
in Rumania, Poland, and the Baltic states in the event of war with
Germany. Following the German assault on Poland in September 1939,
Russia occupied the Baltic states and eastern Poland and thus secured frontiers she would thereafter regard as permanent. The Rus-
sian position became clear as early as July 1941. In talks be-
tween Ivan Maisky, Soviet Ambassador to Great Britain, and General
Wladyslaw Sikorski, Prime Minister of the Polish Government-in-
Exile in London, Maisky stated that the Polish-Soviet frontier
could not be restored to what it had been before the German (and
Russian) attack on Poland. Similarly, Soviet Foreign Minister
Vyacheslav Molotov, meeting with British Foreign Secretary Anthony
Eden in May 1942, pushed for an Anglo-Russian treaty recognizing
Soviet frontiers as they existed immediately before the German invasion of Russia. The final result of the unwavering Soviet position was British and American acceptance, but only after serious
disagreement and much disputation, and then only after the issue
had become enmeshed in the larger question of who would rule in
postwar Poland.

By the time of the Yalta Conference in February 1945, there
was abundant evidence to indicate that Poland would be a thorny
issue. Well in advance of the German attack on Russia, Stalin and
his associates had exhibited contempt for the London-based Polish
Government-in-Exile, and in 1943 broke off diplomatic relations.
The occasion for the action was a German announcement in April
1943 that thousands of Polish officers had been discovered in a
mass grave in the Katyn Forest. They had been executed in 1940,
alleged the Germans, by Russian forces in the area. When the Polish Government-in-Exile demanded an investigation by the International Red Cross, the Soviet Union severed relations and, in
July 1944, turned over administration of liberated Polish territory to the Communist-dominated Polish Committee of National
Liberation (Lublin Committee), a rival authority to the London
Poles.

Against this background Churchill, Roosevelt, and Stalin met
at Yalta in the Russian Crimea. The Polish question had by now become the major testing ground for Allied cooperation. Having gone
to war with Germany in 1939 over an attack on Poland, apprehensive
as always of Russian power in east-central Europe, and having supported and accommodated the Polish Government-in-Exile in London,
the British viewed themselves committed by traditional policy and
indebted by honor and blood to a just settlement of Polish issues.
For the United States, the composition of a Polish government was

proclaimed to be a matter of self-determination. But for Russia, a Polish government friendly to the Soviet Union, and incorporation of eastern Poland into Russia, were regarded as indispensable conditions for creation of a buffer against future attack from the west.

Agreements reached at Yalta on the Polish-Soviet frontier and the composition of a Polish government were loosely drawn. Basically they confirmed Russian possession of eastern Poland and accepted the Communist-dominated Polish Committee of National Liberation as a provisional government that would serve as a nucleus for a government to be "reorganized on a broader democratic basis with the inclusion of democratic leaders from Poland itself and from Poles abroad." In the following months, when it became clear that the "reorganized" government would remain dominated by Communists, Great Britain and the United States protested vigorously. In May 1945, President Truman sent Harry Hopkins, a close adviser to President Roosevelt, to Moscow, where, in the course of six conversations with Stalin between May 26 and June 6, he explained to the Russian leader the reasons for American alarm over developments in eastern Europe. Noting that "the question of Poland per se was not so important as the fact that it had become a symbol of our ability to work out problems with the Soviet Union," Hopkins went on to state that the people and government of the United States "felt that the Polish people should be given the right to free elections to choose their own government and their own system and that Poland should genuinely be independent."

Stalin argued at length that he did not oppose an independent or democratic Poland; he did object to a Poland governed by elements unfriendly to the Soviet Union. The thrust of Stalin's position was that in the years preceding World War II the West had sought to maintain Poland as a *cordon sanitaire* on the Soviet borders, an unremitting anti-Communist stance that had enabled Germans to pour through Poland into the Russian heartland. He implied that the Soviet government could see no reason to permit what was now a rampart to again become a gateway.

In addition to the embroilment over Poland, the legacy of suspicion from the interwar years is also seen in disputes regarding the opening of a second front in Europe after the German invasion of Russia. Reeling under the blows of the Wehrmacht and Luftwaffe, Soviet leaders repeatedly pressed for an Allied cross-Channel attack to relieve the pressure on Russia. Planning was soon underway, particularly in the United States (Operation Sledgehammer), on the assumption that an attack would be necessary if a Russian collapse appeared to be imminent. But memories of the carnage in French trenches during World War I, and the recent nightmare of Dunkirk, led the British consistently to oppose plans for an invasion until such time as German submarine and air power had been neutralized and German land forces in France were at minimum

strength. Furthermore, with Egypt and the Mediterranean lifeline
threatened, the British pushed for action in North Africa (Operation Torch) in 1942 as an alternative to what they envisioned as a
suicidal operation on the European continent. As a result, the
North African and Italian campaigns effectively nullified the possibility of operations in western Europe not only in 1942 but in
1943 as well (Operation Roundup). British and American differences notwithstanding, when Foreign Minister Molotov visited Washington in the spring of 1942, he was apparently led to believe
that a second front in Europe before the end of the year was not
an impossibility. When the front did not materialize, in 1942 or
1943, Soviet leaders suspected the worst. Even if, as hindsight
would seem to indicate, the Anglo-American decision to postpone
operations in western Europe was well-founded, continued delay
after indications to the contrary nourished Soviet fears that the
West hoped to see Germany and Russia claw each other to pieces.

Given this milieu of distrust and divergent objectives, by
the war's end disagreements were flourishing among the Big Three.
In March 1945, Allen Dulles, head of the American Office of Strategic Services in Switzerland, opened talks with Nazi SS General
Karl Wolff for the surrender of German troops in Italy. The contact brought an immediate blast from Stalin, who suspected that
German troops in Italy would be used against Russia while American
and British forces would be free to move to the north and east.
Although the talks were broken off by the end of April 1945, exclusion of Russian representatives from the meetings was not soon
forgotten in Moscow.

Nor did East and West cooperate effectively in the administration of Germany after V-E day. The Allies had agreed at Yalta
that reparations would be exacted from Germany, but a total sum
had not been definitely established. The working out of detailed
plans was assigned to an Allied Reparation Commission to meet in
Moscow. After Germany surrendered in early May 1945, the Soviets
began a massive transfer of goods and equipment from their zone of
occupation to Russia, oblivious to the impact of the action on Germany's ability to become economically self-sustaining.

At the Potsdam Conference, July 17 to August 2, 1945, the entire reparations question was again examined. Russia, with an
occupation zone basically agricultural, was to receive capital
goods from the western zones in return for deliveries to the West
of food and other products from their zone. But Russian insistence that reparations should consist of both capital goods and
removals from current production, and the American refusal to accept that interpretation, stymied the exchange of zonal commodi-
ties. In May 1946, General Lucius D. Clay, American Military
Governor in Germany, terminated deliveries of reparations from the
American zone.

Equally revealing of the Allied inability to cooperate in
Germany was the impotence of the Control Council operating in Berlin. Since unanimity for any action was required among the four
occupying powers represented on the Council, carrying out the
Potsdam decision that the country was to be treated as a single
economic unit and administered uniformly proved to be illusive.
At root, France and Russia, twice invaded by Germany in less than
30 years, were intent upon gaining all the booty and reparations
possible while at the same time crippling the German war-making
potential. Opposed to those objectives was England's traditional
policy of trying to maintain the semblance of a balance of power
on the Continent and the American wish to avoid heavy subsidiza-
tion of the German economy (and reparations) and a desire to reconstruct a viable capitalistic system in central Europe. These
fundamentally antipodal goals were reflected in the operations of
the Control Council, complicating all efforts to unify the economy
and administration of Germany.

Other areas of contention between Russia and the West were
the imposition of Communist domination in Bulgaria, Rumania, and
Hungary; the veto and regional security pacts in debates on the
United Nations Charter during May and June of 1945; and, in the
latter half of 1945, Soviet attempts to establish a Communist-con-
trolled state in northern Iran. Thus by March 1946, Winston
Churchill spoke for a majority of officials in both the United
States and Great Britain when he scored the Russians for the iron
curtain which had descended "from Stettin in the Baltic to Trieste
in the Adriatic," and for the worldwide activity of "Communist
fifth columns." And, lest Churchill's famous address be interpreted as throwing down the gauntlet to Russia, supporters of his
analysis, particularly George F. Kennan, U.S. Charge d'Affaires in
Moscow, claimed that a Stalin election speech delivered a month
earlier had been even more provocative in its suggestion of an ir-
reconcilable conflict between capitalism and Communism.

A State Department request for his comments on the Stalin
speech led Kennan to prepare a lengthy telegram, dated February
22, 1946, in which he asserted that Soviet leaders sought nothing
less than the "total destruction of rival power, never . . . compacts and compromises with it." The telegram was circulated widely within the government, and Kennan drew heavily from its content
and analysis to prepare the famous article of July 1947 in the pe-
riodical *Foreign Affairs*, an article frequently described as offering the rationale for the emerging American policy of containment.

For the remainder of 1946 and into the early months of 1947,
the wartime allies drifted further apart. An American proposal
for the international control of atomic energy was spurned by
Russia on the grounds that it left the United States with the up-
per hand. At a conference of foreign ministers held in Paris in

April-June of 1946, negotiations on peace treaties for Italy and
the Balkan countries snagged on a variety of issues. Russia
wanted $100 million in reparations from Italy and the right to ad-
minister at least one of the former Italian colonies in North
Africa under a trusteeship arrangement, and supported the Yugoslavian claim for the Adriatic port of Trieste. Britain and the
United States advocated a lenient reparations assessment against
Italy, opposed Soviet administration of Italian colonies, and proposed autonomy for Trieste under the supervision of the Security
Council of the United Nations. Western fears that Soviet demands,
if met, would strengthen Communism in Italy and extend Russian influence into the Mediterranean contested with the Soviet belief
that Western solicitude for Italy was aimed at depriving Russia of
reparations and preserving Italy as an investment monopoly for the
capitalist nations.

Compromise on both sides allowed peace treaties to be signed
with Italy and the Balkan countries early in 1947, but it was a
different story with Germany and Austria. Anglo-American policies
in Germany aimed at increasing industrial production in their
zones of occupation, suspending reparations shipments, and moving
toward the administration of their zones as a single economic unit
were seen by the Soviets as moves designed to protect Western economic interests, deny Russia the reparations she deserved, postpone German disarmament, and recreate an anti-Communist state in
central Europe in defiance of Soviet security interests. The
cleavage was publicized in two important policy statements—the
first by Soviet Foreign Minister Molotov in Paris on July 10, 1946;
the second, essentially in reply to Molotov, by American Secretary
of State James F. Byrnes on September 6, 1946, in Stuttgart, Germany. Both statements were largely summaries of the attitudes and
policies already descriptive of the actions of Russia and the United States in Germany, but in each instance the speaker appealed
for support to the German people, claiming that the policies of
the other side boded ill for the future well-being of Germany.
This was not the behavior of parties on the verge of compromise.
By the end of 1946 the prospects for early peace treaties with Germany and Austria had all but expired.

The settlement of problems in all of these areas was, in the
official Anglo-American interpretation of the events, rendered impossible by Soviet postwar aims and Soviet intransigence, necessi-
tating implementation of a containment policy in 1947, as reflected in the Truman Doctrine and the Marshall Plan. For the Soviet
Union, on the other hand, solutions to outstanding political differences were frustrated by Anglo-American policies which, if
implemented, would deny Russia security and the political and economic fruits of a victory purchased at enormous cost in blood and
treasure.

Is it possible to affix blame? Does one side or the other bear a preponderant share of the responsibility for the onset of the cold war? Throughout the late 1940s and into the 1950s, those engaged in trying to answer these questions generally stressed one of the following interpretations:

1. The Soviet Union, committed to worldwide revolutions directed from Moscow, was bent on territorial expansion and subversion of non-Communist governments in violation of wartime agreements.

2. Russia sought the more limited objective of establishing friendly (Communist) governments only in those areas, e.g., eastern Europe, where she had legitimate security interests and thus did not pursue a program of worldwide revolution or broad military expansionism.

3. The policies of the United States were excessively idealistic, and they ignored the fact that balance-of-power arrangements and spheres of influence would necessarily continue to exist.

4. The United States followed a genuine anticolonial policy and worked for the self-determination of all peoples.

Within each of the foregoing categories there were various subgroups. Particularly significant were those focusing on individuals. Franklin D. Roosevelt was criticized for allegedly failing to understand the history of Russian expansion or Communist strategy and tactics, thus making indefensible concessions to Stalin. Roosevelt's naivete, it was argued, produced the "sellout" at Yalta which enabled the Soviet Union to fashion an iron grip on eastern and central Europe and to reassert a primacy in Far Eastern affairs from which it had been dislodged by Japan in the preceding four decades, thus preparing the ground for the "loss of China." Roosevelt, in this interpretation, stood condemned for having permitted Russia to trample on the liberal war aims expressed in the Atlantic Charter of 1941 and the United Nations Declaration of January 1, 1942, signed by all of the Allies fighting against Germany.

Other investigators singled out Winston Churchill as the wartime leader responsible for much of the discord. In his readiness to make balance-of-power deals with Stalin—especially in eastern Europe and the Balkans—and to preserve a tottering British imperial structure, Churchill frustrated American efforts to espouse the cause of colonial peoples everywhere. Churchill's deals

inadvertently paved the way for Russia and Communism to pose as
the only international forces who truly championed the aspirations
of oppressed peoples. A tenacious British defense of discredited
diplomatic gambits reminiscent of the nineteenth century had thus
subverted enlightened American policy which had sought to foster
universal self-determination. Inevitably, due to its longstanding
tradition of friendship with Britain, the United States became
identified with the anti-Soviet, anti-Communist policies of Great
Britain and consequently with the forces of the status quo.

And Josef Stalin was taken to task. In its strongest expression, the indictment of Stalin held that Russian historical experience and Marxist-Leninist dogma were peripheral ingredients when
measured against the ambition, ruthlessness, cunning, and profound
suspicion of the Soviet Union's wartime leader. Distrustful of
British and American military strategy, convinced that American
aid cloaked ulterior aims, certain that his Western allies coveted
destruction of the anticapitalist regime over which he presided,
Stalin envisioned nothing less than the establishment of Russian
primacy in all of Europe and neutralization of Western power in
the Far East. Given the scope of his designs, cooperation with
Stalin was possible only at the cost of endless concessions and,
ultimately, complete surrender to his insatiable appetites.

These various interpretations and subgroups have by no means
been eliminated from discussions of cold war origins, as a number
of the selections in this reader make clear. They are presented
above in the past tense simply to emphasize that investigations
over the last decade have both amplified and modified these traditional assessments. Among the issues explored at length by recent
writers are the exclusion of Russia in 1944-1945 from all but nomi-
nal participation in the commission controlling the Italian occupation, and Soviet suspicions about talks in 1945 between Western
and German representatives for the surrender of German forces in
Italy. Other areas subjected to close scrutiny are the use of the
atomic bombs, Russia's request for a postwar American loan to facilitate economic reconstruction, the termination of Lend-Lease to
the Soviet Union, and disputes over the treatment of and future of
Germany. In each of these areas investigators find that Anglo-
American policies, if not consciously antagonistic to the Soviet
Union, were determined and applied in a manner justifying Russian
doubts.

Particularly damaging to the image of Anglo-American forbear-
ance in the face of Soviet obstructionism is the charge that dropping atomic bombs on Hiroshima and Nagasaki was dictated less by
strategic necessity in the war against Japan than by a desire to
intimidate Russia, thus rendering Soviet leaders more pliable to
Western initiatives. The sources for this argument are outlined
in the selection by Gar Alperovitz. In the same vein, the United
States is accused of purposely blunting Soviet efforts to secure a

large postwar credit, and abruptly cutting off Lend-Lease aid in
May 1945 with the intention of exacting Russian compliance on outstanding political disputes. These issues are examined at length
in the articles by Thomas G. Paterson and George C. Herring, Jr.
Intertwined with these moves was an intractable reparations policy
in 1945-1946 aimed doubly at strengthening the economy of the
western zones of Germany for the benefit of American political-economic goals, and depriving the Soviet Union of the means for economic rehabilitation. Two recent studies of American occupation
policies in Germany, by Lloyd C. Gardner and Wolfgang Schlauch,
are reviewed in the article by John Gimbel. Finally, there are
some who maintain that all of these actions reveal what was—and
remains—the dominant theme in American foreign policy, namely, efforts to create a worldwide economic hegemony, an objective dictated by the very nature of the American capitalistic system.

The editors of this volume believe that significant contributions have been made to our understanding of cold war origins by
advocates of each interpretation delineated above.

The articles in Part 1 give four different perspectives on
the cold war and its origins. Mosely and Bernstein are descriptive and analytical; Bronfenbrenner offers clues to the attitudes
underlying dealings between the people of the two countries, and
Marushkin, a Russian writer, challenges both the facts and the interpretations stressed in many Western works on the subject. In
Part 2, the above-mentioned selections by Alperovitz, Paterson,
Herring, and Gimbel focus on specific areas of conflict. The documents in Part 3 relate directly to important issues raised in the
preceding selections, and give the reader an idea of how participants articulated their differences. The concluding section, Part
4, consists of articles that interpret the literature and evaluate,
reconsider, and argue the variety of interpretations, concepts,
and facts of the cold war. H. Stuart Hughes gives a historian-
participant's evaluation of East-West relations in the immediate
postwar years. Christopher Lasch categorizes the numerous
"schools" of thought, and Charles S. Maier, in the last selection,
discusses both the concepts and the literature in the continuing
debate on cold war origins. The emphasis in the articles is on
disputes centered in Europe. Although all but three of the authors are Americans, the suggested readings appended to each selection contain references to documents and to British and translated
Russian works available in most college libraries.

We do not claim that every area of cooperation and conflict
between Russia and the West is examined in these pages, or that
every possible interpretation is included. Our modest ambition
was to bring together a limited number of outstanding scholarly
investigations into the question of cold war origins, and to repro-
duce them in their entirety, rather than merely offer a compila-
tion of brief excerpts. We believe that students who read the

selections, and sample the suggested readings, will learn the
story of the beginnings of the cold war as it is now known. We
believe, also, that the reader will come to appreciate the difficulties historians face in trying to reconstruct and explain the
relationships between nations.

PART 1

FOUR VIEWS ON COLD WAR ORIGINS

The four articles reprinted in this section are representative of the various interpretations and discussions of the cold war's origins that can be found in the extensive and scattered literature on the subject.

The first selection, by Mosely, is a traditional, conventional American interpretation of cold war origins. It conforms to the official American interpretation. The second, by Bernstein, is representative of the revisionist view, which is heavily influenced by the writings of William A. Williams and Denna F. Fleming and which became increasingly popular in the last half of the 1960s. The third, by Bronfenbrenner, is an attempt to deal systematically with the difficult question of motivation and responsibility by probing into the sociopsychological roots of policy formation and determination. The fourth, by Marushkin, is representative of the Soviet interpretation of the origins of the cold war.

SOVIET-AMERICAN RELATIONS SINCE THE WAR*

Philip E. Mosely

Professor Mosely is a specialist in Russian studies and director of the European Institute at Columbia University. He was the *United States political adviser in the European Advisory Commission in 1944-1945, and at the Potsdam Conference in 1945.* He has *published numerous works in his field, including* The Kremlin and World Politics: Studies in Soviet Policy in Action *(New York, 1960), which contains a reprint of the selection printed below.*
Mosely states the more traditional American interpretation of the origins of the cold war, what Barton Bernstein in the second selection refers to as the general consensus among American scholars. The traditional view assigns the initiatives in the cold war to the Soviet Union, and it interprets U.S. actions to be essentially responses and reactions to Soviet thrusts. Mosely's article is also interesting for its examination of various American and Soviet misconceptions that formed the basis for the polarization of the postwar world. In the light of these misconceptions, Mosely reviews briefly the wartime relations between the two powers, and then focuses on Soviet initiatives and pressures after the Yalta Conference of February 1945. The Soviet initiatives and pressures were designed to achieve the objectives that Stalin and Molotov presented as Russian demands at the Potsdam Conference in July 1945. The crucial period in the collapse of the wartime alliance is therefore between February and July 1945, between the Yalta and the Potsdam Conferences. As the war ended, the alliance began to disintegrate, chiefly as a result of the Soviet Union's post-Yalta policy shift. Mosely dates the American response to Soviet pressures early in 1947. At that time the United States broke with its ancient tradition and offered assistance to the countries lying in the path of Soviet expansionism; it developed the policy of containment.

----

*Reprinted from "Soviet-American Relations since the War," *The Annals* 263 (May 1949), 202-211, with permission of the author and The American Academy of Political and Social Science.

The problem which now dominates all aspects of postwar politics is that of the antagonism between American and Soviet politics. If there is a ballot on admitting new members to the United
Nations, or a decision to be taken on reconstruction in Germany,
it cannot be discussed on the merits of the case. Each position
is taken with an eye to its effect upon the two contending greatest powers.

The extreme polarization of power is reflected along sensitive frontiers, as in Norway and Iran. It cuts across critical
areas of homogeneous nationalities, as in the cases of Germany,
Austria, and Korea. It is paralleled in dangerous fissures within
many national communities and is reflected in the continuing unrest within Soviet satellites and in the struggles of the Communist parties in France and Italy, in Greece and China. The factors of conflict, which have been traced in several articles in
this volume, have been tumultuous and remain dangerous.

The dangers are increased by the fact that both Soviet and
American centers of power are largely self-contained; the outlook
and purposes of each of these powers are generated internally, are
secreted from its own way of life. The intentional or unforeseen
repercussions of their acts affect many other peoples in their
most sensitive interests and aspirations. In addition, each of
these two great powers finds it difficult to arrive at a coherent
judgment of the power and intentions of the other.

Soviet Ideas of the United States

When the Soviet leaders look at America, they think primarily
of its great economic power. No doubt, they are rather well informed of its strength in specific skills and of its inventiveness.
Their insistence upon the validity of a single philosophy prevents
them from understanding the political and social experience and
outlook which form the underpinning of American society. In apply-
ing with extreme rigor the system of piece-rate rewards and penal-
ties to their own workers, they overlook the fact that in America
differential incentives to workers rest on a high minimum standard
of living. Admitting the technical superiority of American industry, always measuring their own achievements against American statistics, the Soviet leaders also believe unshakably that the American economy is certain to be pounded to pieces from within. And
since the United States is now the only other great power, they
wait impatiently for the time when that power will disintegrate
and American policy will be paralyzed by internal stresses.

The duality in the Soviet evaluation of American strength was
clearly shown in the question of a postwar loan. The Soviet representatives were eager to secure a very large loan—figures of six
to ten billion dollars were bandied about—and admitted freely

that Soviet reconstruction would be immensely facilitated by the inflow of American equipment. On the other hand, they were absolutely convinced that this loan was not something for which they would have to make an effort, even an effort to maintain some degree of diplomatic decorum. They were certain that America would come hat in hand, begging them to accept a large loan, solely for the purpose of staving off a catastrophic depression at home. They felt they would be doing a favor to American manufacturers by giving their rickety economic system a few years of grace. Holding these views, the Soviet leaders assumed that their own offensive against American interests and sentiments was in no way incompatible with the obtaining of a loan.

A similar opaqueness has shaped the Soviet leaders' understanding of American policies in the postwar world. They can recognize that Americans are basically oriented inwards and find it hard to be concerned steadily with world affairs. They know that the United States did not take the initiative in starting either of the world wars in this century. From the full and open discussion of policy which goes on in this country, they can see that most disputes revolve around the question of finding the best way to prevent a new war. Yet the Soviet leaders insist that America is the center of a new and active conspiracy to unleash a new world war.

Believing that the Soviet system alone has solved the inner contradictions of industrial society and that it is bound to expand into ever wider areas and some day to encompass the world, the Soviet leaders conclude that any forces which are outside Soviet control are, potentially or in reality, a menace to their ambition and to their regime. Professing to believe that the non-Soviet world envies the achievements of the Soviet Union and desires to destroy their system, they assume that the forces of the non-Soviet world are bound, sooner or later, to coalesce around the strongest non-Soviet power. Power beyond Soviet control and "anti-Soviet" power tend to become identified in their way of thinking.

In 1941 the Soviet leaders fully expected Britain and the United States to sit idly by while Hitler attempted to destroy the Soviet regime, or even to join with him. The prompt support which the Soviets received in a time of greatest danger, the great contributions of supplies, and the constant efforts to promote closer co-operation did not shake their faith in the dogma of "capitalist encirclement." In February 1946 this basic tenet was reaffirmed by Marshal Stalin as the central point in the postwar Soviet program.

Reasoning from Unsound Premises

The trouble about Soviet reasoning is not that it is illogical—it is usually too strictly logical—but that its premises ignore or distort simple facts which are readily discernible to minds which have not been subjected to the process of "Bolshevist hardening." If "lasting peace" is declared to be possible only under the Soviet system, then, logically, only the Soviet Union and its obedient satellites can be considered truly "peace-loving" countries. Whatever "subjective" horror of war may be expressed by "capitalist" leaders, their governments, "objectively" analyzed, are engaged in "warmongering." Anyone who criticizes or opposes Soviet claims and actions is, of course, "spreading anti-Soviet slander," "undermining peace," "promoting fascism," or "destroying Allied unity." This syllogism rests in turn on an assumption, which cannot be questioned or criticized in areas under Soviet control, that a small group of leaders in command of the regime has, through self-appointed apostolic succession to Lenin, a monopoly of wisdom and virtue.

Of course, the faculty of reasoning logically from unprovable hypotheses to untenable conclusions is not confined to any one group of men, although it seems to appear most often under conditions of absolute power. Such a faculty is dangerous when its pronouncements monopolize access to men's minds, including the minds of those who direct or serve the dictatorship.

There is a continual danger in the Soviet leaders' habit of taking action upon a set of facts which appear as facts to them alone. An even more serious danger lies in the marshaling and interpreting of a commonly perceived body of facts in accordance with a rigidly enforced philosophy, adherence to which is the password to authority and responsibility within the Soviet system.

Some American Misconceptions about the Soviet Union

Most Americans cannot make up their minds as to whether the Soviet Union is strong or weak. Because the Soviet war effort was greatly assisted through Lend-Lease, many Americans suppose that the Soviet Union cannot wage a major war on the basis of its own production. This assumption overlooks the fact that up to the turning of the tide at Stalingrad, the Soviet armies had received relatively small quantities of supplies from abroad. Throughout the war, the basic tools of war—artillery, tanks, planes—were almost entirely of Soviet manufacture. It would be short-sighted to suppose that Soviet capacity to wage war is far smaller, or is not actually substantially greater, than it was when the Soviet forces broke the German onslaught.

It is sometimes assumed that a denial of technical equipment
and knowledge derived from the West will slow down or even disrupt
the development of Soviet industry. It must, however, be assumed
that in the production of machine tools the Soviet Union is "over
the hump" in the process of industrialization. Failure to obtain
abroad certain specialized or more modern types of equipment may
delay or hamper but cannot prevent the broad development of Soviet
industry on the basis of skills already acquired. Finally, the
ratio of total industrial power to war potential varies considerably under diverse systems. The Soviet system gives its leaders
great leeway in deciding what proportion of industrial power shall
be directed towards military needs.

A contrary assumption is also advanced that the Soviet leaders may lightheartedly engage in a new trial of strength by war,
as soon as they feel confident of thereby gaining some immediate
and decisive advantage. Their real range of choice seems to lie
somewhere between two extremes. It is unrealistic to suppose that
they would make concessions from their basic program, either to
secure economic aid or to win favor in the eyes of the non-Soviet
world. It is also unreasonable to assume that the urge to extend
their system to new areas will lead them into war without considering the effect of war upon the low Soviet standard of living or
without reflecting on the possibly unpredictable outcome of a war
against a powerful, highly ingenious, and relatively impregnable
enemy.

If the Soviet leaders have, since 1945, steadily weighted
their choice in favor of a relentless political offensive against
the non-Soviet world, this may be due in large part to their habit
of subordinating economic considerations to factors of power. It
may be due to a short-run assumption that the economic advantages
which might be gained immediately through a more conciliatory policy are of minor importance to them when compared with the great
extension of political power on which they are gambling. It may
also be assumed that they have felt sure that a policy of strong
pressure offered no risk to their basic security, since the American military machine was being dismantled with great haste and
there was no other power to challenge their ambitions.

Because the Soviet Government rules through a centralized dictatorship and severely limits the range of suggestion or criticism
allowed to its citizens and to supporters abroad, an American
readily assumes that the system is inherently weak, maintained
only through the constant stimulation of fear. This impression of
political instability has been enhanced by the sensational abandonment of Soviet allegiance by individual citizens and by the much
less publicized refusal of several hundreds of thousands of its
citizens to return to the Soviet Union. To people accustomed to a
regime which periodically submits to the judgment of the voters,
these facts suggest weakness, hence, a necessity for such a regime
to avoid war at all cost.

This interpretation, natural in American eyes, overlooks many
unfamiliar factors: a long tradition of rule by a strong and irresponsible power, the tradition of combining incessant persuasion
with coercion, and absence of conscious formulation of alternative
programs despite widespread discontent with privations and injustices. It would be short-sighted to disparage the substantial
level of disciplined action achieved under the Soviet regime or to
assume that internal discontent would be an important factor, especially in a short test of strength. In any major war, of course,
a defeated and occupied country may undergo a change of regime,
and new currents may come to the surface. In Russia today, or any-
where in Europe, few of these currents would be tender of individual rights.

Popular Appeal of Communism

It is hard for Americans to realize that Communism meets with
acceptance and even fanatical support in many segments of the population. Communism remains a powerful force in France and Italy,
for American gifts and economic recovery do not reach far into the
basic factors making for discontent. Backward countries may be attracted to the Soviet recipe of quick action through dictatorship,
rather than to the American method of piecemeal improvement and
changes brought about through consent. Where problems of overpopu-
lation, absence of technical skills and capital, and age-old accu-
mulations of social and national resentments set discouragingly
high barriers to modernization, the appeal of Communism is bound
to remain strong. There it is judged by its promises of "progress"
—not by the as yet unknown effects which may follow from the quality and direction of the "progress" it offers. The Soviet leaders
choose to regard American democracy as a "conspiracy." It would
be equally dangerous for Americans to assume that their own type
of democracy is universally admired and desired, and that the
strength of Communism resides only in a centralized conspiracy of
force.
Since the Soviet leaders accept the duty of spreading their
system and rejoice at the appearance of each new "people's democracy," it is easily and widely assumed that this political ambition motivates its leaders at all times with an unvarying emotional intensity. It is difficult to judge the emotional intensities
within the Politburo, but it is clear from the record that the
outward pressure of Soviet expansionism has fluctuated rather
widely over the past thirty-one years. This intensity may vary in
the future.
A relative relaxation of the outward thrust may come about in
one of several ways. It may arise from a discouraged recognition
of solid and impassable barriers erected in its path; or it may

develop from the operation of internal factors. In the case of an
ideology which offers the only "scientific" basis for prediction,
repeated failures to predict accurately may result in the growth
of skepticism towards the doctrine of infallibility itself. Or,
when a militant ideology has outlived the generation which formulated it in the heat of revolutionary struggle, and becomes the
property of a generation which docilely received the tradition
ready-made, the fervor of the revolutionary "fathers" may not pass
integrally into the postrevolutionary "sons."
     The written word of revelation may remain sacrosanct, but if
it is believed with, say 10 percent less fervor by a new generation, the compulsion to act hazardously on behalf of the doctrine
may slacken. As a dogma becomes more rigid, it may not evoke the
same desire to act. Since about 1937, Soviet dogma has achieved a
remarkable posture of rigidity, unnatural in a people of quick
mind and ranging curiosity. Meanwhile, since no confident prediction of a slackening of the Soviet urge to messianic expansion can
be made, it has become necessary to act on the assumption that
this urge can be restrained only by constructing external barriers
and setting clear warning signals.

Soviet-American Relations during the War

     During the stress of common danger a limited degree of co-
operation was established between the Soviet Union and the United
States, and a modest amount of combined planning for the postwar
period was accomplished. During the war the American Government
made many efforts, not always well directed, to win the confidence
of a very distrustful group of leaders and to lay the groundwork
of a postwar community of interest. It was agreed to establish
a new security organization, dominated by the great powers, and
specific agreements were reached concerning the postwar occupation
and control of Germany and Austria. Some limited successes were
achieved, and it could not be said with finality that the Soviet
leaders were determined to go their own way in the postwar world
and to ignore completely their allies' constant invitations to cooperative action. It can be said that in this phase the Soviet
Government insisted on safeguarding its own strength, security,
secrecy, and independence of decision, yet was willing, when none
of these factors was directly involved, to make limited commitments to joint action. This phase lasted through the Yalta Conference, which marked the high point in the prospects for closer
understanding and co-operation.
     A fortnight after Yalta there occurred a significant shift
in the emphasis of Soviet policy. While the slogan of "Allied
unity" continued to be chanted in every key by Soviet propagandists, there took place a rapid ebbing in any signs of Soviet

consideration for the interests or hopes of the western Allies. In direct violation of the recently signed Yalta agreements, the Soviet Government proceeded to impose governments of its own choosing upon the smaller countries of eastern Europe. In violation of another part of the Yalta agreement it gave its full support to the minority Lublin regime in Poland, and signed with it a close alliance and a unilateral agreement defining Poland's western boundary, again in disregard of a specific agreement with its allies. At this very time it also backed away, in a significant respect, from implementing the agreement to co-operate with its allies in the postwar control of Germany.

After the signing, in November 1944, of the Allied agreement for establishing joint control over postwar Germany, the three governments of Great Britain, the Soviet Union, and the United States had agreed orally to set up immediately a nucleus of the future control machinery. The three, later four, nucleus control groups could thus, in advance, become accustomed to working together, could adjust their diverse administrative conceptions and establish their twelve working divisions, and would be ready to begin operations within a few days after the German surrender. The Soviet representative on the European Advisory Commission, in London, informed his colleagues that the Soviet nucleus group was being selected, that it was nearly complete, that it was almost ready to join the American and British groups. At Yalta Marshal Stalin agreed to expedite the arrival of the nucleus group, and about ten days later his representative in London informed his American colleague, with obvious satisfaction, that the Soviet group would arrive on a fixed day. Shortly after, the Soviet delegate sent a subordinate to inform the American delegation that the Soviet group was not coming at all. Viewed in retrospect, this reversal was merely one additional sign pointing to a strong trend towards unilateral Soviet policy everywhere in Europe.

Factors in Post-Yalta Shift

There may be several partial explanations for this post-Yalta shift from limited co-operation to an attitude of sharp rivalry. As Soviet troops entered German territory, the dominant voice in Soviet policy may well have passed from the foreign ministry, which had until then been responsible for planning the occupation on the agreed basis of joint Allied action, into the hands of the powerful economic ministries, bent on squeezing every bit of economic relief out of Germany, and of the secret police, responsible directly to the Politburo for enforcing Soviet control in occupied areas. Another factor may have been the strong Soviet expectation of a rapid withdrawal of American forces from Europe.

At Yalta, American officials had insisted that the United
States Government could not commit its people to any specific and
continuing responsibilities in Europe, and that American forces
would be withdrawn across the ocean just as rapidly as the availability of shipping would permit. At that stage the Morgenthau
"Plan," which dominated official thinking about the German problem, showed no trace of any concern for Germany's longer-range
future. Turning Germany into a "pastoral" country would, of
course, have left Communism as the sole hope for German survival.
Knowing after Yalta that American power would be withdrawn with
utmost speed from Europe, the Soviet leaders could also, and did,
treat with contempt American protests, even President Roosevelt's
personal appeals to Stalin, concerning the open and frequent violations of the Yalta agreements on eastern Europe.

The same factors must have encouraged the Soviet leaders,
after digesting the experience of Yalta, to hope that France and
Italy, where the native Communist parties were far stronger and
better organized than in Poland, Hungary, or Rumania, would also
come under Russian Communist domination. In addition, throughout
1944-46 one of the strongest arguments of Communist supporters in
western Europe was that America, though it appeared strong and
friendly, was an unreliable friend, that its armies were nonexist-
ent in time of peace and its economic assistance would melt away
in a postwar economic crisis of its own, while the Soviet Union
would remain close at hand and would know how to reward its adherents and punish its opponents.

As the Moscow Politburo wrote to the obstreperous Belgrade
Politburo in 1948, the way in which the war ended had, "unfortu-
nately," made it impossible for the Soviet Union to establish
"people's democracies" in Italy and France. But if they could not
be established in western Germany, France, and Italy by the expe-
ditious means of Soviet military assistance, the same goal might
still be achieved through combined pressure from within and without, provided American support were withdrawn and American policy
reverted to transoceanic isolationism.

Soviet-American Relations, 1945-47

The new phase, of Soviet initiatives and intensive Soviet
pressure, which began shortly after Yalta, continued into the
spring of 1947. During this period Soviet policy was based on the
assumption that France was beyond recovery, that Britain was done
as a great power, and that the United States was about to isolate
itself from European affairs or fall into economic impotence. At
Potsdam there were still some slight traces of willingness on the
part of Soviet leaders to give a hearing to the views of their allies and to compromise in minor details. But it was at Potsdam

that the Soviet leaders gave frank expression to a program of expansion which, if achieved, would have made their power supreme in
Europe and in the eastern Mediterranean.

To list the Soviet demands, flatly presented or delicately
adumbrated at Potsdam, is to outline the policy which the Soviet
leaders have pursued since 1945 with remarkable persistence. In
Germany they wanted to rewrite the Allied agreement on zones of
occupation by setting up a separate Ruhr region under three-power
control, with a veto assuring them of a high degree of bargaining
power. They wanted to slap a ten-billion-dollar reparations mortgage on Germany, regardless of its effects on the survival of the
German people or on the American taxpayer. A completely unman-
ageable mortgage of this kind would have given them unlimited opportunities to promote the Sovietization of all Germany through
hunger blackmail. Marshal Stalin tried hard to secure a release
from the Yalta agreements concerning eastern Europe and to secure
a carte blanche for whatever he might do there. The Soviet delegation pressed for an immediate confirmation of the Polish-German
boundary which the Soviet Government had laid down; it reluctantly
agreed to consider the boundary as provisional in return for
Allied support of Soviet annexation of part of East Prussia.

The Soviet leaders also made it clear that they wanted control of the Turkish Straits, and expressed their "interest" in the
Dodecanese Islands. They pressed for the immediate removal of
British troops from Greece, and at the same time asked to be relieved of the obligation, signed in 1942, to remove their troops
from northern Iran after the end of the war. Stalin did gain a
definite advantage in this respect, for he now secured consent to
keep his forces in Iran until six months after the end of the war
against Japan—not against Germany as had been assumed until then.
Stalin's main argument was that "it [Iran] is too near Baku."
Marshal Stalin also said he was "definitely interested" in the
Italian colonies, but postponed asking for a trusteeship over
Tripolitania until six weeks later, at the London Conference of
Foreign Ministers. Shortly after Potsdam the Soviet Government
also demanded, without success, an equal share in the occupation
of Japan.

The Potsdam demands were set forth in a matter-of-fact manner, without the propaganda orchestration which was applied after
the going became rough. Nevertheless, they added up to a very substantial program: a strangle hold on the Ruhr and on the entire
German economy; an uncontested domination of the one hundred million people of eastern Europe; domination of the eastern Mediterranean through control of Greece, Turkey, and Tripolitania; and
domination of Iran.

To the great perplexity and anger of the Soviet leaders,
this second phase, outlined at Potsdam, was successful only in

those areas where Soviet forces were on the ground at the close
of the war. Elsewhere the execution of the program was averted
through delaying actions, improvisations, evasion, and by the
growth of an awareness in western Europe and America that Soviet
ambitions had grown far beyond the "natural" sphere of a concern
for security.

In the beginning of the second phase, American opinion was extremely sensitive to any disparagement of Soviet actions or intentions. In the wave of sympathy for Soviet sacrifices in the war,
of enthusiasm for Soviet courage, and in the passionate hope that
a solid basis of Allied understanding had been found, American
sentiment discredited or ignored many facts which, added together,
suggested that the Soviet leaders saw no obstacles in the path of
their ambition to extend and entrench their power in a world which
had been devastated and hollowed out by Nazi brutality and by war.
By the end of this phase, which was marked by the Truman Doctrine
and the Marshall Plan, the pendulum had swung so far, under the
hard impact of evidence of the Soviet challenge for power, that
anyone who admitted the possibility of ever settling any dispute
with the Soviet Government was likely to fall under suspicion of
favoring "appeasement."

The Third Phase

In the third phase, the United States broke with ancient tradition to offer specific assistance and to furnish specific guarantees to countries which lay in the path of Soviet expansionism.
Overcoming its scruples concerning the governments in Greece and
Turkey, it came to their assistance. The alternative would have
been acquiescence in the establishment of a Communist-dominated
regime in Greece and the submission of Turkey to Soviet overlord-
ship, either through Soviet control of the Turkish Straits and of
the highlands of eastern Anatolia, or through the installing of a
"friendly" regime, according to the Soviet definition. By this decision the United States undertook to deter the Soviet Government
from any sudden move to control the eastern Mediterranean.

The United States embarked on a far broader program of
strengthening the economic and social structure of western Europe,
although the program, announced tentatively in June 1947, went
into effect only in 1948. Instead of joining the Committee of
European Economic Co-operation and demanding a large share of American aid for itself and its satellites, the Soviet Government mo-
bilized its supporters in opposition. Its attacks were not fully
consistent. It asserted, on one hand, that the program was only a
bluff and was bound to fail, and in the same breath denounced it
as the spearhead of military aggression directed against the Soviet Union. To offset the attractions of the Marshall Plan among

its satellites, it established the Cominform in September 1947 and rounded out its control of the Soviet bloc by the Communist sei- zure of power in Czechoslovakia in February 1948, and by a pact of mutual assistance with Finland in April. The nervous insistence of the Soviet leaders on complete subservience of subsidiary Commu- nist regimes, and their difficulties in securing a reliable pic- ture of the true situation through their overindoctrinated agents, were high-lighted in the falling away, or rather the kicking away, of the Yugoslav member of the Soviet bloc in June. The Soviet cor- respondence with the Yugoslav Politburo has shown clearly that the only "nationalism" that can be tolerated within the Soviet orbit is Soviet nationalism.

The movement in western Europe for self-protection against Soviet pressure moved steadily forward in 1948 and 1949, from Bevin's speech in January 1948 to the Franco-British agreement for mutual assistance, to the five-power Brussels Pact, and to the signing of the twelve-power North Atlantic Treaty on April 4, 1949. In bolstering western Europe against the massive land power of the Soviet Union, the United States had to choose between two approach- es. It could have encouraged the formation of a Western European Union, in the hope that over a period of years this advanced and populous region would become strong enough to be, in itself, a deterrent to a possible Soviet attack or threat of attack, without becoming too closely bound to American policy. Western Europe might, it was hoped, emerge as a "third force," standing between the Soviet and American centers of power and able to deal effec- tively with both.

In the short run, however, western Europe has proved too weak to make adequate provision for its own security. It requires American support if it is to constitute even a moderately powerful deterrent. In addition, western Europe is unable to cope with the economic and political rehabilitation of western Germany except with American co-operation. In American policy the consolidation of western Europe and the recovery of Germany have become increas- ingly closely associated. In order to provide a firm barrier against Soviet domination of western Europe it has become neces- sary to avert a Soviet domination of all Germany. In order to at- tract western Germany to the side of the Atlantic powers it is necessary to promote the emergence of an effective economic and political regime in western Germany.

Since 1947 the Soviet Union has lost the momentum of military and ideological expansion in Europe, and political initiative has passed to western Europe and the United States. In China, on the other hand, the American effort to bring together Nationalist and Communist forces, to help in the strengthening of an effective central government, capable of active efforts at reform and of protecting China's national independence, was a failure. Parallel to the effort in Germany, there has been a shift in the occupation

of Japan towards more strenuous promotion of economic recovery.
The Soviet Government has constantly denounced American policy in
Germany and Japan as a plot to acquire additional allies for an
attack on the Soviet Union. Since both occupied countries are completely disarmed, these accusations are somewhat wide of the mark.
However, the question of how the security of these two countries
may be assured poses a serious dilemma. Certainly, there are
strong misgivings about permitting any form of rearmament, but it
is doubtful if the United Nations, which they can enter only with
Soviet approval, can offer sufficient assurance of their continued
independence.

Retrospect and Prospect

Looking back to Yalta and Potsdam, the Soviet leaders must
realize that the successes which they anticipated have, in many
instances, eluded their grasp. The hardening of American policy
has been due to successive shocks administered by the Politburo.
Their relative lack of success they owe, in large part, to their
failure to understand the nature of the American polity and the
underlying motives of American action abroad. They have underes-
timated the repugnance with which Americans view the destruction
of the national independence of small but proud peoples. They
have overestimated the elements of instability operating within
the American economy. The mysterious workings of a democratic
public opinion which first praises them to the skies and then
turns on them, while they feel they have remained themselves
throughout, they explain away by reference to a malevolent "conspiracy." Attributing to others their own habits of thought, they
are certain that there is an American "Politburo" which secretly
manipulates the press, the economy, and the Government. The fact
that the location, the membership, and the operations of this Politburo remain undiscoverable they attribute to that well-known
tradition of American ingenuity.
Beyond the building of adequate deterrents to Soviet expansion, American policy has another duty. It has a difficult path
to walk in these next years, strengthening the supports of a tol-
erable democratic peace and at the same time avoiding provocative
actions and gestures. There is no better gift to the Soviet propagandists than speculation in the press by an American officer on
how many atomic bombs it would require to "eliminate" the Soviet
capacity to make war. American policy makers must likewise be prepared to state the terms on which they would be willing to settle
specific problems through negotiation. Such terms have been stated repeatedly with respect to Austria and Korea. When the western
German state is a going concern, the United States and its allies
must be prepared eventually to negotiate for a reunification of

Germany on terms guaranteeing its independence, or else allow the
eastern and western German states to work out terms for their own
unification.

Even after the American people were pitchforked by Japanese
and German aggression into a war for national survival, it was far
from clear that they would accept, after the war, any continuing
responsibilities beyond their ocean borders. In 1945 they assumed
that the United Nations, if firmly supported, would suffice to
keep the peace and that they, as a nation, need have no concern
for developments abroad beyond some temporary assistance in economic recovery. If the Soviet leaders had curbed their own postwar ambitions, they would have profited by a great fund of good
will in America. If, in 1945 and 1946, the Soviet leaders had
been less cocksure of the validity of their "scientific" prognosis
and had met American interests and sentiments a part of the way, a
continuing basis for correct and fairly co-operative relations
might have been laid. This did not occur. The philosophy of
world-wide expansion, which the Soviet leaders had muted down
during the co-operation with Hitler, was turned on full-blast
against their recent allies. In their gamble, the Soviet leaders
threw into the discard those human *imponderabilia* which even Bis-
marck considered as important in the conduct of successful policy
as the possession of great power.

SUGGESTED ADDITIONAL READINGS

Bolles, Blair. "The Fallacy of Containment," *The Nation*, 168
    (March 19, 1949), 327-329. The head of the Washington Bu-
    reau, Foreign Policy Association, discusses the Moscow Con-
    ference, the Marshall Plan, the fall of Czechoslovakia, and
    other topics. Kennan's policy of containment cannot end the
    cold war and neither can Wallace's proposals for more concili-
    ation.

Carr, Albert Z. *Truman, Stalin, and Peace*. Garden City, N. Y.,
    1950. An expert on German reparations on why Stalin started
    the cold war, on the fall of China, on Truman's peaceful in-
    tentions, and on how Germany benefited economically from the
    cold war.

Chamberlin, William H. "The Cold War: A Balance Sheet," *The
    Russian Review*, IX (April 1950), 79-86. A traditionalist
    view of the cold war, emphasizing the importance of contain-
    ment. Cold war originated in the post-Yalta disillusionment,
    began formally in 1946, and emerged full-blown in 1947.

Donnelly, Desmond. *Struggle for the World: The Cold War from Its Origins in 1917*. London, 1965. A British study, dedicated to Bevin and Acheson for standing firm and holding the line against Russian initiatives, pressures, and programs for world domination.

Ingram, Kenneth. *History of the Cold War*. New York, 1955. General survey, noting the suspicions undergirding the wartime coalition and interpreting the cold war as a development not unnatural among sovereign nations with differing interests.

Mackintosh, J. M. *Strategy and Tactics of Soviet Foreign Policy*. London, 1962. A traditional study of Soviet expansion by military force, subversion, and political, economic, and psychological initiatives. By a British expert.

Morgenthau, Hans J. "Peace in Our Time?" *Commentary*, 37 (March 1964), 66-69. A realist's analysis of the cold war as a continuing political struggle, and a discussion of the deterioration of the Soviet position caused by conflicts with China, Soviet difficulties with the satellite states, and Soviet economic problems. All these are opportunities for the West.

Powers, Richard J. "Containment: From Greece to Vietnam—and Back?" *The Western Political Quarterly*, XXII (December 1969), 846-861. A criticism of the policy of containment, which was formulated for Greece, but for the wrong reasons. It continues to be applied in Vietnam, for the same wrong reasons. Much detail on the origins of the Truman Doctrine.

AMERICAN FOREIGN POLICY
AND THE ORIGINS OF THE COLD WAR*

Barton J. Bernstein

Barton J. Bernstein is professor of history at Stanford University. He is currently preparing studies of the Truman administration and of the cold war, and he is also completing a book on the 1952 election. He is editor of and contributor to Towards a New Past: Dissenting Essays in American History *(New York, 1968)* and, with Allen J. Matusow, editor of Twentieth Century America: Recent Interpretations *(New York, 1969).*

Bernstein takes issue with the general consensus, or traditional view, on the origins of the cold war. He states what is classified in the literature as the revisionist view of cold war origins, a view that emerged in the sixties following the two-volume study published by Denna F. Fleming. American foreign policy after World War II was not merely a response to Soviet initiatives and threats; neither was it as innocent and nonideological as the traditionalists would have us believe. American leaders promoted American interests, and they used American power— atomic, economic, and military—to reshape the postwar world to accord with American needs, standards, and conceptions of security. American leaders did these things conscious of the risk that the Soviet Union might be provoked thereby. Bernstein sees the major shift occurring, not in the Soviet Union's post-Yalta initiatives and pressures (as Mosely does), but in the forward policy of President Truman, who listened to W. Averell Harriman, Admiral Leahy, and other tough-minded advisers after April 1945. The Truman initiative is reflected in the sudden cutoff in Lend-Lease shipments, the rigidity and new toughness on Poland, the renewed American interest in pushing for Rumanian and Bulgarian settlements acceptable to the United States, the denial of a postwar reconstruction loan to the Soviet Union, the reversal of the American decision on German reparations after the Yalta Conference, and the use of the atomic bomb in Japan as a lever to influence future Soviet-American relations. The Truman Doctrine, the Marshall Plan, and other similar actions are variations and extensions of the basic policy adopted by Truman and his advisers in the spring of 1945.

----

*Reprinted, without footnotes, by permission of Quadrangle Books from Politics and Policies of the Truman Administration, edited by Barton J. Bernstein. Copyright © 1970 by Quadrangle Books, Inc.

Despite some dissents, most American scholars have reached a
general consensus on the origins of the Cold War. As confirmed
internationalists who believe that Russia constituted a threat to
America and its European allies after World War II, they have endorsed their nation's acceptance of its obligations as a world
power in the forties and its desire to establish a world order of
peace and prosperity. Convinced that only American efforts prevented the Soviet Union from expanding past Eastern Europe, they
have generally praised the containment policies of the Truman Doctrine, the Marshall Plan, and NATO as evidence of America's acceptance of world responsibility. While chiding or condemning
those on the right who opposed international involvement (or had
even urged preventive war), they have also been deeply critical of
those on the left who have believed that the Cold War could have
been avoided, or that the United States shared substantial responsibility for the Cold War.

Whether they are devotees of the new realism or open admir-
ers of moralism and legalism in foreign policy, most scholars have
agreed that the United States moved slowly and reluctantly, in
response to Soviet provocation, away from President Franklin D.
Roosevelt's conciliatory policy. The Truman administration, perhaps even belatedly, they suggest, abandoned its efforts to maintain the Grand Alliance and acknowledged that Russia menaced
world peace. American leaders, according to this familiar interpretation, slowly cast off the shackles of innocence and moved to
courageous and necessary policies.

Despite the widespread acceptance of this interpretation,
there has long been substantial evidence (and more recently a body
of scholarship) which suggests that American policy was neither so
innocent nor so nonideological; that American leaders sought to
promote their conceptions of national interest and their values
even at the conscious risk of provoking Russia's fears about her
security. In 1945 these leaders apparently believed that American
power would be adequate for the task of reshaping much of the
world according to America's needs and standards.

By overextending policy and power and refusing to accept Soviet interests, American policy-makers contributed to the Cold War
There was little understanding of any need to restrain American
political efforts and desires. Though it cannot be proved that
the United States could have achieved a *modus vivendi* with the Soviet Union in these years, there is evidence that Russian policies
were reasonably cautious and conservative, and that there was at
least a basis for accommodation. But this possibility slowly
slipped away as President Harry S. Truman reversed Roosevelt's
tactics of accommodation. As American demands for democratic governments in Eastern Europe became more vigorous, as the new administration delayed in providing economic assistance to Russia and
in seeking international control of atomic energy, policy-makers

met with increasing Soviet suspicion and antagonism. Concluding
that Soviet-American cooperation was impossible, they came to
believe that the Soviet state could be halted only by force or the
threat of force.
　The emerging revisionist interpretation, then, does not view
American actions simply as the necessary response to Soviet challenges, but instead tries to understand American ideology and interests, mutual suspicions and misunderstandings, and to investi-
gate the failures to seek and achieve accommodation.

I

During the war Allied relations were often marred by suspicions and doubts rooted in the hostility of earlier years. It
was only a profound "accident"—the German attack upon the Soviet
Union in 1941—that thrust the leading anti-Bolshevik, Winston
Churchill, and Marshal Josef Stalin into a common camp. This wartime alliance, its members realized, was not based upon trust but
upon necessity; there was no deep sense of shared values or obvious similarity of interests, only opposition to a common enemy.
"A coalition," as Herbert Feis has remarked, "is heir to the sup-
pressed desires and maimed feelings of each of its members." Wartime needs and postwar aims often strained the uneasy alliance.
In the early years when Russia was bearing the major burden of the
Nazi onslaught, her allies postponed for two years a promised second front which would have diverted German armies. In December,
1941, when Stalin requested recognition of 1941 Russian borders as
they had been before the German attack (including the recently annexed Baltic states), the British were willing to agree, but Roosevelt rebuffed the proposals and aroused Soviet fears that her security needs would not be recognized and that her allies might
later resume their anti-Bolshevik policies. So distrustful were
the Allies that both camps feared the making of a separate peace
with Germany, and Stalin's suspicions erupted into bitter accusations in March 1945, when he discovered (and Roosevelt denied)
that British and American agents were participating in secret negotiations with the Germans. In anger Stalin decided not to send
Vyacheslav Molotov, the Foreign Minister, to San Francisco for the
April meeting on the founding of the United Nations Organization.
So suspicious were the Americans and British that they would
not inform the Soviet Union that they were working on an atomic
bomb. Some American leaders even hoped to use it in postwar negotiations with the Russians. In wartime, American opposition to
communism had not disappeared, and many of Roosevelt's advisers
were fearful of Soviet intentions in Eastern Europe. In turn,
Soviet leaders, recalling the prewar hostility of the Western
democracies, feared a renewed attempt to establish a *cordon*

sanitaire and resolved to establish a security zone in Eastern
Europe.

Though Roosevelt's own strategy often seems ambiguous, his
general tactics are clear: they were devised to avoid conflict.
He operated often as a mediator between the British and Russians,
and delayed many decisions that might have disrupted the wartime
alliance. He may have been resting his hopes with the United Nations or on the exercise of America's postwar strength, or he may
simply have been placing his faith in the future. Whatever future
tactics he might have been planning, he concluded that America's
welfare rested upon international peace, expanded trade, and open
markets:

> . . . it is our hope, not only in the interest of our
> own prosperity, but in the interest of the prosperity
> of the world, that trade and commerce and access to ma-
> terials and markets may be freer after this war than
> ever before in the history of the world. . . . Only
> through a dynamic and soundly expanding world economy
> can the living standards of individual nations be ad-
> vanced to levels which will permit a full realization
> of our hopes for the future.

His efforts on behalf of the postwar world generally reflected
this understanding.

During the war Roosevelt wavered uneasily between emphasizing
the postwar role of the great powers and minimizing their role and
seeking to extend the principles of the Atlantic Charter. Though
he often spoke of the need for an open postwar world, and he was
reluctant to accept spheres of influence (beyond the Western hemisphere, where American influence was pre-eminent), his policies
gradually acknowledged the pre-eminence of the great powers and
yielded slowly to their demands. By late 1943 Roosevelt confided
to Archbishop Francis Spellman (according to Spellman's notes)
that "the world will be divided into spheres of influence: China
gets the Far East; the U.S. the Pacific; Britain and Russia,
Europe and Africa." The United States, he thought, would have
little postwar influence on the continent, and Russia would probably "predominate in Europe," making Austria, Hungary, and Croatia
"a sort of Russian protectorate." He acknowledged "that the European countries will have to undergo tremendous changes in order to
adapt to Russia; but he hopes that in ten or twenty years the European influence would bring the Russians to become less barbarous."

In 1944 Roosevelt recognized the establishment of zones of
influence in Europe. The Italian armistice of the year before had
set the pattern for other wartime agreements on the control of

affairs of liberated and defeated European nations. When Stalin requested the creation of a three-power Allied commission to deal with the problems of "countries falling away from Germany," Roosevelt and Churchill first rebuffed the Russian leader and then agreed to a joint commission for Italy which would be limited to information gathering. By excluding Russia from sharing in decision-making in Italy, the United States and Great Britain, later concluded William McNeill, "prepared the way for their own exclusion from any but a marginal share in the affairs of Eastern Europe."

When Roosevelt refused to participate in an Anglo-American invasion of southeastern Europe (which seemed to be the only way of restricting Russian influence in that area), Churchill sought other ways of dealing with Russian power and of protecting British interests in Greece. In May 1944 he proposed to Stalin that they recognize Greece as a British "zone of influence" and Rumania as a Russian zone; but Stalin insisted upon seeking Roosevelt's approval and refused the offer upon learning that the United States would not warmly endorse the terms. When the Soviets liberated Rumania in September they secured temporarily the advantages that Churchill had offered. They simply followed the British-American example in Italy, retained all effective power, and announced they were "acting in the interests of all the United Nations." From the Soviet Union, W. Averell Harriman, the American ambassador, cabled, "The Russians believe, I think, that we lived up to a tacit understanding that Rumania was an area of predominant Soviet interest in which we should not interfere. . . . The terms of the armistice give the Soviet command unlimited control of Rumania's economic life" and effective control over political organization.

With Russian armies sweeping through the Balkans and soon in a position to impose similar terms on Hungary and Bulgaria, Churchill renewed his efforts. "Winston," wrote an associate, "never talks of Hitler these days; he is always harping on the dangers of Communism. He dreams of the Red Army spreading like a cancer from one country to another. It has become an obsession, and he seems to think of little else." In October Churchill journeyed to Moscow to reach an agreement with Stalin. "Let us settle our affairs in the Balkans," Churchill told him. "Your armies are in Rumania and Bulgaria. We have interests, missions and agents there. Don't let us get at cross-purposes in small ways." Great Britain received "90 per cent influence" in Greece, and Russia "90 per cent influence" in Rumania, "80 per cent" in Bulgaria and Hungary, and "50 per cent" in Yugoslavia.

In the cases of Hungary and Bulgaria the terms were soon sanctioned by armistice agreements (approved by the United States) which left effective power with the Soviets. "The Russians took it for granted," Cordell Hull, then Secretary of State, wrote

later, "that . . . Britain and the United States had assigned them
a certain portion of the Balkans, including Rumania and Bulgaria,
as their spheres of influence." In December Stalin even confirmed
the agreement at a considerable price: he permitted British
troops to put down a rebellion in Greece. "Stalin," wrote Churchill later, "adhered strictly and faithfully to our agreement . . .
and during all the long weeks of fighting the communists in the
streets of Athens, not one word of reproach came from *Pravda* or
Izvestia."

At Yalta in February 1945 Roosevelt did not seem to challenge
Soviet dominance in east-central Europe, which had been established by the Churchill-Stalin agreement and confirmed by the armi-
stices and by British action in Greece. What Roosevelt did seek
and gain at Yalta was a weak "Declaration on Liberated Europe"—
that the powers would consult "where in their judgment conditions
require" assistance to maintain peace or to establish democratic
governments. By requiring unanimity the declaration allowed any
one power to veto any proposal that seemed to threaten that
power's interests. In effect, then, the declaration, despite its
statements about democratic governments, did not alter the situation in Eastern Europe. The operative phrases simply affirmed the
principle that the three powers had already established: they
could consult together when all agreed, and they could act together when all agreed. At Yalta the broadly phrased statement provoked little discussion—only a few pages in the official proceedings. Presumably the Russians did not consider it a repudiation
of spheres of influence, only as rhetoric that Roosevelt wanted
for home consumption. Despite later official American suggestions,
the Yalta agreement was not a product of Roosevelt's misunderstanding of the Soviet meaning of "democracy" and "free elections."
Rather, it ratified earlier agreements, and the State Department
probably understood this.

While accepting the inevitable and acknowledging Russian influence in these areas, Roosevelt had not been tractable on the
major issue confronting the three powers: the treatment of postwar Germany. All three leaders realized that the decisions on
Germany would shape the future relations of Europe. A dismembered
or permanently weakened Germany would leave Russia without challenge on the continent and would ease her fears of future invasion.
As Anthony Eden, the British Foreign Minister explained, "Russia
was determined on one thing above all others, that Germany would
not again disturb the peace of Europe. . . . Stalin was determined
to smash Germany so that it would never again be able to make war."
A strong Germany, on the other hand, could be a partial counterweight to Russia and help restore the European balance of power
on which Britain had traditionally depended for protection.
Otherwise, as Henry Morgenthau once explained in summarizing

Churchill's fears, there would be nothing between "the white snows of Russia and the white cliffs of Dover."

The Allied policy on Germany had been in flux for almost two years. At Teheran in 1943 the Allies had agreed in principle (despite Churchill's reluctance) that Germany should be dismembered, and in 1944 Roosevelt and a reluctant Churchill, much to the distress of Foreign Minister Anthony Eden, had agreed on a loosely phrased version of the Morgenthau Plan for the dismemberment and pastoralization of Germany. Not only would the plan have eliminated German military-industrial potential and thereby allayed Russian fears, but by stripping Germany it would also have provided the resources for Russian economic reconstruction. Churchill, despite his fear of Russia and his desire for Germany as a counterweight on the continent, had temporarily agreed to the plan because it seemed to be a prerequisite for increased American economic aid and promised to eliminate German industry as a postwar rival for the trade that the debt-ridden British economy would need. Many in the State and War Departments charged that the plan was economic madness, that it would leave not only Germany but also much of war-torn Western Europe (which would need postwar German production) without the means for economic reconstruction. (Secretary of the Treasury Morgenthau concluded after discussion with many officials that they wanted a strong Germany as a "bulwark against Bolshevism.") Yielding to the pleas of the War and State Departments, Roosevelt decided upon a plan for a stronger postwar Germany, and Churchill, under pressure from advisers, also backed away from his earlier endorsement of the Morgenthau Plan and again acted upon his fears of an unopposed Russia on the continent. At Yalta, he resisted any agreement on the dismemberment of Germany. Stalin, faced with Anglo-American solidarity on this issue, acceded. The final communiqué patched over this fundamental dispute by announcing that the three powers had pledged to "take such steps including the complete disarmament, demilitarization, and dismemberment of Germany as they deem requisite for future peace and security." The strategy of postponement had triumphed. Unable to reach a substantive agreement, the Big Three agreed to submit these problems (and the related, vital issues of reparations and boundaries) to three-power commissions.

Though Yalta has come to represent the triumph of the strategy of postponement, at the time it symbolized Allied accord. Stalin accepted a limitation of the veto power on certain quasi-judicial issues in the U.N. Security Council; Roosevelt conceded to Russia the return of the Kurile Islands, which stretched between Japan and Siberia, and special rights in Dairen and Port . Arthur in Manchuria; Stalin promised to enter the Pacific war within three months of the end of the European conflict. "Stalin," as William McNeill explained, "had conceded something to the British in Yugoslavia; and Churchill had yielded a good deal in Poland."

II

Roosevelt's successor was less sympathetic to Russian aspirations and more responsive to those of Roosevelt's advisers, like
Admiral William Leahy, Chief of Staff to the Commander in Chief;
Harriman; James Forrestal, Secretary of the Navy; and James F.
Byrnes, Truman's choice for Secretary of State, who had urged that
he resist Soviet efforts in Eastern Europe. As an earlier self-
proclaimed foe of Russian communism, Truman mistrusted Russia.
("If we see that Germany is winning the war," advised Senator Truman after the German attack upon Russia in 1941, "we ought to help
Russia, and if Russia is winning we ought to help Germany and in
that way kill as many as possible.") Upon entering the White
House, he did not seek to follow Roosevelt's tactics of adjustment
and accommodation. Only eleven days in the presidency and virtually on the eve of the United Nations conference, Truman moved to a
showdown with Russia on the issue of Poland.

Poland became the testing ground for American foreign policy,
as Truman later said, "a symbol of the future development of our
international relations." At Yalta the three powers had agreed
that the Soviet-sponsored Lublin Committee (the temporary Polish
government) should be "reorganized on a broader democratic basis
with the inclusion of democratic leaders from Poland itself and
from Poland abroad." The general terms were broad: there was no
specific formula for the distribution of power in the reorganized
government, and the procedures required consultation and presumably unanimity from the representatives of the three powers. The
agreement, remarked Admiral Leahy, was "so elastic that the Russians can stretch it all the way from Yalta to Washington without
ever technically breaking it." ("I know, Bill—I know it. But
it's the best I can do for Poland at this time," Roosevelt
replied.)

For almost two months after Yalta the great powers haggled
over Poland. The Lublin Committee objected to the Polish candidates proposed by the United States and Great Britain for consultation because these Poles had criticized the Yalta accord and
refused to accept the Soviet annexation of Polish territory (moving the eastern boundary to the Curzon Line). In early April
Stalin had offered a compromise—that about 80 per cent of the
cabinet posts in the new government should be held by members of
the Lublin Committee, and that he would urge the committee to
accept the leading Western candidates if they would endorse the
Yalta agreement (including the Curzon Line). By proposing a
specific distribution of power, Stalin cut to the core of the
issue that had disrupted negotiations for nearly three months,
and sought to guarantee the victory he probably expected in Poland. Roosevelt died before replying, and it is not clear whether
he would have accepted this 4 to 1 representation; but he had

acknowledged that he was prepared to place "somewhat more emphasis on the Lublin Poles."

Now Truman was asked to acknowledge Soviet concern about countries on her borders and to assure her influence in many of these countries by granting her friendly (and probably non-democratic) governments, and even by letting her squelch anti-communist democrats in countries like Poland. To the President and his advisers the issue was (as Truman later expressed Harriman's argument) "the extension of Soviet control over neighboring states by independent action; we were faced with a barbarian invasion of Europe." The fear was not that the Soviets were about to threaten all of Europe but that they had designs on Eastern Europe, and that these designs conflicted with traditional American values of self-determination, democracy, and open markets.

Rushing back to Washington after Roosevelt's death, Harriman found most of FDR's advisers (now Truman's) sympathetic to a tougher approach. At a special White House meeting Harriman outlined what he thought were the Soviet Union's two policies—cooperation with the United States and Great Britain, and the creation of a unilateral security ring through domination of its border states. These policies, he contended, did not seem contradictory to Russian leaders, for "certain elements around Stalin" misinterpreted America's generosity and desire to cooperate as an indication of softness and concluded "that the Soviet Government could do anything that it wished without having any trouble with the United States." Before Roosevelt's death, Harriman had cabled:

> It may be difficult . . . to believe, but it still may be true that Stalin and Molotov considered at Yalta that by our willingness to accept a general wording of the declaration on Poland and liberated Europe, by our recognition of the need of the Red Army for security behind its lines, and of the predominant interest of Russia in Poland as a friendly neighbor and as a corridor to Germany, we understood and were ready to accept Soviet policies already known to us.

Harriman wanted the American government to select a few test cases and make the Russians realize they could not continue their present policies. Such tactics, he advised, would place Russian-American relations on a more realistic basis and compel the Soviet Union to adhere to the American interpretation of the issues in dispute. Because the Soviet government "needed our [economic assistance] . . . in their reconstruction," and because Stalin did not wish to break with the United States, Harriman thought Truman "could stand firm on important issues without running serious

risks." As early as January 1944 Harriman had emphasized that
"the Soviet Government places the utmost importance on our cooperation" in providing economic assistance, and he had concluded:
"it is a factor which should be integrated into the fabric of our
overall relations." In early April Harriman had proposed that
unless the United States were prepared "to live in a world dominated largely by Soviet influence, we must use our economic power
to assist those countries that are naturally friendly to our concepts." In turn, he had recommended "tying our economic assistance directly into our political problems with the Soviet Union."
     General George Marshall, the Army Chief of Staff, and Sec-
retary of War Henry Stimson, however, recommended caution. Stimson observed "that the Russians perhaps were being more realistic
than we were in regard to their own security," and he feared "that
we would find ourselves breaking our relations with Russia on the
most important and difficult question which we and Russia have got-
ten between us." Leahy, though supporting a firm policy, admitted
that the Yalta agreement "was susceptible to two interpretations."
Secretary of State Edward Stettinius read aloud the Yalta decision
and concluded "that this was susceptible of only one interpretation."
     Having heard his advisers' arguments, Truman resolved to
force the Polish question: to impose his interpretation of the
Yalta agreement even if it destroyed the United Nations. He later
explained that this was the test of Russian cooperation. If Stalin would not abide by his agreements, the U.N. was doomed, and,
anyway, there would not be enough enthusiasm among the American
electorate to let the United States join the world body. "Our
agreements with the Soviet Union so far . . . [have] been a one-
way street." That could not continue, Truman told his advisers.
"If the Russians did not wish to join us, they could go to hell."
("FDR's appeasement of Russia is over," joyously wrote Senator
Arthur Vandenberg, the Republican leader on foreign policy.) Continuing in this spirit at a private conference with Molotov, the
new President warned that economic aid would depend upon Russian
behavior in fulfilling the Yalta agreement. Brushing aside the
diplomat's contention that the Anglo-American interpretation of
the Yalta agreement was wrong, the President accused the Russians
of breaking agreements and scolded the Russian Foreign Minister.
When Molotov replied, "I have never been talked to like that in my
life," Truman warned him, "Carry out your agreement and you won't
get talked to like that."
     At the United Nations conference in San Francisco, when An-
thony Eden, the British Foreign Minister, saw a copy of Truman's
"blunt message" about Poland to Stalin, "he could scarcely believe
his eyes . . . and cheered loudly," reported Vandenberg. But the
policy of firmness was not immediately successful. American-
Russian relations were further strained by the disputes at the

meeting to create the U.N.—over the veto, the admission of fascist Argentina, and the persistent question of Poland. Despite
Soviet objections and Roosevelt's promise at Yalta to exclude Argentina from the U.N., the United States supported the Latin
American state's candidacy for membership. In committee Molotov,
whom Stalin had sent to establish good will with the new President,
tried to block the admission of Argentina until the Lublin Poles
were also admitted, but his proposed bargain was overwhelmingly
defeated. Later in the plenary session, when only three nations
voted with Russia, the Soviets found additional evidence for their
fears of an American bloc directed against their interests. The
Truman administration's action also gave the Soviets more reason
to doubt America's explanations that her interests in Poland were
inspired simply by a desire to guarantee representative, democratic governments. Moreover, because of the American bloc and
Soviet fears that the U.N. (like the League of Nations) might be
used against her, Molotov was at first unwilling to accede to the
demands of the United States and the smaller nations who wished to
exclude procedural questions before the Security Council from the
great power veto.

The Soviets were further embittered when the United States
abruptly curtailed lend-lease six days after V-E Day. Though Truman later explained this termination as simply a "mistake," as
policy-making by subordinates, his recollection was incomplete and
wrong. Leo Crowley, the director of lend-lease, and Joseph Grew,
the Under Secretary of State, the two subordinates most closely
involved, had repeatedly warned the President of the likely impact
of such action on relations with Russia, and the evidence suggests
that the government, as Harriman had counseled, was seeking to use
economic power to achieve diplomatic means. Termination of lend-
lease, Truman later wrote, "should have been done on a gradual
basis which would not have made it appear as if somebody had been
deliberately snubbed." Yet, despite this later judgment, Truman
had four days after signing the order in which to modify it before
it was to be implemented and announced, and the lend-lease administrator (in the words of Grew) had made "sure that the President
understands the situation." The administrator knew "that we would
be having difficulty with the Russians and did not want them to be
running all over town for help." After discussing the decision
with Truman, Grew, presumably acting with the President's approval,
had even contrived to guarantee that curtailment would be a dramatic shock. When the Soviet chargé d'affaires had telephoned
Grew the day before the secret order was to become effective, the
Under Secretary had falsely denied that lend-lease to Russia was
being halted. Harriman, according to Grew's report to the Secretary of State, "said that we would be getting 'a good tough slash-
back' from the Russians but that we would have to face it."

Presumably to patch the alliance, Truman dispatched to Moscow Harry Hopkins, Roosevelt's former adviser and a staunch advocate of Soviet-American friendship. Hopkins denied that Truman's action was an American effort to demonstrate economic power and coerce Russia ("pressure on the Russians to soften them up," as Stalin charged). Instead he emphasized that "Poland had become a symbol of our ability to work out our problems with the Soviet Union." Stalin acknowledged "the right of the United States as a world power to participate in the Polish question," but he stressed the importance of Poland to Soviet security. Within twenty-five years the "Germans had twice invaded Russia via Poland," he emphasized. "All the Soviet Union wanted was that Poland should not be in a position to open the gates to Germany," and that required a government friendly to Russia. There was "no intention," he promised, "to interfere in Poland's internal affairs" or to Sovietize Poland.

Through the Hopkins mission, Truman and Stalin reached a compromise: 70 per cent of the new Polish government (fourteen of twenty ministers) should be drawn from the Lublin Committee. At the time there was reason to believe that such heavy communist influence would not lead to Soviet control. Stalin had reaffirmed the pledge of free elections in Poland, and Stanislaw Mikolajczyk, former Prime Minister of the exile government in London and Deputy Prime Minister in the new coalition government, was optimistic. He hoped (in Harriman's words) that

> a reasonable degree of freedom and independence can be preserved now and that in time after conditions in Europe can become more stable and [as] Russia turns her attention to her internal development, controls will be relaxed and Poland will be able to gain for herself her independence of life as a nation even though he freely accepts that Poland's security and foreign policy must follow the lead of Moscow.

Truman compromised and soon recognized the new Polish government, but he did not lose his hopes of rolling back the Soviets from their spheres of influence in Eastern Europe. Basing most of his case on the Yalta "Declaration on Liberated Europe" (for which he relied on State Department interpretations), Truman hoped to force Russia to permit representative governments in its zones, and expected that free elections would diminish, perhaps ever remove, Soviet authority. Refusing to extend diplomatic recognition to Rumania and Bulgaria, he emphasized that these governments were "neither representative of nor responsive to the will of the people."

"The opportunities for the democratic elements in Rumania and
Bulgaria are not less than, say, in Italy, with which the Governments of the United States and the Soviet Union have already resumed diplomatic relations," replied Stalin, who was willing to ex-
aggerate to emphasize his case. The Russians were demanding a
quid pro quo, and they would not yield. At Potsdam, in late July,
when Truman demanded "immediate reorganization" of the governments
of Hungary and Bulgaria to "include representatives of all significant democratic elements" and three-power assistance in "holding
. . . free and unfettered elections," Stalin pointed to Greece,
again to remind Truman of the earlier agreements. The Russians
were "not meddling in Greek affairs," he noted, adding that the
Bulgarian and Rumanian governments were fulfilling the armistice
agreements while in Greece "terrorism rages . . . against democratic elements." (One member of the American delegation later
claimed that Stalin at one point made his position clear, stating
that "any freely elected government [in Eastern Europe] would be
anti-Soviet and that we cannot permit.") In effect, Stalin demanded that the United States abide by his construction of earlier
agreements, and that Truman acknowledge what Roosevelt had accepted as the terms of the sphere-of-influence agreements—that democratic forms and anti-communist democrats of Eastern Europe be
abandoned to the larger cause of Russian-American concord.

Though the Allies at Potsdam were not able to settle the
dispute over influence in Eastern Europe, they did reach a limited
agreement on other European issues. In a "package" deal the Soviets accepted Italy in the U.N. after a peace treaty could be ar-
ranged; the United States and Great Britain agreed to set the temporary western border of Poland at the Oder-Neisse line; and the
Soviets settled for far less in reparations than they had expected.
The decisions on Germany were the important settlements, and the
provision on reparations, when linked with American avoidance of
offering Russia economic aid, left Russia without the assistance
she needed for the pressing task of economic reconstruction.

Russia had long been seeking substantial economic aid, and
the American failure to offer it seemed to be part of a general
strategy. Earlier Harriman had advised "that the development of
friendly relations [with Russia] would depend upon a generous
credit," and recommended

that the question of the credit should be tied into our
overall diplomatic relations with the Soviet Union and
at the appropriate time the Russians should be given to
understand that our willingness to cooperate wholeheartedly with them in their vast reconstruction problem will
depend upon their behavior in international matters.

In January 1945 Roosevelt had decided not to discuss at Yalta the
$6 billion credit to the Soviet Union, explaining privately, "I
think it's very important that we hold this back and don't give
them any promises until we get what we want." (Secretary Morgenthau, in vigorous disagreement, believed that both the President
and Secretary of State Stettinius were wrong, and "that if they
wanted to get the Russians to do something they should . . . do
it nice. . . . Don't drive such a hard bargain that when you come
through it does not taste good.") In future months American officials continued to delay, presumably using the prospect of a
loan for political leverage. Shortly before Potsdam, the administration had secured congressional approval for a $1 billion
loan fund which could have been used to assist Russia, but the
issue of "credits to the Soviet Union" apparently was never even
discussed.

Shunting aside the loan, the United States also retreated
from Roosevelt's implied agreement at Yalta that reparations
would be about $20 billion (half of which the Soviets would re-
ceive); Truman's new Secretary of State, James F. Byrnes, pointed
out that the figures were simply the "basis" for discussion. (He
was technically correct, but obviously Roosevelt had intended it
as a general promise and Stalin had so understood it. Had it not
been so intended, why had Churchill refused to endorse this section of the Yalta agreement?) Because Byrnes was unwilling to
yield, the final agreement on reparations was similar to the
terms that would have prevailed if there had been no agreement:
the Soviet Union would fill her claims largely by removals from
her own zone. That was the substance of the Potsdam agreement.
The Russians also surrendered any hopes of participating in control of the heavily industrialized Ruhr, and confirmed the earlier
retreat from the policy of dismemberment of Germany. They settled for an agreement that they could trade food and raw materials
from their zone for 15 per cent of such industrial capital equipment from the Western Zones "as is unnecessary for the German
peace economy," and that the allies would transfer from the Western Zones "10 per cent of such industrial capital equipment as is
unnecessary for the German peace economy"—but the agreement left
undefined what was necessary for the economy.

Potsdam, like Yalta, left many of the great questions unre-
solved. "One fact that stands out more clearly than others is
that nothing is ever settled," wrote Lord Alanbrooke, Chief of
the British Staff, in his diary. As he observed, neither the
United States nor Russia had yielded significantly. Russia had
refused to move from the areas that her armies occupied, and the
United States had been vigorous in her efforts, but without offering economic assistance to gain concessions. Though the atomic
bomb may not have greatly influenced Truman's actions in the
months before Potsdam, the bomb certainly influenced his behavior

at Potsdam. When he arrived he still wanted (and expected) Russian intervention in the Japanese war. During the conference he learned about the successful test at Alamogordo. With Russian intervention no longer necessary, Truman's position hardened noticeably. As sole possessor of the bomb, he had good reason to expect easier future dealings with Stalin. For months Stimson had been counseling that the bomb would be the "master card," and Truman, acting on Stimson's advice, even delayed the Potsdam Conference until a time when he would know about the bomb. On the eve of the conference the President had confided to an adviser, "If it explodes, as I think it will, I'll certainly have a hammer on those boys [the Russians]."

III

At Potsdam President Truman was "delighted" when Stimson brought him the news about the bomb on July 16. Upon learning more about the results of the test, Truman (according to Stimson) said "it gave him an entirely new feeling of confidence and he thanked me for having come to the conference and being present to help him in this way." The President's enthusiasm and new sense of power were soon apparent in his meetings with the other heads of state, for as Churchill notes (in Stimson's words), "Truman was evidently much fortified by something that had happened and . . . he stood up to the Russians in a most emphatic and decisive manner." After reading the full report on the Alamogordo explosion, Churchill said, "Now I know what happened to Truman yesterday. I couldn't understand it. When he got to the meeting after having read this report he was a changed man. He told the Russians just where they got off and generally bossed the whole meeting."

"From the moment [when we learned of the successful test] our outlook on the future was transformed," Churchill explained later. Forced earlier to concede parts of Eastern Europe to the Russians because Britain did not have the power to resist Soviet wishes and the United States had seemed to lack the desire, Churchill immediately savored the new possibilities. The Prime Minister (Lord Alanbrooke wrote in his diary about Churchill's enthusiasm)

was completely carried away . . . we now had something in our hands which would redress the balance with the Russians. The secret of this explosive and the power to use it would completely alter the diplomatic equilibrium. . . . Now we had a new value which redressed our position (pushing out his chin and scowling); now we could say, "If you insist on doing this or that well. . . ." And then where were the Russians!

Stimson and Byrnes had long understood that the bomb could influence future relations with Russia, and, after the successful test, they knew that Russian entry was no longer necessary to end the Japanese war. Upon Truman's direction, Stimson conferred at Potsdam with General Marshall and reported to the President that Marshall no longer saw a need for Russian intervention. "It is quite clear," cabled Churchill from Potsdam, "that the United States do not at the present time desire Russian participation in the war against Japan."

"The new explosive alone was sufficient to settle matters," Churchill reported. The bomb had displaced the Russians in the calculations of American policy-makers. The combat use of the bomb, then, was not viewed as the only way to end the Far Eastern war promptly. In July there was ample evidence that there were other possible strategies—a noncombat demonstration, a warning, a blockade. Yet, before authorizing the use of the bomb at Hiroshima, Truman did not try *any* of the possible strategies, including the three most likely: guaranteeing the position of the Japanese Emperor (and hence making surrender conditional), seeking a Russian declaration of war (or announcement of intent), or waiting for Russian entry into the war.

As an invasion of the Japanese mainland was not scheduled until about November 1, and as Truman knew that the Japanese were sending out "peace feelers" and that the main obstacle to peace seemed to be the requirement of unconditional surrender (which threatened the position of the Emperor), he could wisely have revised the terms of surrender. At first Under Secretary of State Grew and then Stimson had urged Truman earlier to revise the terms in this way, and he had been sympathetic. But at Potsdam Stimson found that Truman and Byrnes had rejected his advice. As a result the proclamation issued from Potsdam by the United States, Great Britain, and China retained the demand for unconditional surrender when a guarantee of the Emperor's government might have removed the chief impediment to peace.

Nor was Truman willing to seek a Russian declaration of war (or even an announcement of intent). Even though American advisers had long believed that the *threat* of Russian entry might be sufficient to compel Japanese capitulation, Truman did not invite Stalin to sign the proclamation, which would have constituted a statement of Russian intent. There is even substantial evidence that Truman sought to delay Russian entry into the war.

Pledging to maintain the position of the Emperor, seeking a Russian declaration of war (or announcement of intent), awaiting Russian entry—each of these options, as well as others, had been proposed in the months before Hiroshima and Nagasaki. Each was available to Truman. Why did he not try one or more? No *definite* answer is possible. But it is clear that Truman was either incapable or unwilling to reexamine his earlier assumption (or decision) of using the bomb. Under the tutelage of Byrnes and Stimson, Truman had come to assume by July that the bomb should be used, and perhaps he was incapable of reconsidering this strategy because he found no compelling reason not to use the bomb. Or he may have consciously rejected the options because he wanted to use the bomb. Perhaps he was vindictive and wished to retaliate for Pearl Harbor and other atrocities. (In justifying the use of the bomb against the Japanese, he wrote a few days after Nagasaki, "The only language they seem to understand is the one we have been using to bombard them. When you have to deal with a beast you have to treat him as a beast.") Or, most likely, Truman agreed with Byrnes that using the bomb would advance other American policies: it would end the war before the Russians could gain a hold in Manchuria, it would permit the United States to exclude Russia from the occupation government of Japan, and it would make the Soviets more manageable in Eastern Europe. It would enable the United States to shape the peace according to its own standards.

At minimum, then, the use of the bomb reveals the moral insensitivity of the President—whether he used it because the moral implications did not compel a reexamination of assumptions, or because he sought retribution, or because he sought to keep Russia out of Manchuria and the occupation government of Japan, and to make her more manageable in Eastern Europe. In 1945 American foreign policy was not innocent, nor was it unconcerned about Russian power, nor did it assume that the United States lacked the power to impose its will on the Russian state, nor was it characterized by high moral purpose or consistent dedication to humanitarian principles.

IV

Both Secretary of War Stimson and Secretary of State Byrnes had foreseen the importance of the bomb to American foreign policy. To Stimson it had long promised to be the "master card" for diplomacy. After Hiroshima and Nagasaki Byrnes was eager to use the bomb as at least an "implied threat" in negotiations with Russia, and Truman seems to have agreed to a vigorous course in trying to roll back Russian influence in Eastern Europe.

Truman seemed to be rejecting Stimson's recommendations that international control of atomic energy be traded for important Russian concessions—"namely the settlement of the Polish, Rumanian, Yugoslavian, and Manchurian problems." In his report on the Potsdam Conference the day after the second bomb, the President asserted that Rumania, Bulgaria, and Hungary "are not to be spheres of influence of any one power" and at the same time proclaimed that the United States would be the "trustees" of the atomic bomb.

Following Truman's veiled threat, Byrnes continued his efforts to roll back the Soviet Union's influence. Assisted by a
similar protest by the British, who clearly recognized the power
of the bomb, he gained postponement of the Bulgarian elections,
charging that the government was not "adequately representative of
important elements . . . of democratic opinion" and that its arrangements for elections "did not insure freedom from the fear of
force or intimidation." In Hungary, Russia also acceded to similar Anglo-American demands and postponed the scheduled elections.
It is not unreasonable to conclude that the bomb had made the Russians more tractable. "The significance of Hiroshima was not lost
on the Russians," Alexander Werth, British correspondent in the Soviet Union, later reported. "It was clearly realized that this
was a New Fact in the world's power politics, that the bomb constituted a threat to Russia. . . . Everybody . . . believed that although the two [atomic] bombs had killed or maimed [the] . . .
Japanese, their real purpose was, first and foremost, to intimidate Russia."

Perhaps encouraged by his successes in Bulgaria and Hungary,
Byrnes "wished to have the implied threat of the bomb in his pock-
et during the [September] conference" of foreign ministers in
London. Stimson confided to his diary that Byrnes

> was very much against any attempt to cooperate with Rus-
> sia. His mind is full of his problems with the coming
> meeting . . . and he looks to having the presence of the
> bomb in his pocket . . . as a great weapon to get through
> the thing he has. He also told me of a number of acts of
> perfidy . . . of Stalin which they had encountered at
> Potsdam and felt in the light of those that we would not
> rely upon anything in the way of promises from them.

The London conference ended in deadlock, disbanding without
even a joint communiqué. Despite American possession of the bomb,
Molotov would not yield to American demands to reorganize the governments of Bulgaria and Rumania. In turn, he demanded for Russia
a role in the occupation government of Japan, but Byrnes rebuffed
the proposal. Unprepared for this issue, Byrnes was also unwilling or unable to understand Soviet anxieties about the security of
their frontiers, and he pressed most vigorously for the reorganization of the Rumanian government. He would not acknowledge and perhaps could not understand the dilemma of his policy: that he was
supporting free elections in areas (particularly in Rumania) where
the resulting governments would probably be hostile to the Soviet
Union, and yet he was arguing that democracy in Eastern Europe was
compatible with Soviet demands for security. Unable to accept

that Byrnes might be naive, Molotov questioned the Secretary's sincerity and charged that he wanted governments unfriendly to the Soviet Union. From this, Byrnes could only conclude later, "It seemed that the Soviet Union was determined to dominate Europe."

While the United States in the cases of these Eastern European nations chose to support traditional democratic principles and neither to acknowledge its earlier agreements on spheres of influence nor to respect Russian fears, Byrnes would not admit the similarity between Russian behavior in Rumania and British action in Greece. As part of the terms of his agreement with Churchill, Stalin had allowed the British to suppress a revolutionary force in Greece, and as a result the Greek government could not be accurately interpreted as broadly representative nor as a product of democratic procedures. Yet, as Molotov emphasized, the United States had not opposed British action in Greece or questioned the legitimacy of that government, nor was the United States making a reversal of British imperialism in Greece a condition for the large loan that Britain needed.

Some American observers, however, were aware of this double standard. In the northern Pacific and in Japan, America was to have the deciding voice, but in Eastern Europe, emphasized Walter Lippmann, "we invoke the principle that this is one world in which decisions must not be taken unilaterally." Most Americans did not see this paradox, and Byrnes probably expressed crystallizing national sentiment that autumn when he concluded that the dispute with Russia was a test of whether "we really believed in what we said about one world and our desire to build collective security, or whether we were willing to accept the Soviet preference for the simpler task of dividing the world into two spheres of influence."

Despite Byrnes's views, and although he could not secure a reorganization of the Rumanian government, communist influence was weakened in other parts of Eastern Europe. In Budapest free elections were held and the Communist party was routed; and early in November, just two days after the United States recognized Hungary, the Communists lost in the national elections there. In Bulgaria elections took place in "complete order and without disturbance," and, despite American protests, a Communist-dominated single ticket (representing most of the political parties) triumphed.

While the Soviet Union would not generally permit in Eastern Europe conditions that conformed to Western ideals, Stalin was pursuing a cautious policy and seeking accommodation with the West. He was willing to allow capitalism but was suspicious of American efforts at economic penetration which could lead to political dominance. Though by the autumn of 1945 the governments in Russia's general area of influence were subservient in foreign policy, they varied in form and in degree of independence—democracy in Czechoslovakia (the only country in this area with a democratic tradition), free elections and the overthrow of the Communist party in

Hungary, a Communist-formed coalition government in Bulgaria, a broadly based but Communist-dominated government in Poland, and a Soviet-imposed government in Rumania (the most anti-Russian of these nations). In all of these countries Communists controlled the ministries of interior (the police) and were able to suppress anti-Soviet groups, including anti-communist democrats.

Those who have attributed to Russia a policy of inexorable expansion have often neglected this immediate postwar period, or they have interpreted it simply as a necessary preliminary (a cunning strategy to allay American suspicions until the American Army demobilized and left the continent) to the consolidation and extension of power in east-central Europe. From this perspective, however, much of Stalin's behavior becomes strangely contradictory and potentially self-defeating. If he had planned to create puppets rather than an area of "friendly governments," why (as Isaac Deutscher asks) did Stalin "so stubbornly refuse to make any concessions to the Poles over their eastern frontiers?" Certainly, also, his demand for reparations from Hungary, Rumania, and Bulgaria would have been unnecessary if he had planned to take over these countries. (America's insistence upon using a loan to Russia to achieve political goals, and the nearly twenty-month delay after Russia first submitted a specific proposal for assistance, led Harriman to suggest in November that the loan policy "may have contributed to their [Russian] avaricious policies in the countries occupied or liberated by the Red Army.")

Russian sources are closed, so it is not possible to prove that Soviet intentions were conservative; nor for the same reason is it possible for those who adhere to the thesis of inexorable Soviet expansion to prove their theory. But the available evidence better supports the thesis that these years should be viewed not as a cunning preliminary to the harshness of 1947 and afterward, but as an attempt to establish a *modus vivendi* with the West and to protect "socialism in one country." This interpretation explains more adequately why the Russians delayed nearly three years before ending dissent and hardening policies in the countries behind their own military lines. It would also explain why the Communist parties in France and Italy were cooperating with the coalition governments until these parties were forced out of the coalitions in 1947. The American government had long hoped for the exclusion of these Communist parties, and in Italy, at least, American intimations of greater economic aid to a government without Communists was an effective lever. At the same time Stalin was seeking to prevent the revolution in Greece.

If the Russian policy was conservative and sought accommodation (as now seems likely), then its failure must be explained by looking beyond Russian actions. Historians must reexamine this period and reconsider American policies. Were they directed toward compromise? Can they be judged as having sought adjustment?

Or did they demand acquiescence to the American world view, thus thwarting real negotiations?

There is considerable evidence that American actions clearly changed after Roosevelt's death. Slowly abandoning the tactics of accommodation, they became even more vigorous after Hiroshima. The insistence upon rolling back Soviet influence in Eastern Europe, the reluctance to grant a loan for Russian reconstruction, the inability to reach an agreement on Germany, the maintenance of the nuclear monopoly—all of these could have contributed to the sense of Russian insecurity. The point, then, is that in 1945 and 1946 there may still have been possibilities for negotiations and settlements, for accommodations and adjustments, if the United States had been willing to recognize Soviet fears, to accept Soviet power in her areas of influence, and to ease anxieties.

V

In October 1945 President Truman delivered what Washington officials called his "getting tough with the Russians" speech. Proclaiming that American policy was "based firmly on fundamental principles of righteousness and justice," he promised that the United States "shall not give our approval to any compromise with evil." In a veiled assault on Soviet actions in Eastern Europe, he declared, "We shall refuse to recognize any government imposed on any nation by the force of any foreign power." Tacitly opposing the bilateral trading practices of Russia, he asserted as a principle of American foreign policy the doctrine of the "open door"—all nations "should have access on equal terms to the trade and the raw materials of the world." At the same time, however, Truman disregarded the fact of American power in Latin America and emphasized that the Monroe Doctrine (in expanded form) remained a cherished part of American policy there: ". . . the sovereign states of the Western Hemisphere, without interference from outside the Western Hemisphere, must work together as good neighbors in the solution of their common economic problems."

"Soviet current policy," concluded a secret report by the Deputy Director of Naval Intelligence a few months later, "is to establish a Soviet Monroe Doctrine for the area under her shadow, primarily and urgently for security, secondarily to facilitate the eventual emergence of the USSR as a power which could not be menaced by any other world combination of powers." The report did not expect the Soviets ". . . to take any action during the next five years which might develop into hostilities with Anglo-Americans," but anticipated attempts to build up intelligence and potential sabotage networks, "encouragement of Communist parties in all countries potentially to weaken antagonists, and in colonial areas to pave the way for 'anti-imperialist' disorders and revolutions

as a means of sapping the strength of . . . chief remaining European rivals, Britain and France." "Present Soviet maneuvers to
control North Iran," the report explained, were conceived to "push
. . . from their own oil . . . and closer to the enemy's oil."
There was no need to fear military expansion beyond this security
zone, suggested the report, for the Soviet Union was economically
exhausted, its population undernourished and dislocated, its industry and transportation "in an advanced state of deterioration."
Despite suggestions that Soviet policy was rather cautious, Truman
was reaching a more militant conclusion. "Unless Russia is faced
with an iron fist and strong language," asserted Truman to his Secretary of State in January, "another war is in the making. Only
one language do they understand—'how many divisions have you'
. . . I'm tired of babying the Soviets."

   During the winter months Byrnes, Senator Vandenberg, and John
Foster Dulles, a Republican adviser on foreign policy, publicly attacked Russian policies. Vandenberg warned "our Russian ally"
that the United States could not ignore "a unilateral gnawing away
at the status quo." After these attacks, Churchill, accompanied
by the President, delivered at Fulton, Missouri, a speech that announced the opening of the Cold War. "From Stettin in the Baltic
to Trieste in the Adriatic, an iron curtain has descended across
the Continent," declared the former British war leader. Condemning the establishment of "police governments" in Eastern Europe
and warning of "Communist fifth columns or . . . parties elsewhere," Churchill, with Truman's approval, called for an Anglo-
American alliance to create "conditions of freedom and democracy
as rapidly as possible in all [these] countries." The Soviet
Union, he contended, did not want war, only "the fruits of war and
the indefinite expansion of their power and doctrines." Such dangers could not be removed "by closing our eyes to them . . . nor
will they be removed by a policy of appeasement." While he said
that it was "not our duty *at this time* . . . to interfere forcibly
in the internal affairs" of Eastern European countries, Churchill
implied that intervention was advisable when Anglo-American forces
were strengthened. His message was clear: ". . . the old doctrine of the balance of power is unsound. We cannot afford . . .
to work on narrow margins, offering temptations to a trial of
strength."
   This was, as James Warburg later wrote, the early "idea of
the containment doctrine . . . [and] the first public expression
of the idea of a 'policy of liberation,'" which Dulles would
later promulgate. Truman's presence on the platform at Fulton implied that Churchill's statement had official American endorsement,
and though the President lamely denied afterward that he had known
about the contents of the speech, he had actually discussed it
with Churchill for two hours. Despite official denials and brief,
widespread popular opposition to Churchill's message (according to

public opinion polls), American policy was becoming clearly militant. It was not responding to a threat of immediate military danger; it was operating from the position of overwhelming power, and in the self-proclaimed conviction of righteousness.

Undoubtedly Truman had also agreed with the former Prime Minister when Churchill said at Fulton:

> It would . . . be wrong and imprudent to intrust the secret knowledge of experience of the atomic bomb, which the United States, Great Britain and Canada now share, to the world organization. . . . No one in any country has slept less well in their beds because this knowledge and the method and raw material to apply it are at present . . . in American hands. I do not believe that we should all have slept so soundly had the positions been reversed and some Communist or neo-Fascist state monopolized, for the time being, these dread agencies. . . . Ultimately, when the essential brotherhood of man is truly embodied and expressed in a world organization, these powers may be confided to it.

Here, in classic form, was a theme that would dominate the American dialogue on the Cold War—the assertion of the purity of Anglo-American intentions and the assumption that the opposing power was malevolent and had no justifiable interests, no justifiable fears, and should place its trust in a Pax Americana (or a Pax Anglo-Americana). Under Anglo-American power the world could be transformed, order maintained, and Anglo-American principles extended. Stalin characterized Churchill's message as, "Something in the nature of an ultimatum: 'Accept our rule voluntarily, and then all will be well; otherwise war is inevitable.'"

VI

Churchill's assurances notwithstanding, Russia had reason to fear the atomic bomb, particularly after Byrnes's efforts to use it as an "implied threat." For Byrnes the nuclear monopoly seemed to promise the possibility of creating on American terms a lasting structure of peace. Since this monopoly would last at least seven years, according to his estimates, America could achieve its objectives and presumably avoid an arms race. (A few days after Hiroshima, Byrnes instructed J. Robert Oppenheimer, the nuclear physicist, that "for the time being . . . international agreement was not practical and that he and the rest of the gang should pursue their work [on the hydrogen weapon] full force.")

Byrnes's strategy was briefly and unsuccessfully challenged
by another member of the administration, Henry Stimson. Earlier
Stimson had hoped that America's possession of the bomb could lead
to the offer of a partnership with the Russians in return for a
quid pro quo—"the settlement of the Polish, Rumanian, Yugoslavian,
and Manchurian problems," and liberalization of the Soviet regime.
Russia would have to roll back her curtain of secrecy and move toward an open society, reasoned Stimson, for "no permanently safe
international relations can be established between two such fundamentally different national systems." The bomb, he believed,
could not be shared until Russia liberalized her regime, and he
hoped that the need for international controls would pry back the
lid of secrecy. But his conversations with Harriman at Potsdam
had made Stimson pessimistic about Russia's easing her restrictions, and after the bombing of Japan, as he watched Byrnes's
strategy unfolding, he moved more strongly toward international
cooperation. On September 5 the Secretary of War met with the
President, explaining

> that both my plan and Byrnes's plan contained chances
> which I outlined and I said that I thought that in my
> method there was less danger than in his and also we
> would be on the right path towards establishment of an
> international world, while on his plan we would be on
> the wrong path in that respect and would be tending to
> revert to power politics.

Rejecting his earlier idea of using possession of the bomb
"as a direct lever" to produce "a change in Russian attitudes toward individual liberty," Stimson urged the President to invite
the Soviet Union to share the secret "upon a basis of cooperation
and trust."

> It is true [he wrote to the President] if we approach
> them now, as I would propose, we may be gambling on their
> good faith and risk their getting into production of
> bombs sooner than they would otherwise. To put the mat-
> ter concisely, I consider the problem of our satisfactory
> relations with Russia as not merely connected with but
> virtually dominated by the problem of the atomic bomb.
> Except for the problem of the control of that bomb, those
> relations, while vitally important, might not be immedi-
> ately pressing. The establishment of relations of mutual
> confidence between her and us could afford to await the
> slow process of time. But with the discovery of the bomb,

they become immediately emergent. *Those relations may
be irretrievably embittered by the way in which we approach the solution of the bomb with Russia. For if we
fail to approach them now and merely continue to negotiate with them, having this weapon rather ostentatiously
on our hip, their suspicions and their distrust of our
purposes and motives will increase.*

"The chief lesson I have learned in a long life," concluded Stimson, "is the only way you can make a man trustworthy is to trust
him; and the surest way you can make a man untrustworthy is to
distrust him and show your distrust." A week after learning that
Byrnes planned to use the bomb as an "implied threat," Stimson
warned Truman that a direct and forthright approach should be made
before using "*express or implied threats* in our peace negotiations."
     While Byrnes was at the unsuccessful London conference in mid-
September, Stimson was lining up support for his new approach.
The President seemed to approve of Stimson's memorandum. Truman
"thought that we must take Russia into our confidence," wrote Stimson in his diary. Dean Acheson, the Under Secretary of State,
also seemed "strongly on our side in the treatment of Russia,"
Stimson recorded. Robert P. Patterson, Stimson's Under Secretary
who was scheduled to replace the Secretary upon his retirement
later in the month, was convinced (in Stimson's words): "The saf-
est way is not to try to keep the secret. It evidently cannot be
kept . . . and that being so it is better to recognize it promptly
and try to get on [better] terms with the Russians."
     At a special cabinet meeting on September 21, Stimson out-
lined his proposal: "(1) that we should approach Russia at once
with an opportunity to share on proper *quid pro quo* the bomb and
(2) that this approach to Russia should be to her directly and not
through the . . . [United Nations] or a similar conference of a
number of states." He received support from Patterson, Robert Han-
negan, the Postmaster General, Henry Wallace, the Secretary of Commerce, and Acheson, who was representing the State Department in
Byrnes's absence. Explaining that he could not "conceive of a
world in which we were hoarders of military secrets from our Allies, particularly this great Ally," Acheson (reported Forrestal)
"saw no alternative except to give the full information to the Russians . . . for a *quid pro quo*."
     Forrestal, Fred Vinson, the Secretary of the Treasury, Tom
Clark, the Attorney General, and Clinton Anderson, the Secretary
of Agriculture, opposed sharing the secret. Vinson compared it to
the decision at the end of World War I to sink ships, and Anderson
emphasized that the President must retain the confidence of the nation in his ability to "handle Russia." He warned that giving up
information on atomic energy and the bomb would dangerously weaken

that confidence. Forrestal, apparently the most vigorous opponent, objected to any attempt to "buy [Russian] understanding and sympathy. We tried that once with Hitler." Concluding that "trust had to be more than a one-way street," he recommended that the United States exercise "a trusteeship over the . . . bomb on behalf of the United Nations."

Twelve days later, on October 3, Truman publicly announced his decision: the United States would seek international control of atomic energy but would not share the secret of the bomb. Byrnes, who had just returned from the London conference, resisted even this plan: he opposed the sharing of any information with the Russians. Since he believed that his diplomacy had been frustrated by Russian secrecy and suspicions, he did not see how inspection could operate. Convinced that the United States should delay until it had achieved a "decent" peace, he urged the President to stall. He realized that the United States was relying more heavily on the bomb and sharply cutting back conventional forces, and he was unwilling to risk yielding nuclear mastery.

For more than two months the American government delayed even approaching the Russians. "The insistence by the inventors of mankind's most horrible weapon on withholding the secret from their ally has produced a most evident reaction in Moscow," reported the *New York Times*. It also led to Molotov's uneasy public boasting in November that Russia too would develop the bomb. ("We will have atomic energy and many other things too.") Finally, four months after Hiroshima, at the Moscow Conference of Foreign Ministers in late December, Byrnes invited Russia to join in recommending that the United Nations establish a commission on atomic energy.

During the next five months, while the Cold War intensified, the Truman administration organized to formulate a policy. In March it released a preliminary study (the Acheson-Lilienthal report) which sought to minimize the problems of inspection by recommending the establishment of an international Atomic Development Authority (ADA), which would control all significant nuclear activities. The ADA would be established in stages, and at each stage the United States would provide the necessary information, with the specific information on the bomb withheld until the final stage.

Probably this plan would have been unacceptable to the Russians. It would have left the secret of the bomb as an American trust for at least a few years, and it would have meant Russia's relinquishing possible control of a source of great economic potential to an international authority dominated by Western powers. In its emphasis, however, the report also conflicted with the desires of many American officials. It stressed generosity and negotiations when most were emphasizing fear and suspicion. It saw no need for punishment. A violation by any nation, under the

proposed arrangements, would have been obvious and would have been
a warning to other nations, and all would have returned at that
point to big-power politics. The plan emphasized the necessity of
international control and was willing to countenance small risks
for world security when most emphasized the primacy of American security. ("We should not under any circumstances throw away our
gun until we are sure that the rest of the world can't arm against
us," asserted Truman.)

The final American plan was formulated and presented by Bernard Baruch, whom Truman had appointed as American representative
to the U.N. Atomic Energy Commission. It emphasized "sanctions"
and "condign punishments," and called for the elimination of the
Security Council veto on matters of atomic energy. The issue of
the veto was unnecessary; if any nation violated the treaty after
the sharing of atomic energy, what action could be vetoed? In
turn, until the nations reached the last stages of the plan, a violation, whatever the situation in the U.N., would lead to the withdrawal of other nations from the plan. Also, rather than following Stimson's advice and first approaching the Soviets privately
on control of atomic energy, Baruch insisted upon negotiations in
the public forum where positions could easily harden. Lacking the
flexibility of the earlier plan but relying upon similar stages,
the Baruch plan guaranteed the United States a nuclear monopoly
for some years. Thus it left the United States with the option of
using the bomb for leverage or even blackmail. While Byrnes and
Truman may no longer have wanted to use the bomb as an "implied
threat," its value was clear to the Joint Chiefs of Staff who had
so counseled Baruch. The atomic bomb, "because of its decisive
power is now an essential part of our military strength," explained General Carl Spaatz, the Air Force Chief of Staff. "Our
monopoly of the bomb, even though it is transitory, may well prove
to be a critical factor in our efforts to achieve [peace]." Separately the military chiefs had outlined the strategy which the
Baruch plan followed: "We should exploit [the nuclear monopoly]
to assist in the early establishment of a satisfying peace. . . .
It will be desirable for international agreements concerning the
atomic bomb to follow the European peace treaties and definitely
to precede the time when other countries could have atomic bombs."

Though the Western world generally viewed the plan as mag-
nanimous and interpreted Russia's objections as further evidence
of her refusal to negotiate sincerely, the Soviet criticisms were
actually quite reasonable. The Baruch plan in its early stages
did endanger Soviet security. Russia would have had to allow investigations of natural resources and mapping of the interior—
thus surrendering a principal military advantage. The Baruch plan,
charged Molotov, "proceeds from the desire to secure for the United States the monopolistic possession of the bomb." (Vandenberg
had reportedly told Molotov privately, "We have the atomic bomb

and we are not going to give it up. We are not going to compromise or trade with you. We are not going to give up our immortal
souls.") American leaders, as the Soviets understood, were demanding absolute security for their own nation and refusing to trust
Russia at the same time that they were demanding that the Soviets
trust the United States and risk the possibility of having the
American nuclear monopoly frozen.

The Russian plan, on the other hand, was clearly unacceptable
to American leaders. It called for nuclear disarmament and the
sharing of secrets first while delaying the establishment of controls. In effect it asked the United States to surrender its nuclear advantage and promised that the nations could thereafter
wrestle with the problems of controls. For the Truman administration the Russian plan was further evidence of Soviet insincerity.
American leaders could not understand objections to the suspension
of the veto, nor, perhaps why the Soviets feared a plan that could
guarantee the American monopoly. Yet Baruch had been explicitly
counseled earlier on the advantages of the monopoly, Byrnes had
tried to exploit the monopoly, and presumably Truman had understood it. Perhaps because these men so thoroughly believed that
their intentions were honorable, that their aim was to establish a
just and lasting peace, and that the United States would never use
the bomb first, they could not grant the validity of Soviet objections.

VII

As the great powers moved toward a stalemate on atomic energy,
the dispute over Germany contributed to the growing mistrust. At
the root of many of the difficulties were the French. Though not
a signatory to the Potsdam declaration, they had a zone in Germany
and were frustrating efforts at cooperation. They feared a revived Germany, preferred to weaken their enemy of the last three
wars, and hoped also to profit at her expense. Seeking to annex
territory west of the Rhine, they also wanted to participate in
control of the Ruhr and to dismember Germany. When the French
were blocked in the four-power council, they vetoed proposals for
interzonal trade and economic unification. The other Western powers tolerated these obstructions, but the Russians believed the
actions were American-inspired. "After six months of French ob-
struction," a high Russian official told James Warburg in the summer of 1946, "we began to suspect that this was a put-up-job—that
you did not like the bargain you had made at Potsdam and that you
are letting the French get you out of it."

"Our first break with Soviet policy in Germany came over
reparations," later wrote Lieutenant General Lucius Clay, Deputy
Military Governor of the American zone. With the German economy

in disorder and the United States and Britain contributing food to
their zones while the Soviet Union made its zone live on its own
resources and pay reparations, Clay in May terminated reparations
deliveries to the Russians from the American zone. "This situation could not be permitted to continue as it represented indirect
payment for deliveries to the Soviet Union." This, Clay wrongly
contended, violated the Potsdam agreement by withdrawing reparations from a deficient economy. (Despite the provision in the
Potsdam protocol that Germany would be treated as "one economic
unit," the poorly worded, rather muddled agreement also provided
that the Russians should take reparations from their own zone and
that these reparations were not contingent upon the import-export
balance of the Western zones. In arguing for the plan adopted at
Potsdam, Byrnes had explained that the Russians "would have no
interest in exports and imports from our zone.")

Lashing out at the United States after Clay's decision, the
Russians charged that the Potsdam agreement had been violated.
And Russian policy toward Germany soon changed. On July 10, the
day after Molotov attacked the Western zonal authorities for failing to destroy fascism and its economic base, the cartels and
landed estates, he reversed his tactics and made a bid for German
support. Implying that the Morgenthau plan still shaped Western
policy, he urged the development of peaceful basic industries in a
politically unified Germany. The sudden emphasis on greater industrialization followed abruptly upon Soviet demands for less industrialization. Perhaps the reversal was simply a cynical response to fears of continuing Western violations. Whatever its
inspiration, the speech seemed to be an attempt to kindle antagonism against the West.

Byrnes promptly countered with a proposal for economic (but
not political) unification, which the Russians could not accept
without halting reparations. When France and Russia refused to
participate, the British and Americans moved to create a bizonal
economy. Because of the failure to establish a unified economy,
explained Byrnes in his famous Stuttgart speech of September, the
United States no longer felt bound by the earlier agreement to
maintain a low level of industry. He emphasized that a prosperous
Germany was essential to European recovery. In addition, he
called into question the temporary Neisse River boundary with Poland and implied that the United States would support a return of
the eastern territory to Germany. By affirming that the United
States would stay in Germany "as long as there is an occupation
army," he declared in effect that the country would not be abandoned to Russia. The government of Germany, he promised, would be
returned to the people so that there could be a "peaceful, democratic" nation which would remain free and independent. "It is
not in the interest of the German people or in the interest of
world peace that Germany should become a pawn or a partner in a

military struggle for power between the East and West," concluded
the Secretary. Yet, as the Potsdam agreement crumbled and the
United States and Russia quarreled, Germany would remain a key issue in the Cold War struggle.

VIII

How do American actions since V-J Day appear to other
nations? [asked Secretary of Commerce Henry Wallace in
a private letter to the President in mid-July 1946].
I mean by actions the concrete things like $13 billion
for the War and Navy departments, the Bikini tests of
the atomic bomb [begun just before Baruch presented his
proposal at the U.N.] and continued production of bombs,
the plan to arm Latin America with our weapons, production of B-29s and planned production of B-36s, and the
effort to secure air bases spread over half the globe
from which the other half of the globe can be bombed.
. . . it follows that to the Russians all of the
defense and security measures of the Western powers
seem to have an aggressive intent. Our actions to expand our military security system . . . appear to them
as going far beyond the requirements of defense. I
think we might feel the same if the United States were
the only capitalistic country in the world, and the
principal socialistic countries were creating a level
of armed strength far exceeding anything in their previous history. From the Russian point of view, also,
the granting of a loan to Britain and the lack of tangible results on their request to borrow for rehabilitation purposes may be regarded as another evidence of
the strengthening of an anti-Soviet bloc.
Finally, our resistance to her attempts to obtain
. . . her own security system in the form of "friendly"
neighboring states seems, from the Russian point of view,
to clinch the case. . . . Our interest in establishing
democracy in Eastern Europe, where democracy by and
large has never existed, seems to her an attempt to re-
establish the encirclement of unfriendly neighbors which
was created after the last war and which might serve as
a springboard for still another effort to destroy her.

Wallace could not reverse the course of American policy, and
Truman was not sympathetic to the letter, later claiming that Wallace had proposed "surrendering" to the Soviet Union. In September

the Secretary of Commerce openly criticized the administration's policies while Byrnes was in Paris negotiating peace treaties for the Balkan states. Calling for cooperation between the two great powers, Wallace warned against a "'get tough with Russia' policy. . . . The tougher we get the tougher the Russians will get." While recommending "an open door for trade throughout the world" as the way to promote peace and prosperity, he contended that the United States should recognize that "we have no more business in the *political* affairs of Eastern Europe than Russia has in the *political* affairs of Latin America, Western Europe, and the United States."

Perhaps Wallace was naive to think that economics and politics could be so easily separated, and clearly he did not understand that Russia, particularly after American efforts to use a loan to pry open trade, feared Western economic penetration of Eastern Europe. "In the situation which is likely to prevail in Poland and the Balkan states . . . the United States can hope to make its influence felt only if some degree of equal opportunity in trade [and] investment . . . is preserved," the State Department had advised earlier. Though trade need not lead to political dominance, the Soviets not unreasonably expressed fears of American economic power. (At Potsdam Stalin had thwarted Truman's attempts to open the Danube to free navigation and to create a multination commission for the river with American representation.) If the "'principles of equality' are applied in international life," Molotov had argued, "the smaller states will be governed by the orders, injunctions, and instructions of strong foreign trusts and monopolies." Molotov had already seen the United States withhold aid from Poland when it would not accede to American demands for the "open door," and the State Department had insisted that the Czech government in order to be eligible for a loan must accept "the United States proposals for the expansion of world trade and employment." And Molotov knew that the United States had tried to use its economic power to coerce the Soviet Union into creating an "open door" in Eastern Europe and changing her own state-regulated trade. While negotiating a loan of $3.75 billion for Great Britain, at a low interest rate and without demanding liquidation of the Empire, the United States had falsely claimed to have lost for five months the Soviet request for a loan of $1 billion. The Truman administration belatedly offered in February to consider the Soviet Union's request, then insisted upon more stringent terms than for the British loan—Russia would have to reject state-trading and bilateralism, accept multilateralism, join the American-dominated World Bank and International Monetary Fund, reveal secret information about her economy, and disclose the terms of the favorable trade treaties that she had imposed on the nations of Eastern Europe.

Though Wallace never seemed to understand specifically why these demands were unacceptable to the Soviet Union, he did not want to use American economic power to coerce the Russians. Freer trade, he believed, would advance world peace and prosperity only if nations negotiated agreements without economic blackmail. As early as March he had sufficiently distrusted the American negotiators on the loan to urge the President to appoint a group more sympathetic to the Soviet Union. Truman, by his later admission, "ignored" Wallace's request, and in July, just before Wallace's lengthy lecture, the President had foreclosed the possibility of a loan.

Still believing that Truman was an unknowing captive of Secretary Byrnes and his cohorts, Wallace sought to carry the battle on foreign policy into the public forum. But, often naive and perhaps foolishly optimistic, he could not provoke a dialogue within the administration on a policy that had long been endorsed by the President. Eight days after his speech Wallace was fired for publicly criticizing foreign policy, and the last dissenter against Truman's foreign policy left the cabinet. By then, negotiations on atomic energy were proving useless, and the American staff was casting about for new ways to compel Russian approval. A much-respected foreign service officer, George Kennan, offered his analysis. The Russians, he suggested, had probably concluded "that we will do nothing" if they did not agree to the American proposal. Under such circumstances he proposed that the United States "begin a series of moves designed to convince the Russians of our serious intent and of the consequences if they choose to continue their present course."

IX

As early as February 1946 Kennan had formulated the strategy—later called "containment"—which became acknowledged official policy in 1947 and was dramatically expressed in the Truman Doctrine. In explaining Soviet behavior Kennan expressed the emerging beliefs of American leaders about Soviet irrationality and the impossibility of achieving agreements. Kennan disregarded the history of Western hostility to the Soviet Union and concluded that Soviet policy was *unreasonably* based upon a fear of Western antagonism. Russian leaders, he warned, had a "neurotic view of world affairs. And they have learned to seek security only in patient but deadly struggle for total destruction of rival power, *never in compacts and compromises with it.*"

Soviet power, however, "is neither schematic nor adventuristic," he said. "It does not take unnecessary risks. For this reason it can easily withdraw—and usually does—when strong resistance is encountered at any point. Thus, if the adversary has sufficient force and makes clear his readiness to use it, he rarely has to do so." (In an extended development of the same theme in 1947, Kennan warned that the Soviets move "inexorably along the prescribed path, like a persistent toy automobile wound up and headed in a given direction, stopping only when it meets unanswerable force." It was necessary to "confront the Russians with unalterable counterforce at any point where they show signs of encroaching," to stop the Russians with "superior force.")

Read eagerly by policy-makers, Kennan's message seemed to represent only a slight shift in emphasis from Byrnes's policies. In 1945 and early 1946 the Secretary sought through diplomacy (and apparently "implied threats") to roll back Soviet influence in Eastern Europe. Kennan apparently accepted the situation in Eastern Europe, seemed to recommend military resistance to future expansion, and, by implication, supported a stronger military force and foreign bases. In late 1946, as Byrnes moved reluctantly toward accepting the governments of Eastern Europe, he seemed temporarily to accede to Soviet power there. But he never surrendered his hope of pushing the Soviets back, and he was prepared to resist Soviet expansion. The containment doctrine, by urging continued pressure and predicting that Soviet power would either mellow or disintegrate, promised the success that Byrnes sought; but the doctrine, according to Kennan's conception, did not emphasize the heavy reliance upon armaments and alliances that developed. (Though Kennan never explicitly discussed in his famous cable the issue of economic aid to the Soviet Union, it was clear from his analysis and from his other recommendations that disintegration could be speeded by denying economic assistance.) To the goals that Byrnes and most American officials shared, Kennan added a tactic—patience.

The policies of Byrnes and Kennan were based upon what Walter Lippmann diagnosed as "a disbelief in the possibility of a settlement of the issues raised by . . . [the Cold War. The government] has reached the conclusion that all we can do is 'to contain' Russia until Russia changes." This conclusion, wrote Lippmann, was unwarranted and dangerous.

The history of diplomacy is the history of relations among rival powers which did not enjoy political intimacy and did not respond to appeals to common purposes. Nevertheless, there have been settlements . . . to think that rival and unfriendly powers cannot be brought to a settlement is to forget what diplomacy is about.

Giving up diplomacy, the government prepared to declare publicly a war of ideologies—the struggle between the forces of
light and darkness. On March 12, just a year after Churchill's
Iron Curtain speech, the President officially proclaimed the containment policy as the Truman Doctrine: ". . . it must be the
policy of the United States to support free peoples who are re-
sisting subjugation by armed minorities or by outside pressures."
In urging financial aid for Greece and Turkey, the administration
relied upon arguments that would become a familiar part of the
American Cold War rhetoric. Truman justified opposition to the
Greek revolution by defining it not as a revolution but as a
struggle between totalitarianism and freedom. The insurgents, he
believed, were communist-directed and represented part of the Soviet scheme for expansion. Their victory in Greece would probably
lead to the victory of communism in other European countries, and
the spread of communism automatically undermined the foundations
of world peace and hence the security of the United States.
    Though there is still considerable controversy about the sit-
uation in Greece, it was a dangerous oversimplification to view
the conflict as a struggle between freedom and totalitarianism.
Greece, as many American liberals then emphasized, was not a free,
democratic nation, and indeed many of the guerrillas were not communists. Rather than being part of the Soviet design for expansion (as American policy-makers wrongly believed), the revolution
was opposed by Stalin and it apparently continued despite his opposition. In effect the United States was blocking a revolutionary group, often led by communists and aided by neighboring communist states, which was seeking to overthrow a corrupt, harsh,
British-imposed government.
    Partly because American policy-makers wrongly viewed com-
munism as monolithic and Soviet-directed, they preferred a repres-
sive but anti-communist regime to a pro-communist or communist
regime. Because many were coming to view communism as a radical
evil, as simply a totalitarianism of the left (and identifying it
with Hitler's Nazism), they felt justified in taking vigorous action to halt its advance. Their vaguely formulated assumption
seemed to be that communism, once it gained control, would never
relax its grip or even ease restraints on liberty; but other forms
of repression were milder and would probably yield, ultimately con-
forming more closely to American democratic aspirations. Significantly, though there were occasional admissions that Greece was
not really democratic, American policy-makers did not broaden the
public dialogue and adequately explain that they were supporting
counter-insurgency to keep open the options for democracy. Rather,
in terms reminiscent of the earlier discussion about the Balkans,
they publicly discussed the conflict in unreal terms distorted by
ideology, as a struggle between freedom and tyranny.

There were of course other reasons why the administration was concerned about Greece and Turkey, for these nations controlled the sea trade to the Middle East and were close to important oil resources on which Anglo-American interests depended. The United States wanted to retain access to these vital resources and to keep them out of the Soviet sphere of influence. "These raw materials have to come over the sea," Forrestal explained privately, and "that is *one* reason why the Mediterranean must remain a free highway." In an earlier draft of Truman's speech, advisers had stressed that Greece and Turkey were areas of great natural resources which "must be accessible to all nations and must not be under the exclusive control or domination of any single nation." But, significantly, this theme was removed from the speech, and neither the private nor public arguments that followed generally emphasized such a narrow conception of national economic interest. Instead, American policy-makers painted a larger and more frightening picture: a defeat in Greece, by sapping the will of anti-communists elsewhere and encouraging their communist enemies, would lead to the collapse of governments in Western Europe and, through a mixture of infiltration, subversion, and indirect aid, even to the fall of Africa and Asia. "If Greece and then Turkey succumb, the whole Middle East will be lost," explained William Clayton, the Under Secretary of State for Economic Affairs. "France may then capitulate to the Communists. As France goes, all Western Europe and North Africa will go."

The specter of expanding communism did not simply outrage American humanitarianism; more seriously, it seemed to threaten the national interest in the largest sense. For some it simply meant that world resources—populations and materials for war— would fall to the enemy and might give it the strength to conquer the United States. (During the years when America relied upon a nuclear monopoly for protection, this view was certainly unrealistic in the short run and dubious even in the long run.) For others there was another and more subtle fear, not of attacks on the United States but of the menace of expanding communism to the American economy: it could cut off supplies of raw materials for America and curtail trade, eliminating markets for investment capital and for surpluses.

Such restrictions would compel a drastic readjustment of the American economy and greatly reduce the standard of living. Unless communism was halted, according to this view, it might economically encircle the United States and disorder the American economic system. "If these countries [Greece and Turkey] and the other countries should adopt closed economies," warned Clayton, "you can imagine the effect that it would have on our foreign trade . . . it is important that we do everything we can to retain those export markets." Looking at the economic crises in the world in early 1947, Joseph Jones, a major draftsman of the Truman

Doctrine speech, explained the fears of the administration. If
the British Empire, Greece, France, and China "are allowed to spiral downwards into economic anarchy, then at best they will drop
out of the United States orbit and try an independent nationalis-
tic policy; at worst they will swing into the Russian orbit." The
result, he predicted, would be a disastrous depression, far worse
than the Great Depression.

"A large volume of soundly based international trade is essential if we are to achieve prosperity, build a durable structure of
world economy and attain our goal of world peace and security," explained Harry S. Truman. Linking national prosperity to international peace and prosperity, American leaders acknowledged their
nation's overwhelming economic power and assumed that it was essential to the advancement of world peace and prosperity. According
to this analysis, the conditions necessary for American economic
expansion also promoted international economic and political good
health, *directly* (through the flow of benefits from America) and
indirectly (because other economies would emulate the American).
In turn, however, nations like Russia, which engaged in state-trading and bilateralism, endangered the world economy and the American economy. "Nations which act as enemies in the marketplace,"
explained Clayton, "cannot long be friends at the council table."

"If, by default, we permit free enterprise to disappear in
the other nations of the world, the very existence of our own
economy and our own democracy will be threatened . . ."—these
were the words penned by some of Truman's assistants in an earlier
draft of the Truman Doctrine speech. Not only did most American
leaders believe that communism threatened the American economy,
but they often expressed the belief that traditional freedoms
rested upon the prevailing forms of the economy. Dean Acheson
explains:

> Under a different system in this country, you could use
> the entire production of the country in the United States.
> If you wished to control the entire trade and income of
> the United States, which means the life of the people,
> you could probably fix it so that everything produced
> here would be consumed here, but that would completely
> change our Constitution, our relations to property,
> human liberty, our very conceptions of law.

"Foreign trade is vitally necessary to an expanding American
economy," Truman explained. "Our system cannot survive in a contracting economy," Less than a week before announcing the Truman
Doctrine, the President offered a more complete analysis of the
American political economy, of the relation of cherished freedoms
to corporate capitalism:

There is one thing that Americans value even more than peace. It is freedom. Freedom of worship—freedom of speech—freedom of enterprise. It must be true that the first two of these freedoms are related to the third. . . . So our devotion to free enterprise has deeper roots than a desire to protect the profits of ownership. It is part and parcel of what we call American.

. . . The pattern of trade that is *least* conducive to freedom of enterprise is one in which decisions are made by governments.

. . . If this [international] trend is not reversed, the Government of the United States will be under pressure . . . to fight for markets and raw materials. And if the Government were to yield to this pressure, it would shortly find itself in the business of allocating foreign goods among importers and foreign markets among exporters, and telling every trader what he could buy or sell. . . . It is not the American way.

Opposition among policy-makers to communist expansion in the immediate postwar years sprang from a cluster of related attitudes —humanitarianism, expectation of military attack in the short or long run, and the fear of economic encirclement. It is this fear of economic danger, so closely linked to the political economy of American liberalism, which has often constituted much of the basis for American intervention in other lands. American efforts, as William Appleman Williams has emphasized, have frequently been directed toward maintaining an economic open door. To do so, at times the United States has been compelled to subdue or limit challenges, and in the postwar years the most serious challenges were communist. The justification usually offered—that these challenges are totalitarian—is not false but, rather, often incomplete.

X

The fear of communism, often mixed with a misunderstanding of Munich and the sense that compromise may be appeasement, has led policy-makers generally to be intransigent in their response to communism. They have allowed their fears to distort their perceptions and their ideology to blur reality. This is part of the legacy of the Truman administration in the development of the Cold War.

In these years American liberal democracy became visibly defensive. Though espousing humanitarian ideals and proclaiming the value of self-determination, Americans have often failed to exhibit a tolerance or understanding of the methods of other people in pursuing social change and establishing governments in their own (non-American) way. Revolutions have been misunderstood, seldom accepted, never befriended. Fearing violence, respecting private property, and believing in peaceful reform, Americans have become captives of an ideology which interprets revolution as dysfunctional and dangerous to American interests. Opposing these radical movements in the name of freedom, America has turned often to oligarchies and dictators instead. By falsely dividing the world into the free and the unfree, and by making alliances in the name of freedom (not security) with the enemies of freedom, America has often judged world events by the standards of the crusade against communism, and thus it has been unable to understand the behavior and problems of the underdeveloped nations. It is this defective world view, so visible in the early Cold War, that has led some to lament that the American self-conception has lost its utopian vision.

SUGGESTED ADDITIONAL READINGS

Feis, Herbert. *From Trust to Terror*: *The Onset of the Cold War, 1945-1950*. New York, 1970. A traditionalist survey of the main issues in the deterioration and collapse of the wartime alliance and the early cold war, by a master of organization and lucid expression. Heavy emphasis on the German occupation.

Fleming, Denna F. *The Cold War and Its Origins*. Garden City, N.Y., 1961. The pioneering revisionist study of the cold war's origins, which Fleming dates from 1917. Based on published records and newspapers. Very critical of U.S. policies. Two volumes, of which Volume 1 relates to Bernstein's topic.

Gardner, Lloyd C. *Architects of Illusion*: *Men and Ideas in American Foreign Policy, 1941-1949*. Chicago, 1970. A revisionist study of the men who made and influenced American policy during and after World War II, and an essay on the history of the cold war. Chapters on Bullitt, FDR, Truman, Byrnes, Clayton, Marshall, Baruch, Acheson, Clay, and Forrestal.

Herz, Martin F. *Beginnings of the Cold War*. Bloomington, Ind., 1966. A thorough study of American-Soviet relations from the Yalta to the Potsdam Conferences. Based on published records, made more lucid by Herz's former service in the Department of State. Excellent on the Polish question.

LaFeber, Walter. *America, Russia, and the Cold War, 1945-1966*. New York, 1967. A survey, mildly revisionist, with major emphasis and strength on the cold war rather than on its origins.

McNeill, William H. *America, Britain, and Russia: Their Co-operation and Conflict, 1941-1946*. London, 1953. An early study of the collapse of the wartime alliance, still valuable for its comprehensive coverage and interesting insights. Especially good for its attention to the British role, which many other writers tend to slight.

Williams, William A. *The Tragedy of American Diplomacy*. New York, 1962. Critical analysis of American foreign policy, by the "dean of the revisionists" and the teacher of many of them. Chapter 6, "The Nightmare of Depression and the Vision of Omnipotence," is especially pertinent to Bernstein's analysis.

THE MIRROR IMAGE IN SOVIET-AMERICAN
RELATIONS: A SOCIAL PSYCHOLOGIST'S REPORT*

Urie Bronfenbrenner

*Professor Urie Bronfenbrenner is a social psychologist in the
Human Development and Family Studies Department at Cornell University. He has visited the Soviet Union every year for the past ten
years and has published numerous articles based on his observations and research there. Among his works are "Allowing for
Soviet Perceptions,"* in Roger Fisher, ed., International Conflict
and Behavioral Science: The Craigville Papers *(New York, 1964),*
pp. 161-178, *and* Two Worlds of Childhood: U.S. and U.S.S.R.
(New York, 1970).

*Bronfenbrenner sees postwar American-Russian relations as a
reflection of the images that Russians and Americans have of themselves and of each other. At first glance, Bronfenbrenner's approach may appear to be unique or tangential to the discussion of
cold war origins. His emphasis on the social-psychological basis
for policy nevertheless touches one of the fundamental issues in
the debate on cold war origins, especially the debate between the
traditionalists and the revisionists. Few authors discuss these
questions formally (although Mosely does so in identifying the
misconceptions), but all of them analyze specific events, incidents, issues, and developments from implied or unstated assumptions about motives and causes. Bronfenbrenner's attempt to deal
with the deeper sociopsychological motivations for policy is thus
an important contribution to the discussion of the cold war, and
it is basic to the discussion of responsibility.*

I should explain by way of introduction that I was in the Soviet Union during the summer of 1960, about a month after the U2
incident. The primary purpose of my trip was to become acquainted
with scientific developments in my field, which is social psychology. But in addition to visiting laboratories at universities and
institutes, I wanted also to become acquainted with *living* social
psychology—the Soviet people themselves. It was my good fortune

----
*Reprinted by permission of The Society for the Psychological
Study of Social Issues from *Journal of Social Issues,* XVII, No. 3
(1961), 45-56.

to be able to speak Russian. I was traveling with a tourist visa on a new plan which permitted me to go about alone without a guide. Accordingly, after spending the first two or three days of my visit in a particular city at scientific centers, I would devote the remaining days to walking about the town and striking up conversations with people in public conveyances, parks, stores, restaurants, or just on the street. Since foreigners are a curiosity, and I was obviously a foreigner (though, I quickly learned, not obviously an American), people were eager to talk. But I also went out of my way to strike up conversations with people who weren't taking the initiative—with fellow passengers who were remaining silent, with strollers in the park, with children and old people. Or I would enter a restaurant deciding in advance to sit at the third table on the left with whoever should turn out to be there. (In Soviet restaurants it is not uncommon to share a table with strangers.)

These conversations convinced me that the great majority of Russians feel a genuine pride in the accomplishments of their system and a conviction that communism is the way of the future not only for themselves but for the rest of the world as well. For several reasons my Soviet journey was a deeply disturbing experience. But what frightened me was not so much the facts of Soviet reality as the discrepancy between the real and the perceived. At first I was troubled only by the strange irrationality of the Soviet view of the world—especially their gross distortion of American society and American foreign policy as I knew them to be. But then, gradually, there came an even more disquieting awareness—an awareness which I resisted and still resist. Slowly and painfully, it forced itself upon me that *the Russian's distorted picture of us was curiously similar to our view of them—a mirror image*. But of course our image was real. Or could it be that our views too were distorted and irrational—a mirror image in a twisted glass?

It was—and is—a frightening prospect. For if such reciprocal distortion exists, it is a psychological phenomenon without parallel in the gravity of its consequences. For this reason, the possibility deserves serious consideration.

The Mirror Image Magnified

Let us then briefly examine the common features in the American and Soviet view of each other's societies. For the Russian's image I drew mainly not on official government pronouncements but on what was said to me by Soviet citizens in the course of our conversations. Five major themes stand out.

1. *They* are the aggressors.

The American view: Russia is the warmonger bent on imposing
its system on the rest of the world. Witness Czechoslovakia, Berlin, Hungary, and now Cuba and the Congo. The Soviet Union consistently blocks Western proposals for disarmament by refusing
necessary inspection controls.

The Soviet view: America is the warmonger bent on imposing
its power on the rest of the world and on the Soviet Union itself.
Witness American intervention in 1918, Western encirclement after
World War II with American troops and bases on every border of the
USSR (West Germany, Norway, Turkey, Korea, Japan), intransigence
over proposals to make Berlin a free city, intervention in Korea,
Taiwan, Lebanon, Guatemala, Cuba. America has repeatedly rejected
Soviet disarmament proposals while demanding the right to inspect
within Soviet territory—finally attempting to take the right by
force through deep penetration of Soviet air space.

2. Their government exploits and deludes the people.

The American view: Convinced communists, who form but a
small proportion of Russia's population, control the government
and exploit the society and its resources in their own interest.
To justify their power and expansionist policies they have to perpetuate a war atmosphere and a fear of Western aggression. Russian elections are a travesty since only one party appears on the
ballot. The Russian people are kept from knowing the truth
through a controlled radio and press and conformity is insured
through stringent economic and political sanctions against deviant
individuals or groups.

The Soviet view: A capitalistic-militaristic clique controls
the American government, the nation's economic resources, and its
media of communication. This group exploits the society and its
resources. It is in their economic and political interest to maintain a war atmosphere and engage in militaristic expansion. Voting in America is a farce since candidates for both parties are
selected by the same powerful interests leaving nothing to choose
between. The American people are kept from knowing the truth
through a controlled radio and press and through economic and political sanctions against liberal elements.

3. The mass of their people are not really sympathetic to the regime.

The American view: In spite of the propaganda, the Soviet
people are not really behind their government. Their praise of
the government and the party is largely perfunctory, a necessary
concession for getting along. They do not trust their own sources
of information and have learned to read between the lines. Most
of them would prefer to live under our system of government if
they only could.

The Soviet view: Unlike their government, the bulk of the
American people want peace. Thus, the majority disapproved of

American aggression in Korea, the support of Chiang Kai Shek, and, above all, of the sending of U2. But of course they could do nothing since their welfare is completely under the control of the ruling financier-militaristic clique. If the American people were allowed to become acquainted with communism as it exists in the USSR, they would unquestionably choose it as their form of government. ("You Americans are such a nice people; it is a pity you have such a terrible government.")

    4. *They* cannot be trusted.

The American view: The Soviets do not keep promises and they do not mean what they say. Thus while they claim to have discontinued all nuclear testing, they are probably carrying out secret underground explosions in order to gain an advantage over us. Their talk of peace is but a propaganda maneuver. Everything they do is to be viewed with suspicion since it is all part of a single coordinated scheme to further aggressive communist aims.

The Soviet view: The Americans do not keep promises and they do not mean what they say. Thus they insist on inspection only so that they can look at Soviet defenses; they have no real intention of disarming. Everything the Americans do is to be viewed with suspicion (e.g., they take advantage of Soviet hospitality by sending in spies as tourists).

    5. *Their* policy verges on madness.

The American view: Soviet demands on such crucial problems as disarmament, Berlin, and unification are completely unrealistic. Disarmament without adequate inspection is meaningless, a "free Berlin" would be equivalent to a Soviet Berlin, and a united Germany without free elections is an impossibility. In pursuit of their irresponsible policies the Soviets do not hesitate to run the risk of war itself. Thus it is only due to the restraint and coordinated action of the Western alliance that Soviet provocations over Berlin did not precipitate World War III.

The Soviet view: The American position on such crucial problems as disarmament, East Germany, and China is completely unrealistic. They demand to know our secrets before they disarm; in Germany they insist on a policy which risks the resurgence of a fascist Reich; and as for China, they try to act as if it did not exist while at the same time supporting an aggressive puppet regime just off the Chinese mainland. And in pursuit of their irresponsible policies, the Americans do not hesitate to run the risk of war itself. Were it not for Soviet prudence and restraint, the sending of U2 deep into Russian territory could easily have precipitated World War III.

    It is easy to recognize the gross distortions in the Soviet views summarized above. But is our own outlook completely realistic? Are we correct, for example, in thinking that the mass of

the Soviet people would really prefer our way of life and are unen-
thusiastic about their own? Certainly the tone and tenor of my
conversations with Soviet citizens hardly support this belief.

But, you may ask, why is it that other Western observers do
not report the enthusiasm and commitment which I encountered?

I asked this very question of newspaper men and embassy officials in Moscow. Their answers were revealing. Thus one reporter
replied somewhat dryly, "Sure, I know, but when a communist acts
like a communist, it isn't news. If I want to be sure that it
will be printed back home, I have to write about what's wrong with
the system, not its successes." Others voiced an opinion expressed most clearly by representatives at our embassy. When I reported to them the gist of my Soviet conversations, they were grateful
but skeptical: "Professor, you underestimate the effect of the police state. When these people talk to a stranger, especially an
American, they *have* to say the right thing."

The argument is persuasive, and comforting to hear. But perhaps these very features should arouse our critical judgment.
Indeed, it is instructive to view this argument against the background of its predecessor voiced by the newspaperman. To put it
bluntly, what he was saying was that he could be sure of getting
published only the material that the *American people wanted to
hear*. But notice that the second argument also fulfills this objective, and it does so in a much more satisfactory and sophisticated way. The realization that "Soviet citizens *have* to say the
right thing" enables the Western observer not only to discount
most of what he hears, but even to interpret it as evidence in direct support of the West's accepted picture of the Soviet Union as
a police state.

It should be clear that I am in no sense here suggesting that
Western reporters and embassy officials deliberately misrepresent
what they know to be the facts. Rather I am but calling attention
to the operation, in a specific and critical context, of a phenomenon well known to psychologists—the tendency to assimilate new
perceptions to old, and unconsciously to distort what one sees in
such a way as to minimize a clash with previous expectations. In
recent years, a number of leading social psychologists, notably
Heider, Festinger, and Osgood, have emphasized that this "strain
toward consistency" is especially powerful in the sphere of social
relations—that is, in our perceptions of the motives, attitudes,
and actions of other persons or groups. Specifically, we strive
to keep our views of other human beings compatible with each other.
In the face of complex social reality, such consistency is typical-
ly accomplished by obliterating distinctions and organizing the
world in terms of artificially-simplified frames of reference.
One of the simplest of these, and hence one of the most inviting,
is the dichotomy of good and bad. Hence we often perceive others,
be they individuals, groups, or even whole societies, as simply

"good" or "bad." Once this fateful decision is made, the rest is easy, for the "good" person or group can have only desirable social characteristics and the "bad" can have only reprehensible traits. And once such evaluative stability of social perception is established, it is extremely difficult to alter. Contradictory stimuli arouse only anxiety and resistance. When confronted with a desirable characteristic of something already known to be "bad," the observer will either just not "see" it, or will reorganize his perception of it so that it can be perceived as "bad." Finally, this tendency to regress to simple categories of perception is especially strong under conditions of emotional stress and external threat. Witness our readiness in times of war to exalt the virtues of our own side and to see the enemy as thoroughly evil.

Still one other social psychological phenomenon has direct relevance for the present discussion. I refer to a process demonstrated most dramatically and comprehensively in the experiments of Solomon Asch, and known thereby as the "Asch phenomenon." In these experiments, the subject finds himself in a group of six or eight of his peers all of whom are asked to make comparative judgments of certain stimuli presented to them, for example, identifying the longer of two lines. At first the task seems simple enough; the subject hears others make their judgments and then makes his own. In the beginning he is usually in agreement, but then gradually he notices that more and more often his judgments differ from those of the rest of the group. Actually, the experiment is rigged. All the other group members have been instructed to give false responses on a predetermined schedule. In any event, the effect on our subject is dramatic. At first he is puzzled, then upset. Soon he begins to have serious doubts about his own judgment, and in an appreciable number of cases, he begins to "see" the stimuli as they are described by his fellows.

What I am suggesting, of course, is that the Asch phenomenon operates even more forcefully outside the laboratory where the game of social perception is being played for keeps. *Specifically, I am proposing that the mechanisms here described contribute substantially to producing and maintaining serious distortions in the reciprocal images of the Soviet Union and the United States.*

My suggestion springs from more than abstract theoretical inference. I call attention to the possible operation of the Asch phenomenon in the Soviet-American context for a very concrete reason: I had the distressing experience of being its victim. While in the Soviet Union I deliberately sought to minimize association with other Westerners and to spend as much time as I could with Soviet citizens. This was not easy to do. It was no pleasant experience to hear one's own country severely criticized and to be constantly out-debated in the bargain. I looked forward to the next chance meeting with a fellow Westerner so that I could get much-needed moral support and enjoy an evening's invective at

the expense of Intourist and the "worker's paradise." But though
I occasionally yielded to temptation, for the most part I kept
true to my resolve and spent many hours in a completely Soviet environment. It was difficult, but interesting. I liked many of
the people I met. Some of them apparently liked me. Though mistaken, they were obviously sincere. They wanted me to agree with
them. The days went on, and strange things began to happen. I
remember picking up a Soviet newspaper which featured an account
of American activities in the Near East. "Oh, what are they doing
now!" I asked myself, and stopped short; for I had thought in
terms of "they," and it was my own country. Or I would become
aware that I had been nodding to the points being made by my Soviet companion where before I had always taken issue. In short,
when all around me saw the world in one way, I too found myself
wanting to believe and belong.

And once I crossed the Soviet border on my way home, the process began to reverse itself. The more I talked with fellow Westerners, especially fellow Americans, the more I began to doubt the
validity of my original impressions. "What would you expect them
to say to an American?" my friends would ask. "How do you know
that the person talking to you was not a trained agitator?" "Did
you ever catch sight of them following you?" I never did. Perhaps
I was naive. But, then, recently I reread a letter written to a
friend during the last week of my stay. "I feel it is important,"
it begins, "to try to write to you in detail while I am still in
it, for just as I could never have conceived of what I am now ex-
periencing, so, I suspect, it will seem unreal and intangible once
I am back in the West." The rest of the letter, and others like
it, contain the record of the experiences reported in this account.

In sum, I take my stand on the view that there *is* a mirror
image in Soviet and American perceptions of each other and that
this image represents serious distortions by *both* parties of realities on either side.

The Mirror Image Projected

And if so, what then? Do not distortions have adaptive func-
tions? Especially in war is it not psychologically necessary to
see the enemy as thoroughly evil and to enhance one's self image?
And are we not engaged in a war, albeit a cold war, with the Soviet Union?

But is not our hope to bring an end to the cold war and,
above all, to avoid the holocaust of a hot one? And herein lies
the terrible danger of the distorted mirror image, for *it is characteristic of such images that they are self-confirming*; that is,
each party, often against its own wishes, is increasingly driven
to behave in a manner which fulfills the expectations of the other.

As revealed in social psychological studies, the mechanism is a
simple one: If A expects B to be friendly and acts accordingly,
B responds with friendly advances; these in turn evoke additional
positive actions from A, and thus a benign circle is set in motion.
Conversely, where A's anticipations of B are unfavorable, it is
the vicious circle which develops at an accelerating pace. And as
tensions rise, perceptions become more primitive and still further
removed from reality. Seen from this perspective, the primary danger of the Soviet-American mirror image is that it impels each nation to act in a manner which confirms and enhances the fear of
the other to the point that even deliberate efforts to reverse the
process are reinterpreted as evidences of confirmation.

Manifestations of this mechanism in Soviet-American relations
are not difficult to find. A case in point is our policy of restricting the travel of Soviet nationals in the United States by
designating as "closed areas" localities that correspond as closely as possible to those initially selected by Soviet authorities
as "off limits" to Americans in the USSR. As was brought home to
me in conversations with Soviet scientists who had visited the
United States, one of the effects of this policy is to neutralize
substantially any favorable impressions the visitor might otherwise get of American freedoms.

To take another example in a more consequential area: in a
recent issue of *Atlantic Monthly* (August 1960), Dr. Hans Bethe, an
American physicist who participated in negotiations at the Geneva
Conference on nuclear testing, reports that our tendency to expect
trickery from the Soviets led us into spending considerable time
and energy to discover scientific loopholes in their proposals
which could have permitted them to continue nuclear tests undetect-
ed. As a result, our scientists did succeed in finding a theoretical basis for questioning the effectiveness of the Soviet plan.
It seems that if the Soviets could dig a hole big enough, they
could detonate underground explosions without being detected.
Says Dr. Bethe:

> I had the doubtful honor of presenting the theory
> of the big hole to the Russians in Geneva in November
> 1959. I felt deeply embarrassed in so doing, because
> it implied that we considered the Russians capable of
> cheating on a massive scale. I think they would have
> been quite justified if they had considered this an
> insult and walked out of the negotiations in disgust.
>   The Russians seemed stunned by the theory of the
> big hole. In private, they took Americans to task for
> having spent the last year inventing methods to cheat
> on a nuclear test cessation agreement. Officially, they
> spent considerable effort in trying to disprove the

theory of the big hole. This is not the reaction of a
country that is bent on cheating.

But the most frightful potential consequence of the mirror
image lies in the possibility that it may confirm itself out of existence. For if it is possible for either side to interpret concessions as signs of treachery, it should not be difficult to recognize an off-course satellite as a missile on its way. After all,
we, or they, would be expecting it.

But it is only in the final catastrophe that the mirror image
is impartial in its effects. Short of doomsday, we have even more
to lose from the accelerating vicious circle than do the Soviets.
Internally, the communist system can justify itself to the Soviet
people far more easily in the face of external threat than in
times of peace. And in the international arena, the more the United States becomes committed to massive retaliation and preventive
intervention abroad the more difficult it becomes for uncommitted
or even friendly nations to perceive a real difference in the foreign policies of East and West.

The last point calls attention to still another weakness of
the stance of the West in the hall of twisted mirrors. In the progressive exchange of moves and countermoves, it is the Soviet
Union that has taken the initiative. It is they who choose the
time, the place, and the weapons; and pressed by the anxiety of
being a move behind, we hasten to retaliate, almost invariably on
the terms of their choosing. They act, and we react. The result
is often a greater gain for them than for us.

Finally, we should take note of another debilitating effect
of the mirror image; it not only preoccupies us with a false reality but blinds us to the true one. Thus so long as we remain vic-
tims of the reassuring belief that the Soviet Union can acquire
adherents only by force, *we are likely to underestimate the positive appeal, especially to economically backward countries, of
communism not only as an ideology but as a technology that seems
to work.* The Soviets themselves are certainly not blind to the
effectiveness of this appeal and use it to considerable advantage.
But because of our own deprecatory image of the constructive potential of communist ideas and methods, and our lack of any mis-
sionary zeal of our own, we are slow even to retaliate in this
peaceful sphere of competition between systems. Rather we continue to concentrate our efforts on bigger and better nuclear weapons.
In our anxiety to be prepared for the hot war, we risk losing the
cold war and finding ourselves a minority in a world dominated by
communism ideologically and economically.

Breaking the Mirror Image

How can we avoid such awesome consequences? One step seems clearly indicated: we must do everything we can to break down the psychological barrier that prevents both us and the Russians from seeing each other and ourselves as we really are. If we can succeed in dispelling the Soviet Union's bogeyman picture of America, we stand to gain, for to the same degree that militant communism thrives in a context of external threat, it is weakened as this threat is reduced. And as the *raison d'etre* for sacrifice, surveillance, and submission disappears there arises opportunity for the expression of such potential for liberalization as may still exist in Russian society.

But we rejoice too soon. Before we can hope to make any progress in changing the views of the Russians, we must learn to see reality ourselves. And here the first requirement is *exposure*. We must be willing and eager to look. And so long as the Soviets continue to encourage American tourism and exchange, such looking remains possible on a grand scale; estimates of the number of American tourists in the Soviet Union last summer range from 8000 to 15,000.

But mere looking is not enough. One must be able to see what is there. Many a traveler returns from the USSR with little beyond confirmations of his prior expectations of black or white, as the case may be. How can we enhance the possibility of seeing something else besides the expected when it is there? One possibility is to encourage travel on an even larger scale by persons who have a legitimate basis for interacting and finding common ground with the Russians on ideologically neutral matters—in science, culture, industry and commerce. In the course of such interactions it should be easier for us to become aware of the actual realities of Soviet life—both good and bad. And in selecting persons for such exposure, we should pick those who have status and influence back home so that their accounts cannot be readily dismissed as the irresponsible ramblings of incompetents and fellow travelers.

But, you may say, all this is obvious, and hardly requires any radical reorientation of American policy. True, but this is only the first step, and the next may not be so easy. For, if we are truly serious about exposing ourselves to the realities of the Soviet society and its people, then we must be willing to go much further than we have in permitting and encouraging Soviet citizens to travel in the United States. We should, for example, revise our immigration and travel restrictions, even in the absence of reciprocal concessions by the USSR. Indeed, to compete with the Soviets in this sphere, we would have to provide interpreters, set up conferences with opposite numbers, make travel arrangements. It would be a major enterprise.

And would it be worth it, since the Soviet Government permits
only a small number to come, and only convinced communists at that?
But is it not precisely these from whom we have the most to learn
and whom it is most important for us to influence?

And here we come face to face with the even more challenging
problem of bringing about a more realistic view of America in the
Soviet Union. Despite the formidable barriers, opportunities for
communication do exist. One of my many surprises in the Soviet
Union was the fact that over half of the people with whom I talked
mentioned having heard Russian language broadcasts from the West.
But along with this encouraging discovery came a disturbing one,
for I learned that the Russians' distorted views were a product
not only of their propaganda but, ironically, also our own. For,
in line with the mirror image psychology, our broadcasts to Russia
apparently present a distorted, one-sided picture of ourselves.
Thus the comments I heard about our foreign language programs—
even from persons favorably disposed toward the United States—
were hardly reassuring. Our reporting, they said, was much less
objective than that of the BBC. In our presentations, America was
always good; the Soviet Union always bad. Beyond that, many of
our broadcasts seemed to have as their objective not furthering
understanding of America but fomenting revolution in the USSR.
And we kept emphasizing our military might and our determination
to further American interests around the world.

Since I heard no broadcasts myself, I am in no position to
judge to what extent these descriptions may be exaggerated. But
to the extent that they are true at all, they illustrate the reality of the mirror image phenomenon and the dangers it entails.
*For so long as our foreign broadcasts, diplomatic pronouncements
and overt acts in the international arena give one-sided emphasis
to our nuclear prowess, our readiness for massive retaliation, and
our determination to defend American interests wherever they may
be, we only confirm the image of aggressive intransigence in the
eyes not only of the communist world—but what is perhaps more important—the non-committed nations as well.*

Let me be absolutely clear about what I am saying. I am *not*
arguing against military preparedness. On the contrary, it is essential that we be strong, and that the Russians know it. Nor do
I deny that we are contributing a great deal in the interests of
peace and of the welfare of other nations of the world. I believe
we should do much more, but even this is not my main concern.
What I wish to express most forcefully, and here I speak as a
psychologist, is my fear that *we are being incredibly naive in the
one-sided picture we present of ourselves to the outside world—
naive to the point that we further the cause of our adversary and
run the risk of driving the uncommitted world into the communist
camp*. We accomplish this awesome irony by dramatizing our aggressive stance and underplaying and even bungling opportunities to

present ourselves as a nation committed to peace, human values, and the economic and social welfare of the world. Passing over our tragic ineptness in the handling of the U2 incident, consider the more recent examples of the fanfare with which we announced our launching of a nuclear missile submarine. Proudly we beamed to the whole world the official statement that this single vessel could release more destruction than was represented by the combined explosive power of all the munitions fired by both sides in World War II. Surely we could do little more to confirm to the Russian people (and other nations as well) what the Soviet government has been telling them for years about American aggressiveness.

But our greatest error is one of omission. For we fail to recognize the importance of giving not just equal but even greater prominence to events expressing our concern for human welfare, justice, and peace. Consider, for example, the psychological impact abroad of a public statement by the President, also made with great fanfare, that the United States, in the interests of furthering peaceful relations between nations, has unilaterally waived all restrictions on the travel of Soviet and satellite nationals within our borders. Other possibilities come to mind at a more consequential level. We could be making a great deal more, for example, of the closing down of some of our overseas bases. Suppose that we were to announce to the world, again with all the magnificent hoop-la at our command, that in the interests of decreasing world tensions, we were not only abolishing these bases but, to preserve the economy of the host countries, were turning the installations over to the United Nations for use as centers for exploring peaceful uses of atomic energy, international universities, and the like.

Of course the Soviets would immediately denounce such measures as obvious propaganda gestures. But if we really did what we said, the Soviet leaders would know it. And what is more, the pressure would now be on the Soviet Union to match our initiative. And in this manner, the way is opened to transforming the vicious circle into a benign one.

Finally, there remains the most risky possibility of all: taking the Russians at their word in selected instances. This would have to be done with the greatest caution and with careful weighing of alternative consequences. Nevertheless, our analysis argues the wisdom of moving even in this dangerous direction. For if our theory of the distorted mirror image is correct, it follows that proposals that seem, *and actually are*, genuine concessions for one side, will not appear to be genuine concessions to the other, and vice versa. In short, meeting the other party half way will never be enough. The only way to break the impasse is for one party or the other to be willing to take what it views as a calculated risk.

But one thing should be clear. Dispelling the image of the
Soviet bogeyman will not dispel the Soviet danger. On the contrary, disabused of our delusions, we should be able to see the
danger more clearly. The competition and conflict with the communist world will continue. But at least the battle will be over
differences that are real, and hence less likely to propel us
toward mutual annihilation.

SUGGESTED ADDITIONAL READINGS

Bailey, Thomas A. *America Faces Russia*. Ithaca, N.Y., 1950.
    A general survey.

Burnette, O. Lawrence, Jr., and William Converse Haygood, eds.
    A Soviet View of the American Past. Glenview, Ill., 1960.
    An annotated translation of the section on American history
    in the *Great Soviet Encyclopedia*. After Roosevelt's death,
    "reactionary circles" in the United States spurned coopera-
    tion with Russia and launched the cold war.

Filene, Peter G., ed. *American Views of Soviet Russia, 1917-1965*.
    Homewood, Ill., 1968, esp. pp. 141-250. An excellent collec-
    tion of editorial, personal, and documentary comments on
    postrevolutionary Russia.

Mitrokhin, Lev N. "American Mirages," *Views of America*, ed.
    Alan F. Westin, et al. New York, 1966, pp. 106-111. An in-
    dictment of American values by a Soviet writer who visited
    the United States with youth delegations in 1960 and 1961.

Nekrasov, Viktor. *Both Sides of the Ocean: A Russian Writer's
    Travels in Italy and the United States*, trans. Elias
    Kulukundis. New York, 1964, esp. pp. 91-191. A Soviet
    writer's account of a visit to the United States in 1960.
    Nekrasov subsequently fell into disfavor at home for his
    less critical views on the United States than, for example,
    those of Mitrokhin.

Williams, William A. *American-Russian Relations, 1781-1947*. New
    York, c. 1952. A general survey with emphasis on the early
    twentieth century.

AMERICAN FALSIFIERS
AND THE FACTS OF HISTORY*

B. Marushkin

International Affairs *is an English-language monthly journal published in Moscow for distribution abroad. It regularly features articles, theoretical essays, excerpts from memoirs, and documents. It has, for example, published Soviet documents on the Yalta and Potsdam Conferences. No biographical information on B. Marushkin is available to the editors.*

Marushkin's article, which concentrates on U.S. historians and their treatment of Soviet-American relations during the war, contains the essential elements of the Soviet interpretation of the cold war's origins. They are also found in the Stalin and Zhdanov speeches, reprinted elsewhere in this reader. Americans never abandoned their intentions to destroy socialism, despite the wartime alliance and the overt cooperation it occasioned. The war, nevertheless, proved the strength and vitality of socialism as a historical force. The American claim to exclusive postwar world leadership did not accord with the realities of Russian power and socialist vitality in 1945. Americans since then have ignored what the war proved: They have minimized the Russian contribution and the Russian victories in the war, and they have ascribed obvious Russian successes and gains to American blunders, mistakes, naivete, and innocence, and to U.S. failure to push a political program during the war. In addition, they have adopted a series of policy doctrines designed to contain, deter, and roll back Communism, and thus correct the mistakes of the past. The cold war is therefore a postwar American program designed to accomplish what the United States failed to do during the war: weaken Russia and socialism by delaying the second front, by occupying key territories formerly held by Fascists (especially Berlin, Vienna, and Prague), and by other means. According to Marushkin, U.S. historians contribute to the postwar American program by falsifying the history of the war for American readers. Only a few American historians (the revisionists) recognize the new aggressive tendencies in U.S. foreign policy after Roosevelt's death in 1945. They are also the ones who understand that the United States tried to turn Fascist aggression against the Soviet Union before and during World War II and that the United States dropped the atomic bomb on Hiroshima and Nagasaki to intimidate the Soviet Union.

----

*Reprinted, without footnotes, from *International Affairs* (Moscow), June 1970, pp. 15-22.

The outcome of the Second World War provided convincing evidence that there is no force in the world that can destroy socialism and alter the course of historical development. The lessons of the last world war demonstrate the law-governed and irreversible nature of the changes taking place in the world; today these lessons serve as a stern warning to all imperialist aggressors.

The aggressive circles of American imperialism, still unwilling to reconcile themselves to the results of the Second World War and hoping to see them revised, bend every effort to pervert and distort the history of the war and to bury the lessons of the war in oblivion. For the past 25 years, American bourgeois historiography, fulfilling the social task set it by the U.S. ruling circles, has produced a huge amount of literature on the Second World War and has developed a large number of conceptions.

There is a direct connection between this semi-official historical science and the foreign policy of the United States. With the aim of disguising and "justifying" their aggressive policy, the ruling circles of the U.S. invariably turn to the "arguments" of a history that has been accordingly doctored. Thus, distortion of the history of the Second World War in American bourgeois historiography has become one of the elements of U.S. foreign policy strategy.

The American historian L. Morton wrote that: ". . . because of the needs of the policy-maker, there is a strong tendency to orient scholarship towards current problems and to use the products of scholarship in support of policy." This idea is expressed even more concretely by Chicago University Professor H. Morgenthau, who states that besides the military-industrial complex, there is also in the United States an "academic-political complex" which defends the interests of the ruling circles in the historical sciences. This kind of dependence of bourgeois history on the policy of the ruling circles manifests itself both in writings on the history of the Second World War and in works on U.S. foreign policy in the postwar years.

It is true that during the Second World War some American bourgeois historians assessed Soviet military victories with a certain degree of objectivity. For instance, in his book *The Road to Teheran*, F. R. Dulles stressed that "the Soviet armies were spectacularly dispelling the myth of German invincibility and giving the people of the United Nations a revived confidence in ultimate victory."

However, during and immediately after the war, there was evidence of a tendency to give a false interpretation to past events; this tendency grew in the postwar period and today it clearly predominates in American bourgeois historical science.

Even during the war, according to H. Feis, the U.S. War Department enlisted the services of historians to write its official history. After the war, Harry Barnes notes in the book *Perpetual War for Perpetual Peace*, the U.S. government again asked the historians "to prepare an acceptable official history of world events and American policy."

During the cold war period, a conception was formulated in American historical literature according to which the U.S.S.R.'s decisive role in the Second World War was denied, while the U.S. role was exaggerated. The supporters of this conception tried to ignore the established fact that the Soviet Union's struggle against the fascist aggressors changed the course of the war and that the Soviet-German front was the main front of the war. They continually stressed that the United States was the "arsenal of democracy" and that it was America's economic and military might that predetermined the outcome of the war.

A typical example of this line was A. Schlesinger's book *The Rise of Modern America*, in which the author pays almost no attention to the U.S.S.R.'s entry into the Second World War. For him, the "breaking point" of the war came not in the middle, but at the end of 1941, that is, after the U.S. entered the war. He also ignores the significance of the Soviet Army's victory near Moscow, mentioning only in passing that the "Reds" had ". . . captured some territory around Leningrad and Moscow." Yet he goes out of his way to play up the "mobilisation of American might" for "all-out participation" in the war, although it is well known that the U.S.A. did not actually fight against Germany for a long time.

However hard he tries, Schlesinger cannot completely ignore the facts of the heroic struggle of the Soviet people against the fascist aggressors. But in mentioning, again in passing, the "mounting Russian successes," he extols the role of lend-lease and exaggerates the significance of Allied air bombings of Germany. After a one-sentence remark about the battle of Stalingrad, Schlesinger focuses his attention on a description of the Allied operations, particularly in connection with the opening of the second front. Such a description of the events of the Second World War cannot, of course, be called objective.

Why U.S. foreign policy makers subscribed to the conception outlined above is easy to see when we recall that immediately after the war the U.S.A. openly claimed world leadership. The ruling circles "substantiated" such claims on the basis of the false conception of the U.S.A.'s "decisive role" in the Second World War, from which they derived the no less false thesis of America's "inevitable" "leading role" in the postwar world. In 1945, the President of the United States, Harry Truman, stated outright, "Whether we like it or not, we must recognise that the victory which we have won has placed upon the American people the continuing burden of responsibility of world leadership."

These claims to world leadership were subsequently repeated in one form or another by almost every high U.S. government

official, despite the fact that both past and current history show
unequivocally that they are groundless and without prospect. Thus
in 1965, Secretary of State Dean Rusk said: "This has become a
very small planet. We have to be concerned with all of it—with
all its land, waters, atmosphere, and with surrounding space."
Somewhat more cautious, but still quite definite, was the statement made in April 1969 by Secretary of State William Rogers:
"The United States is the world's greatest military and economic
and technological power; and there is no way to isolate ourselves
from the responsibilities that go with that position."

Truman himself not only made wide use of the fruits of the
falsifiers' efforts, but did everything to promote their work. In
a message to the American Historical Association, he noted that
the main task of U.S. foreign policy was the fight against communism and that, in this connection, "the work of American historians is of the utmost importance." Bourgeois historiography, in
turn, had a clear idea of the nature of the social task set it by
the country's ruling circles. Conyers Read, one of the American
Historical Association's presidents, wrote: "Total war, whether
it be hot or cold, enlists everyone and calls upon everyone to assume his part. The historian is no freer from his obligation than
the physicist."

Observing the evolution of historical science in the U.S.A.,
University of California Professor John Hicks stated: ". . . the
techniques of history writing have changed markedly in recent
years . . . the historian need no longer pretend in his writing a
degree of impartiality he cannot possibly feel."

These, then, are the political and methodological lines along
which semi-official historical science in the U.S.A. develops.
Works published by the Defense Department consistently make apolo-
getic assessments of the strength of the U.S. war machine created
during the war years, of its "growing successes" on many fronts,
and of the skill of the American generals.

Some American bourgeois historians acknowledge that the
U.S.S.R.'s armed struggle against Germany was important; however,
they usually qualify this by saying that it was important only insofar as it won the time needed to set the economic and military
resources of the United States into motion. Thus, in his book *The
Historian and the Army*, K. Greenfield asserts that the opening of
the second front in the West in essence "completed the work of utter destruction that the Soviet forces and the air-bombing of Germany had begun." And H. Feis echoes this view in his work *Churchill, Roosevelt, Stalin*: ". . . the damage done by the Western
forces to the Germany Army was comparable to the performance of
the Red Army."

Other American bourgeois historians go even further and deny
altogether the decisive role of the Soviet Army in ensuring victory over Germany. For example, in the October 1947 issue of

Foreign Affairs, W. Langer wrote that the very "idea that during
1942 and 1943 they [the Russians—*B. M.*] were carrying the major
share of the burden was essentially a mistaken one." J. Pratt,
in *A History of United States Foreign Policy*, concludes that one
of Washington's basic errors during the war was to overestimate
the significance of the U.S.S.R. as an ally of the United States.
    Some American historians follow the example of their West
German colleagues and argue that the German defeat was brought by
an accidental coincidence of such factors as Hitler's "fatality,"
the unusually cold winter of 1941-1942, the "vast Russian expan-
ses," and "Russia's lack of good roads." They thus attempt to
pass over in silence the heroism and staunchness of the Soviet
people and the superiority of the socialist system over the capitalist one.
    But no matter how bourgeois scholars try to juggle the facts
of history, their tricks are easily exposed by simply referring
to the official documents and materials of the Western governments
themselves—especially the U.S. government. Thus, in a letter
dated June 26, 1941, to Admiral Leahy, President Roosevelt noted
that the entry of the U.S.S.R. into the war "will mean the liberation of Europe from Nazi domination." After Germany attacked the
U.S.S.R., the then U.S. Ambassador to Moscow, J. Davies, wrote
that in his opinion ". . . the extent of the resistance of the Red
Army would amaze and surprise the world, and . . . his [Hitler's]
troubles would just begin." In his book *Roosevelt and the Russians*, Secretary of State Edward Stettinius wrote: ". . . the
American people should remember that they were on the brink of
disaster in 1942. If the Soviet Union had failed to hold on its
fronts, the Germans would have been in a position to conquer Great
Britain. They would have been able to overrun Africa, too, and
in this event they could have established a foothold in Latin
America."
    Many prominent American statesmen of the war period saw a di-
rect connection between the U.S.S.R.'s struggle against fascism
and the security of the United States. They understood that the
liberation of Europe depended on the outcome of this struggle and
attached due importance to the military operations of the Soviet
Army. "We must ever remember," wrote Secretary of State Cordell
Hull in his memoirs, "that by the Russians' heroic struggle
against the Germans they probably saved the Allies from a negotiated peace with Germany. Such a peace would have humiliated the
Allies and would have left the world open to another Thirty Years
War." After the war, General George C. Marshall wrote that the
heroic stand of the Soviet people saved the United States a war
on her own soil.
    But the most convincing refutation of the fabrications of
American bourgeois historiography was provided by the events of
the war itself. The fact is that from the middle of 1941 to the

beginning of 1944, between 153 and 201 German divisions were de-
ployed on the Soviet-German front, and this amounted to between
55 and 72 per cent of all the German forces. During that same period, the British and American troops in North Africa and Italy
faced between 0.9 and 6.1 per cent of the German divisions. In a
telegram to General MacArthur in May 1942, Franklin D. Roosevelt
said: "In the matter of grand strategy I find it difficult this
spring and summer to get away from the simple fact that the Russian armies are killing more Axis personnel and destroying more
Axis material than all the other twenty-five United Nations put
together."

For a long time the Soviet Union was in fact fighting Germany and her satellites single-handed, while the U.S.A. and Britain, despite their promise to open a second front in Western Europe in 1942, kept delaying the landing of their troops. On
January 20, 1943, British Prime Minister Winston Churchill told
his War Cabinet: ". . . it must be admitted that all our military
operations taken together are on a very small scale compared with
the mighty resources of Britain and the United States, and still
more with the gigantic effort of Russia."

Even after the opening of the second front in June 1944, the
Soviet Army faced 239 German and German satellite divisions, while
the Allied armies had to deal with only 81 divisions. Thus,
throughout the war the overwhelming majority of the most efficient
and best equipped troops of Germany and her satellites were fighting on the Soviet-German front.

In the course of the war, the Soviet Union destroyed the main
forces of Germany and her satellites. The fascist forces suffered
10,000,000 casualties on the Soviet-German front, while their total casualties in the war were 13,600,000. "It is the Russian
Army," said Churchill in August 1944, "which has done the main
work of ripping the guts out of the German Army . . . there was no
force in the world . . . that would have been able to maul and
break the German Army. . . ."

The foreign policy course of the U.S.A. was and still is to a
significant degree determined by a dislike for the results of the
Second World War and the desire to revise them. Denying the legitimacy of the Soviet Union's victory in the Second World War and
the revolutionary transformations in the postwar world which it en-
gendered, American imperialism built and continues to build various foreign policy doctrines such as those of "deterring," "rolling back," and "eroding" communism.

Following these guidelines, many American historians assert
that socialism was able to strengthen its positions in Europe and
Asia mainly because of U.S. military-strategic errors, the nature
of the international commitments assumed by the U.S.A. during the
war, and the excessive scrupulousness it displayed in carrying

them out. It is easy to see that such assertions are aimed at providing "historical" grounds for the aggressive course taken by U.S. foreign policy towards the socialist states. Writing in the July 1954 issue of *Atlantic*, Hanson W. Baldwin, a prominent military commentator, stated: "Our World War II actions, policies, and agreements were in many cases so naively trusting, politically superficial, or limited in outlook as to make it not only possible, but easy, for Soviet Communism to turn them to its advantage. . . . We fought to win and we forgot that wars must have political aims. . . . We substituted one enemy for another; and today's enemy, Soviet Russia, is more threatening than the old."

The gist of this kind of thinking is as follows: on entering the Second World War, the U.S.A. upset the "balance of power" in Europe and Asia. By throwing its weight on the side of the Allies, it prevented Germany and Japan from bleeding and weakening the U.S.S.R., and thereby opened the way for the U.S.S.R.'s "military predominance" in Europe and Asia.

Also being criticised is the position that the Allies had taken in insisting on the unconditional surrender of Germany and Japan. "It meant," Hanson W. Baldwin wrote, "the creation of vacuums of power, the complete destruction of two nations—Germany and Japan—which in modern history had been the traditional counterpoise to Soviet Russia." Former President Dwight D. Eisenhower felt that Roosevelt's insistence on Germany's unconditional capitulation was an error that prolonged the war.

Many American bourgeois historians contend that the U.S.A. made a mistake in opening the second front in France, instead of following Churchill's plan to strike at "the soft underbelly" of Europe—the Balkans. Invasion via the underbelly, J. Pratt wrote in the book mentioned above, "might have brought Anglo-American armies into Central Europe, where they could have countered Soviet domination in that area."

In their attempts to minimise the significance of the Soviet Army's victories at the final stage of the war, American historians declare that the U.S.A. "permitted" the U.S.S.R. to take Berlin and liberate Prague and Vienna. In its July 22, 1959, issue, *U.S. News & World Report* reflected this viewpoint by asking: "Should the U.S. and British troops have pressed on to capture Berlin ahead of the Russians? Should the Americans have gone on east to Prague in Czechoslovakia? Should they have beaten the Red Army in a race for Vienna?"

That there are no grounds for the thesis advanced in the postwar years, that the Soviet victories at the concluding stage of the war were a result of the failure of U.S. ruling circles to pursue political aims in the war, becomes all the more obvious when we again turn to the facts and documents of the war years. From them we learn that at the beginning of the war, the State Department formed a committee to study and prepare future U.S. policy.

After Japan attacked Pearl Harbor, Franklin Roosevelt instructed
his Secretary of State to set up an Advisory Committee on Post-War
Foreign Policy. During the war, this committee compiled a large
volume of recommendations for the government. Thus, it was not
that no attention was given to the political aims of the war, but
that the committee's recommendations, which were supposed to facilitate the achievement of those aims, were often built on erroneous
appraisals and assumptions. Specifically, the U.S. ruling circles
thought that the U.S.S.R. would be so weakened by the war that by
using their atom bomb monopoly they could impose their will on the
U.S.S.R. at international negotiations.

It is no secret that U.S. strategic planning itself was subordinated to political aims. From a purely military point of view
for example, the second front in Europe could have been opened
much earlier than it was. The Allied troop landing in Normandy in
June 1944 was conditioned by political considerations. And Churchill's notorious plan for an Allied invasion of Europe through the
Balkans was also rejected for political reasons.

"Any assumption that the political consequences of an 'underbelly' attack would have been advantageous is of somewhat doubtful
validity . . .," noted J. McCloy, who was Assistant Secretary of
War at the time. ". . . If the Western Allies' main effort had
been through the Mediterranean, it is likely that even more of
Northern and Western Germany would have been occupied by Soviet
troops than at present. It is doubtful if the United States and
Great Britain would ever have been able to maintain substantial
numbers of troops in both Germany and Southeastern Europe."

Political considerations predominated in U.S. ruling circles
to an even greater extent over military considerations at the final stage of the war. Harry Truman, by then in the White House,
was well known as an advocate of a policy of letting the U.S.S.R.
and Germany exhaust each other. He wrote in his memoirs: "I
could feel with Churchill and fully share his views on the problem
that lay ahead." As for Churchill, it is known that he proposed
at the very end of the war that a "new front" be opened against
the U.S.S.R., that "this front in Europe should be as far east as
possible," and that for this purpose Berlin, Prague, and Vienna
should be occupied.

Following these lines, the Supreme Command of the Anglo-American forces set as its goal to occupy as much of the territory
held by the fascist armies as possible, and above all such centres
as Berlin, Prague, and Vienna. In May 1944, the Headquarters of
the Allied Forces taking part in Operation Overlord had Berlin
down as the final objective of this offensive. This decision was
confirmed in September 1944, but because of the possibility that
Berlin would be taken by Soviet forces, the Supreme Anglo-American
Command planned an alternative offensive: in the north, to the

Baltic ports; in the centre towards Leipzig-Dresden; and in the
south, towards Augsburg-Munich.

On March 25, 1945, the Commander-in-Chief of the Allied Expe-
ditionary Forces, D. Eisenhower, set the main direction for their
advance: Erfurt-Leipzig-Dresden, to make contact with the Soviet
forces on the Elbe southwest of Berlin. This operation was assigned to an army group under the command of General Omar Bradley.
The army under Field Marshal Montgomery was to move towards the
Baltic to "cut off Denmark." And the army group under General
Devers was instructed to advance into the Danube valley until contact was made with the Soviet forces in Austria.

Eisenhower's decision caused irritation in Britain, where it
was assessed as abandonment of all intention to take Berlin. "All
prospect also of the British entering Berlin with the Americans is
ruled out," noted Churchill on March 31, 1945, in a letter to General H. Ismay. Hoping to alter the situation, he demanded that
the Allied armies break through to Central and even Eastern Europe
no matter what the cost, and thereby prevent the Soviet Army from
liberating that region.

The Supreme Allied Command, however, being on the scene of
action, clearly saw the weaknesses of Churchill's plans. As F.
Pogue wrote in his book *The Supreme Command*, ". . . it appeared
clear that the U.S. forces could not possibly outrace the Russians
for the German capital." On April 7, 1945, Eisenhower wrote to
George Marshall: "I am the first to admit that the war is waged
in pursuance of political aims, and if the Combined Chiefs of
Staff should decide that the Allied effort to take Berlin out-
weighs purely military considerations in this theatre, I would
cheerfully readjust my plans and my thinking so as to carry out
such an operation."

The U.S. military command did not shut its eyes to the political consequences that the presence of Allied armies in Europe at
the end of the war could have, and it was not against adopting a
"position of strength" in relation to its ally—the U.S.S.R. But
under the circumstances it considered it possible to establish
only the Allied left flank on the Baltic coastline near Luebeck
"to prevent Russian occupation of Schleswig-Holstein." The Allied
forces moved in the direction where there was least enemy resistance and, consequently, where it was possible to capture the
greatest amount of territory.

Thus, the course of the war in Europe is enough to refute any
assertions that the government and the military command of the
U.S.A. ignored the political aims of the war. The truth of the
matter is that there was a huge gap between these aims—which were
invariably kept in mind—and the possibility of their achievement.

The changes that occurred in Europe after the Second World War
were the natural result of the victory of progressive and peace-
loving forces over the forces of fascism and reaction; in no way

were they the consequence of miscalculations on the part of the
U.S. leaders. The outcome of the war in Europe was decided by the
military, political, and ideological superiority of the U.S.S.R.
And this was something, as George Kennan wrote, that the U.S.A.
could do nothing about: "And there is no reason to suppose that,
had we behaved differently . . . the outcome of military events in
Europe would have been greatly different than it was."

The Second World War showed that fruitful and mutually advantageous cooperation between the Soviet Union and the United States
of America is possible. President Roosevelt explicitly mentioned
this, and it was confirmed by Secretary of State Cordell Hull:
"President Roosevelt and I saw alike with regard to Russia . . .
we also felt we could work with Russia."

The foreign policy course set by the Truman Administration
meant a rejection of the policy of cooperation with the Soviet
Union. Expressing the interests of the country's ruling circles,
American bourgeois historiography began its falsification of history; it began to slander the Soviet Union and to accuse it of aggressive intentions and of beginning the cold war.

The U.S. government strongly opposes any attempts made by
individual American historians to question the semi-official conceptions that are being spread; it uses, in the words of Hans
Morgenthau, "the full powers of persuasion and intimidation," including its means of mass propaganda, to snuff out disagreement
with the official point of view. It is highly significant that in
July 1969, President Nixon came out publicly against the "school
of thought" which argues that the United States is also "responsible for the tensions in the world."

Most active in the campaign to falsify the nature of the relationships between the Allies in the Second World War is the
school represented by Ch. Beard, H. Barnes, G. Morgenstern, Ch.
Tansill, and others, which bases its conceptions on the views of
former head of the American military mission in Moscow, J. Deane.
The last-named insisted that the U.S.A. had gone too far in its
cooperation with the U.S.S.R., and for this reason he called the
alliance between Russia and America "the strange alliance." But
whereas Deane criticised only the extent of the cooperation, this
group of historians questions the advisability of having entered
into an alliance at all with a "potential enemy," contending that
this alliance was not only strange, but also a mistake.

It is clear from its general trend that American semi-official historiography holds essentially the same view. In his book
The American Approach to Foreign Policy, D. Perkins states that
during the war the U.S.A. "sincerely supported" the U.S.S.R.,
rendering it "colossal assistance," and making "exceptional concessions."

Assertions to the effect that the U.S. ruling circles had a "sincere desire" to cooperate with the U.S.S.R. are not corroborated either by the deeds of these circles during the war, or by the materials and documents that became known after the war. The facts indicate that the U.S. ruling circles calculated that the Soviet Union would be weakened as a result of its long and exhausting struggle with Germany and her satellites, and that it would lose its significance as a world power for a long time.

This is what was behind the delays in lend-lease deliveries and the slowness in opening the second front in Europe. At the end of 1944, when the superiority of the Soviet Union's forces became apparent, Deane strongly recommended that Washington re-examine its lend-lease policy. "I feel certain that we must be tougher," he wrote. Also insisting that the U.S. take "a firm and definite stand" in respect to the U.S.S.R. was the U.S. Ambassador in Moscow, Averell Harriman.

At a White House meeting in April 1945—at which Harriman was present—it was decided to implement these recommendations. The new President, Harry Truman, suggested a firm attitude towards Russia. In July 1945, General H. Arnold was already saying that ". . . our next enemy would be Russia." The same view was held by Assistant Secretary of State J. Grew, who said: "A future war with Soviet Russia is as certain as anything in this world can be certain."

The government of the U.S.S.R., on the other hand, proceeding from the common interests of the Allies, acted in an entirely different manner. The Soviet Union not only carried the main burden of the struggle against the fascist armies, but also aided the Allies with material resources. The Soviet Union responded without hesitation to Allied requests for support when the interests of the common struggle with the fascist powers demanded it. The success of the Allied Normandy landing was facilitated to a large extent by the broad Soviet offensive on the Eastern front that was timed to coincide with it.

American military figures who took part in the Second World War give testimony diametrically opposed to the latest assertions made by American bourgeois historians that cooperation with the U.S.S.R. was "impossible." "In fact," wrote Admiral Leahy in his book *I Was There*, "on almost every political problem the Russians had made sufficient concessions for an agreement to be reached. . . ." Former U.S. Secretary of War Stimson admitted that "the Russians were magnificent allies. They fought as they promised." Thus, the attempts made by semi-official American historiography to blame the cold war on the "non-compromising" attitude of the Soviet Union and its "unwillingness" to cooperate with the West are utterly groundless.

This conclusion is also reached by objective American historians on the basis of careful analysis of historical material. For example, D. Fleming, W. Williams, D. Horowitz, G. Alperowitz, and

others recognise that the cold war was brought about by the upsurge in the aggressive tendencies in U.S. foreign policy after
Franklin Roosevelt's death. This was evident specifically in the
use of atomic blackmail and the pressure brought to bear on the
Soviet Union. In his work *The Cold War and Its Origins*, D. Fleming, on the basis of detailed study of international relations
after the October Revolution in Russia, concluded that responsibility for the appearance and continuation of the cold war lies
wholly with the Western powers, and first of all with the U.S.A.
It was the Western powers that wanted to turn fascist aggression
against the U.S.S.R., Fleming stresses, and then put off opening
the second front in Europe for almost three years, hoping to see
their war ally weakened. The United States, he continues, dropped
the atom bomb on Hiroshima and Nagasaki not so much to win the war
against Japan, as to intimidate the Soviet Union. The U.S. pursued a diplomacy of atomic blackmail and intimidation with respect
to the U.S.S.R., hoping thereby to win military, economic, and political concessions.

Chairman of the U.S. Senate Foreign Relations Committee William Fulbright points out that the basic flaw in U.S. Foreign policy and also the basic reason why it suffers failure after failure
is that it is built on "favourite myths" and not on reality. "In
its efforts to cope with the Soviet challenge, the West, I think,
has too often devised its policies in terms of facile and misleading analogies with the conflicts of the past, tending at times to
perceive identity of motive and design where there is only similarity in appearance or detail." It is not, of course, only a
matter of superficial errors or arbitrary interpretation of the
past; it is also a matter of the deliberate falsification of history and disregard for the objective laws of mankind's development.
And these laws—as the events of the postwar years show so convinc-
ingly—do not operate in the interests of capitalism.

Progressive American historian W. Williams compares history
to "a mirror in which, if we are honest enough, we can see ourselves as we are as well as the way we would like to be." The unwillingness of the ruling circles of the U.S.A. to use the mirror
of history to see the country as it really is is the basic reason
for the prolonged crisis in U.S. foreign policy and its evident
lack of prospect.

SUGGESTED ADDITIONAL READINGS

Clemens, Diane Shaver. *Yalta*. New York, 1970. Outstanding study
of the Yalta Conference and its immediate aftermath. Uses
Russian sources and materials.

Deutscher, Isaac. "Twenty Years of Cold War," *Ironies of History:
Essays on Contemporary Communism*. London, 1966, pp. 148-163.
A lecture delivered at various teach-ins in the United States.
Extremely critical of American myths that Russia was bent on
physical or military attack, that Russia could not develop
nuclear power, that Communism and subversion are one and the
same, and that a tough policy is the only alternative to
appeasement.

Fleming, Denna F. "When Did the Cold War Begin?" *The Nation*, 206
(January 8, 1968), 53-55. Interpretive review of Halle's *The
Cold War as History* and Horowitz's *Containment and Revolution*.
Objects to Halle's emphasis on Russian initiatives for the
cold war and contrasts the Russian moves with the Truman Doctrine (a declaration of war), the failure to open a second
front, the use of the atomic bomb for political purposes, and
the Munich Conference (at which Britain and France tried to
turn Hitler's expansionist policies eastward).

Horowitz, David, ed. *Containment and Revolution: Western Policy
towards Social Revolution, 1917 to Vietnam*. London, 1967.
A collection of essays and articles by revisionists and other
critics of the policy of containment, with a preface by Ber-
trand Russell. Topics include U.S. intervention in Russia,
1917-1920; World War I and the cold war; Taft's critique of
containment; Greece and containment; U.S. China policy; and
U.S. intervention in Vietnam.

Horowitz, David. *The Free World Colossus: A Critique of American
Foreign Policy in the Cold War*. London, 1965. Revisionist
survey and critique. Chapters 5 ("The Cold War Begins"), 6
("Retrospect"), and 15 ("The Atomic Bomb") contain good summaries of the revisionist views on cold war origins.

Kolko, Gabriel. *The Politics of War: The World and United States
Foreign Policy, 1943-1945*. New York, 1968. Massive study of
U.S. wartime foreign policy, essentially from Teheran to Potsdam. Strongly revisionist and highly critical of the United
States. Marred by its ponderous style, its loose constructions, its generalizations from scant research (see German
policy), and its speculations disguised as conclusions.

Marzani, Carl. *We Can Be Friends*. New York, 1952. An angry book
by a victim of postwar Red hunters. The cold war is an American conspiracy concocted by Truman, Harriman, Leahy, Forrestal, Byrnes, Vandenberg, and others to frighten the American
people into believing Russia wanted war.

Starobin, Joseph R. "Origins of the Cold War: The Communist Dimension," *Foreign Affairs*, 47 (July 1969), 681-696. An ex-Communist criticizes revisionists for ignoring developments in the world Communist movement, which Starobin sees as a prime cause of the cold war.

PART 2

SELECTED ISSUES EXAMINED

The articles in this section focus on four specific issues important to an understanding of Soviet-American relations in the years 1945 and 1946. The first article, by Herring, is a careful examination of why and how American Lend-Lease aid to Russia was terminated shortly after the German surrender. Gar Alperovitz, in the second article, investigates the decision to drop the atomic bomb on Japan and concludes that it can only be fully understood in the context of American-Russian relations. In the third article, Paterson argues that the United States lost a significant opportunity to test Russia's willingness to cooperate in the postwar period by using economic power as a weapon rather than as a diplomatic tool. The final selection, by Gimbel, questions the conclusions of two revisionist interpretations of American occupation policies in Germany.

LEND-LEASE TO RUSSIA AND THE
ORIGINS OF THE COLD WAR, 1944-1945*

George C. Herring, Jr.

George C. Herring, Jr., is an associate professor in the History Department at the University of Kentucky. He is currently at work on a manuscript dealing with American aid to Russia in the period 1941 to 1946.

Revisionist historians have interpreted the sudden termination of American Lend-Lease aid to the Soviet Union in May 1945 as evidence that the fledgling Truman administration set out to coerce Russia economically. The object was to force political concessions in Europe from Soviet leaders. Herring takes issue with that position. He argues that during the war other states received Lend-Lease only after filing lengthy justifications of their needs, but "Soviet requests were accepted at face value." The procedure emphasized President Roosevelt's hope that generosity in dealing with the Russians would foster amicable postwar relations between the two countries. Although increasingly urged by his advisers to use Lend-Lease as an instrument for exacting Russian cooperation, Roosevelt "refused to approve any basic changes in Soviet Lend-Lease policy."

The war ended in Europe soon after Truman became President. Legal limitations on the nonmilitary use of Lend-Lease and domestic political pressures demanded modification of Roosevelt's policies. Roosevelt would have faced the same situation had he lived on. On May 11, 1945, Truman signed a memorandum ordering curtailment of Lend-Lease to the Soviet Union. The order did not terminate all Lend-Lease to Russia immediately, but its implementation on May 12, 1945, was so literal and rigid that it "caused consternation at San Francisco, in the state department, and in the Russian embassy." Attempts to mollify the Russians by countermanding the harsher features of the order did not succeed in removing the suspicion that the Truman administration was using economic pressure to intimidate the Soviet Union. Herring agrees that the abruptness of the American action was regrettable and tactless, but, he asserts, not until cold war positions had hardened did the Lend-Lease issue emerge as a causative factor for those endeavoring to explain the origins of the conflict.

----

*Reprinted, without footnotes, from *The Journal of American History*, LVI (June 1969), 93-114, by permission of the Organization of American Historians and the author.

On May 11, 1945, three days after the cessation of hostilities against Germany, President Harry S. Truman ordered a drastic
cutback in lend-lease aid to the Soviet Union. The following day,
civilian and military officials, zealously executing the directive,
halted loadings in port and even recalled several ships at sea
bound for Russia. Truman's order naturally evoked loud protests
from the Soviets. The Grand Alliance was disintegrating. Joseph
Stalin interpreted the reduction of lend-lease as an American attempt to extort political concessions through economic pressure.

The full story behind this important policy decision has not
been told. In his *Memoirs*, Truman denied any intention of coer-
cing the Russians. With the war in Europe ended, he argued, large-
scale lend-lease shipments to the Soviet Union were no longer le-
gally justifiable. The cutback applied to all nations, not just
Russia; he had not intended the May 12 reduction to be so severe.
When he had learned that his order had been interpreted too rigidly, Truman recalled, he had quickly corrected the mistake; and
shipments to Russia had been resumed on as large a scale as possible.

Those revisionist historians who have placed major responsibility for the Cold War on the United States have challenged Truman's explanation of the May 11 order and have cited the lend-
lease cutback as one of the first of a series of provocative acts
by his administration to coerce the Russians. The fullest exposi-
tion of the revisionist thesis has been offered by Gar Alperovitz.
He pinpoints the lend-lease cutback as the central element in Truman's "strategy of an immediate showdown" with the Soviets. Shortly after Truman took office, Alperovitz contends, Truman abandoned
Franklin D. Roosevelt's policy of friendship and conciliation toward the Russians and embarked upon a "powerful foreign policy
initiative aimed at reducing or eliminating Soviet influence from
Europe." The drastic reduction of lend-lease after V-E Day was
designed to achieve this objective. Alperovitz cites numerous conversations among Truman's advisers as evidence to prove that their
major concern in cutting back lend-lease was the Soviet Union.
The legal limitations on the use of lend-lease after V-E Day, he
argues, were not rigid and were used by the administration only as
a pretext for an act whose essential purpose was to coerce the Russians. A more flexible line on later Soviet requests for aid was
taken only because the showdown strategy failed to produce a Soviet surrender and because the atomic bomb seemed to provide an
instrument of coercion more powerful than economic pressure.

The availability of new documentary evidence permits a detailed examination of the decision of May 11, 1945, to cut back aid
to Russia. This evidence indicates that neither Truman's apology
nor the revisionists' critique provides an adequate explanation
for the decision. A full study of this important and controversial decision which places it in the context of American lend-lease

policy for Russia and other Allied nations, considers it against
the domestic political background in the United States during the
summer of 1945, and studies it in the light of the emerging conflict in Soviet-American relations, makes it possible to correct
several misconceptions regarding the decision itself and to evaluate more accurately the significance of the lend-lease question in
the origins of the Cold War.

To place the May 11 decision in perspective, it is necessary
to consider the unique manner in which aid to Russia had been administered since its inception in 1941. After the Nazi invasion
of Russia, Roosevelt attached special military importance to assisting the Soviets. He considered it essential to provide maximum support to operations on the Russian front; and until a second
front could be opened, lend-lease was the only means of support
available. During the course of the war, he seems also to have
believed that American generosity in assisting the Russians would
help break down the ingrained Soviet suspicion of the West, that
it would convince the Russian leaders of American good will, and
that it would provide a firm foundation for the Soviet-American
cooperation upon which he came to base his hopes for a lasting
peace.

For these reasons, Roosevelt assigned highest priority to aid
to Russia and took a close personal interest in the implementation
of the Russian lend-lease program. Throughout the war he repeatedly impressed upon his aides the urgency of maintaining a steady
and an increasing flow of supplies to the Soviets. When supply
shortages or administrative red tape threatened to delay shipments,
he exerted his personal influence to break the bottleneck. He relentlessly drove his subordinates to find sufficient shipping to
transport supplies to Russia, and he even established a special
committee, responsible directly to him and headed by his confidant
Harry Hopkins, to oversee Soviet aid.

Under the President's direct supervision, lend-lease to Russia was given a unique status. Lend-lease officials required
other recipients of aid to file elaborate evidence which justified
their need for and indicated their ability to use each item requested. Quarterly programs were established on the basis of this
evidence, but these programs did not represent binding commitments.
They were always subject to modification on the basis of changes
in the availability of equipment or transport and changes in the
strategic situation. As the military position of the Allies improved after mid-1944 and American troops took on a greater burden
of the fighting, lend-lease to most nations was sharply reduced.

None of these limitations applied to Russian lend-lease. Soviet requests were accepted at face value; no supporting evidence
was required. These requests, compiled into annual programs
called protocols, were represented as binding commitments and
limited only by the availability of supplies and shipping.

Difficulties in transporting supplies to Russia imposed severe
limitations on the lend-lease program until 1943, but as the shipping crisis eased, protocol commitments steadily increased and
were often exceeded.

Roosevelt vigorously resisted any efforts to modify this unconditional aid policy. He rejected the proposals of air force
officers to limit aircraft shipments to the Russians and quashed
the army's efforts to get a *quid pro quo* in return for lend-lease
aid. He politely ignored the warnings of his ambassador to Russia, Admiral William H. Standley, that the Soviets were taking
advantage of his generosity. At the first meeting of the President's Soviet Protocol Committee, Hopkins stated that the unconditional aid policy had been established with some misgivings, but
after extensive deliberation. It would be maintained, he continued, and should not be brought up for reconsideration.

In 1944, however, as the Soviets took the offensive in Europe
and political disputes began to divide the Allies, a number of
Roosevelt's advisers questioned with increasing vigor the unconditional aid policy. The Russian military position was no longer
desperate, and the Soviets seemed to be exploiting American generosity. They had ordered much equipment which they could not use
and which reportedly had been wasted. They had requested vast
quantities of industrial equipment which could not be made operational before the end of the war and which was obviously intended
for postwar reconstruction. They were giving or selling to other
countries American supplies or items similar to those received under lend-lease in order to boost their own political influence in
Eastern Europe and the Middle East.

The continued secretiveness of the Soviets suggested to some
Americans that Roosevelt's policy had not succeeded in breaking
the wall of suspicion which separated Russia from the West. More
ominously, the pattern of Soviet policy toward Eastern Europe in
1944 seemed to indicate not only that the unconditional aid policy
had failed to secure Russian-American friendship but also that it
may have encouraged a more aggressive attitude on the part of the
Soviets and deprived the United States of a bargaining lever to
influence the shape of the postwar world. The President's advisers in Moscow, Ambassador W. Averell Harriman and Major General
John H. Deane, chief of the United States Military Mission, warned
their superiors in late 1944 that American generosity had been interpreted by the Soviets as a sign of weakness. Deane cautioned
General George C. Marshall that gratitude could not be banked in
the Soviet Union and that the administration's policy of cooperation with Russia could not work unless it was based on mutual
respect.

Both Deane and Harriman as well as officials in Washington
urged the President to modify the unconditional aid policy, to correct abuses that had developed, and to make clear to the Russians

what the United States expected in return for its assistance. Harriman advised against drastic changes and proposed the adoption of
a "firm but friendly *quid pro quo* approach." Deane, Harriman, and
Secretary of the Navy Frank Knox suggested that the Russians
should be required to justify their requests and to give limited
concessions (in the form of improved communications and the exchange of weather and intelligence information) in return for lend-
lease aid. Moreover, Harriman urged that serious consideration be
given to the use of lend-lease aid as a bargaining lever to protect American interests in Eastern Europe.

Roosevelt adamantly opposed Harriman's proposal to use lend-
lease aid as an instrument of pressure. The President explained
to a group of congressional leaders on January 11, 1945, that the
Russians had preponderant power in that region and that the United
States was in no position to force the issue. In any event, he
continued, a reduction or termination of aid to Russia would hurt
the Allied war effort as much as it hurt the Soviets. Further, as
Cordell Hull recalled in his memoirs, he and the President feared
that a termination of aid would threaten the prospect of a satisfactory postwar relationship with the Russians; even if Stalin did
give in to American threats, there was no reason to expect that he
would uphold his promises after the war ended and he no longer
needed American aid.

Despite rising protest within the administration, the President refused to approve any basic changes in Soviet lend-lease
policy. Official remonstrances were submitted against Soviet re-
transfers of lend-lease materials to other countries, and an effort was made to prevent shipment of industrial equipment which
could not be made operational before the war ended, but these represented only minor changes. While the British lend-lease program
was being reduced steadily, the United States exceeded protocol
commitments to Russia; and Roosevelt continued to give Soviet lend-
lease top priority.

Roosevelt, who earnestly desired the Soviet Union to enter
the war against Japan and to participate in a postwar collective
security organization, apparently feared that any changes in lend-
lease policy might jeopardize these objectives. In a very real
sense, the President was a captive of his own decisions. Having
once adopted a unique policy of economic assistance, he probably
felt he could not modify it without risking a break in the tenu-
ous relationship he had built with the Soviets over a three-year
period.

In an effort to cement this relationship, the President endorsed an ingenious plan for a lend-lease credit to bridge the
gap between the end of lend-lease and the beginning of a comprehensive program of postwar aid for Russia. Based on section 3(c)
of the Lend-Lease Act of 1943, this so-called 3(c) agreement allowed a steady flow of industrial equipment to Russia even if the

equipment did not contribute directly to the war effort or could
not be made operational before the end of the war. The agreement
permitted the Russians to submit orders for large quantities of
industrial equipment; orders shipped before the war ended would be
provided on lend-lease; orders after that date, on credit.

The 3(c) offer, later extended to other nations, was origi-
nated specifically for the Soviet Union and is a clear indication
of the importance Roosevelt attached to economic aid as an instrument of Soviet-American amity. The termination of the 3(c) negotiations with the Soviets on March 24, 1945, is the only evidence
that the course of Soviet policy after Yalta may have caused him
to reconsider his economic policies. This evidence, however, is
not at all conclusive. After months of haggling over terms, the
Russians showed no inclination to accept the American offer and
were seemingly confident that, if they persisted, they could get
a better deal. By late March, American aid officials feared that
the initiation of a 3(c) agreement so near the end of the war
would be construed by Congress as a use of lend-lease for postwar
purposes. Hence, Acting Secretary of State Joseph C. Grew and
Foreign Economic Administrator Leo T. Crowley advised Roosevelt
that the 3(c) offer should be withdrawn; the President concurred.

Withdrawal of the 3(c) agreement cannot be taken as positive
evidence that Roosevelt had decided to alter his policy toward the
Soviets. Nor is there any evidence of how he intended to proceed
after V-E Day, although it was clear to those administering lend-
lease that legal limitations would require substantial adjustments
in all programs when hostilities in Europe ceased. To keep within
the law, the Joint Chiefs of Staff and the Foreign Economic Administration had developed detailed plans which provided for a sharp
reduction in lend-lease shipments to all countries after V-E Day
and limited subsequent shipments for use only in the war against
Japan. To avoid misunderstandings, Harriman had sought to include
in the Fourth Soviet Supply Protocol (covering the period from
June 1944 to June 1945) some provision for adjustment in the event
of a German collapse. But Roosevelt had declined to approve these
plans and in September 1944 had ordered all further planning
stopped. He offered no more guidance on the question.

Within several weeks after Truman assumed the presidency, it
was clear that modifications in the Soviet aid program could not
be postponed. The men to whom Truman turned for advice—those
most intimately acquainted with the intricate operation of the
lend-lease mechanism and those most knowledgeable about Soviet-
American relations—agreed, although for different reasons, that
the unconditional aid policy could no longer be justified. Crowley and the military officials responsible for handling the lend-
lease program emphasized that the end of war in Europe would make
it impossible to support continued shipments to Russia on the prevailing scale. Harriman, who had played a key role in shaping

American-Soviet lend-lease policy from the accession of Truman to
V-J Day, stressed diplomatic considerations.

In his dispatches from Moscow in early April and in discussions in Washington following Roosevelt's death, Harriman dramatized the breakdown in Soviet-American relations since Yalta. The
Soviets' blatant violation of the Yalta agreements and the ruthless manner in which they extended their control over Eastern Europe left no doubt in Harriman's mind that they placed friendship
with the United States secondary to the pursuit of their own interests. The extent of Soviet ambitions was uncertain, but, Harriman warned, the devastation of Europe posed a real danger that the
Russians might dominate the continent. Harriman attributed the
breakdown in cooperation at least in part to American policy. He
was certain that the Soviets had interpreted as a sign of weakness
the continued generous and considerate attitude that the United
States had taken toward them despite their "disregard of our requests for cooperation in matters of interest to us."

Harriman emphasized that cooperation with the Soviets could
be achieved only if the United States dealt with the Russians on
a "realistic basis" and adopted a position of firmness in defense
of its own interests. Soviet-American cooperation could be secured only if the United States made it plain to the Russians that
they could not expect cooperation on terms "laid down by them."
In addition, he recommended a concerted American effort to improve
relations with the other Allied nations, to make them less dependent upon the Soviets, and to demonstrate to the Soviets that they
could not play the Western nations off against each other. A
close understanding among the other Allied nations, he argued,
might force the Soviets to abandon their unilateral policies and
to cooperate with the West.

Specifically, Harriman urged that the United States begin immediately to adopt a position of firmness toward the Soviets, to
select several cases where their actions were intolerable, and to
make them realize that they could not continue their "present attitude except at great cost to themselves." He suggested taking
strong stands at first on minor issues in order to avoid giving
the impression of a "major change in policy." He also favored a
gradual reorientation of American foreign economic policy toward
"taking care of our western Allies and other areas under our responsibility first, allocating to Russia what may be left." He
was hopeful that such a reorientation would help restore stability
in Western Europe as a bulwark against Soviet expansion, that it
would cement American relations with the Allies, and that it would
discourage the Soviets from persisting in their unilateral policies. Russia's essential military requirements should be met, but
the unconditional aid policy and the protocol system should be
ended.

Harriman urged continued efforts toward friendship with the Soviets, but always on a *"quid pro quo* basis." Truman agreed. "The only way to establish sound relations between Russia and our- selves," he remarked on April 20, was "on a give and take basis." Both men were confident that a tougher policy would not cause a break with the Soviets because the Russians urgently needed Ameri- can aid for postwar reconstruction.

The Truman administration carefully considered the possible military repercussions of a firmer posture toward Russia. The end of war in Europe was imminent, and it was agreed at a meeting on April 23 that no harm would be done the war effort if the Russians slowed down or ceased operations in Europe. The war with Japan posed a more difficult problem. By late April, army planners had scaled down considerably earlier estimates of Japan's capacity to resist; this rendered Russian entry into the war less vital. More- over, Harriman and Deane had repeatedly affirmed that the Soviets would enter the war to promote their own interests in Asia regard- less of what the United States did. Marshall and Secretary of War Henry Stimson remained unconvinced and insisted at the April 23 meeting that the United States still needed Russian assistance to win the war and should not jeopardize that objective by a hard line on other issues. The consensus of Truman's advisers, however, seems to have been that Soviet entry into the war, while still de- sirable, was not essential and that, in any case, a tougher line on political issues would probably not affect Russian actions.

The decision to modify the unconditional aid policy reflected the Truman administration's belief that Soviet-American coopera- tion could be established only if the United States adopted a stronger posture in its relations with the Russians. But, it should be emphasized, the policy would have been modified even had Roosevelt lived or had Russian-American relations been amicable. The exigencies of domestic politics and the legal limitations on the use of lend-lease aid left no alternative. Congress insisted that lend-lease must be used exclusively for military purposes and could not be used directly or indirectly for postwar relief, reha- bilitation, or reconstruction. Truman and his advisers were keen- ly aware that any deviation from that position might provoke a rebellion in Congress and endanger acceptance of the proposed United Nations.

The lend-lease program had enjoyed broad popular support in the first years of the war, but opposition mounted in 1944 and 1945. The increasing expense of underwriting a global war, the widespread fear that the nation's resources were being exhausted, and the growing concern for America's economic well-being in the postwar era all contributed to that opposition. Businessmen re- sented continued government regulation of the economy and foreign trade, and rumors of waste and misuse of American supplies by re- cipient nations found a receptive audience as the American people

began to feel the pinch of wartime shortages. Anti-New Deal congressmen played on these fears by denouncing lend-lease as the
most colossal dole of all time and by predicting that it was only
the "opening handout" of a "world-wide W.P.A."

Americans grudgingly accepted the necessity of continuing
lend-lease to win the war. But there was general agreement that
it must cease with the termination of hostilities. This viewpoint
was clearly reflected in Congress. The Lend-Lease Act was extended in 1944 and 1945, but the debates grew louder and the majorities smaller. With each extension, Congress reiterated that lend-
lease was an instrument of war only and must be used for no other
purposes. It must not extend "1 minute or $1 into the post-war
period," Senator Arthur Vandenberg warned in 1944.

The administration repeatedly assured the American people
that lend-lease would be continued only so long as and to the extent that it contributed to the defeat of the Axis. But recurrent
rumors to the contrary fed popular suspicions. Fears were first
raised in the summer of 1944 by reports that the British had requested a postwar extension of lend-lease. Then came rumors of a
deal between Roosevelt and Winston Churchill at Quebec which involved six billion dollars of lend-lease for Britain after the defeat of Germany. Reports of a Russian request for postwar aid and
leaks on the 3(c) negotiations with Russia and France heightened
suspicions, and the publication of a final 3(c) agreement with
France in February 1945 brought the issue to a head.

When the administration presented the Lend-Lease Act for renewal in February 1945, it made a concerted effort to allay these
fears. Crowley, defending the bill before House and Senate com-
mittees, repeatedly stated that lend-lease would be used only to
prosecute the war and that any programs for postwar foreign aid
would be sent to Congress for separate consideration. He carefully explained that the administration had made no commitments
for postwar assistance and emphasized that the Phase II agreement
with Britain, and the French 3(c) agreement involved only war supplies and included adequate safeguards to protect American interests.

Democrats in the House and Senate accepted Crowley's assurances without challenge, but Republicans, both isolationists and
internationalists, remained skeptical and demanded absolute guarantees that the authority granted the President under lend-lease
would not be abused. House Republicans forced the administration
to accept an amendment to the act which explicitly stated that
lend-lease could not be used for postwar purposes. An exception
was made that allowed execution of the 3(c) agreements.

H. R. 2013 encountered still more difficulties in the Senate.
Senator Robert A. Taft of Ohio argued that the exception in the
House amendment nullified the effect of the amendment and permit-
ted the President to send "indefinite amounts" of supplies abroad

for postwar reconstruction under the guise of lend-lease. Taft proposed an amendment to eliminate the exception from the House amendment, thus requiring all lend-lease shipments to stop the instant the war ended. The Taft amendment gained vocal support in the Senate not only from isolationist Republicans William Langer, Kenneth Wherry, and Hugh Butler but also from Vandenberg and Joseph Ball, leaders of the internationalist wing of the party. The vote on the amendment followed partisan lines, and it was defeated by the narrowest of margins—a tie vote. Vice-President Truman voted and broke the tie.

The debates on the extension of lend-lease in 1945 and the vote on the Taft amendment had a significant impact on the future formulation of lend-lease policy. The determination of Republicans to prevent any abuse of the lend-lease authority forced the administration to make unequivocal commitments. The implications of the debate extended far beyond the immediate issue of lend-lease to the entire internationalist program of Presidents Roosevelt and Truman. The vote on the Taft amendment especially was interpreted as foreshadowing a possible resurgence of isolationism in the Senate and underscored the need for caution lest the experience of 1919 and 1920 be repeated.

This lesson was not lost on those who participated in the proceedings. Crowley had made emphatic pledges to Congress, and he repeatedly demonstrated his determination to honor them. The army officers who were responsible for getting lend-lease appropriations from Congress recognized that adjustments had to be made in the program after V-E Day so that they could defend themselves before Congress. Most important, Truman, who had cast the tie-breaking vote against the Taft amendment and signed the bill into law on April 17, was deeply impressed by the debate. Facing the difficult task of steering Roosevelt's peace program through the Senate, Truman was acutely aware of the need to respect congressional sensitivities on lend-lease.

As V-E Day approached, there was no question but that the Russian lend-lease program had to be reduced. Shipments to the European theater would have to be cut off as quickly as possible and future commitments limited to those for Russian military operations in the Far East. Soviet requests for aid would have to be handled on the same basis as requests from other nations; requisitions would be accompanied by full information which justified need and would be approved on the basis of availability of supplies, the urgency of competing requests, and contribution to the war effort. This revised procedure would end the privileged status enjoyed by the Russians since 1941 and would entail a sharp reduction in lend-lease shipments. It would also indicate to the Soviets that the open-ended generosity of the Roosevelt era had ended and that henceforth Russian-American relations would be on a reciprocal basis.

It does not follow, however, that the administration intended to use economic aid as an instrument to coerce the Soviets into
surrendering on the Eastern European question. Revisionists have
argued that the special attention given Russian lend-lease by the
administration in April and May of 1945 is clear indication that
the revisions were designed primarily to pressure the Russians.
It was in fact the unique status given Soviet aid by the Roosevelt
administration that necessitated special handling as V-E Day approached.

It is quite true that some state department officials discussed the possibility of using lend-lease as an instrument of coercion. Harriman himself had suggested that same possibility in
1944. Those responsible for initiating the policy change were
more cautious, however, because they feared that a rupture on the
lend-lease issue might jeopardize the delicate negotiations then
taking place at San Francisco on the Polish question and the organizational structure of the United Nations. At San Francisco on
May 9, the day that Soviet Foreign Minister Vyacheslav Molotov
left for Moscow with the Polish issue and the dispute over voting
in the Security Council deadlocked, Harriman and Secretary of
State Edward R. Stettinius, Jr., discussed the possible impact of
the lend-lease reduction on other issues. They agreed that the
United States should impress upon the Soviets the gravity for Russian-American relations of the Polish issue, but no acts of pressure should be "suggested or considered" until after the San Francisco Conference. The necessary adjustments in the lend-lease
program would be executed as tactfully as possible and "without
any hint of relationship with the Polish or other political problems with the Soviet Union." Stettinius advised the state department the same day that the United States should take a firm approach toward the Soviets on lend-lease and other issues, but
should avoid "any implication of a threat or any indication of
political bargaining."

On May 10, 1945, Harriman conferred with Truman on the proposed changes in lend-lease policy. The same day, Harriman met
with representatives of all departments and agencies involved in
the Soviet aid program to discuss the preparation of a memorandum
for the President's signature which would precisely define the new
policy. Regarding current commitments under the Fourth Protocol,
it was agreed that the United States would supply only those
items required for Soviet operations in the Far East and equipment
needed to complete industrial plants already partially delivered.
Other current and future programs would be evaluated in the context of competing demands and in terms of overall military situation, and all subsequent Soviet requests would have to be supported by information which justified need.

On May 11, representatives of the state department and the
Foreign Economic Administration drafted a memorandum for the

President based on these principles. After securing Harriman's approval, Acting Secretary of State Grew and Crowley presented the memorandum to Truman. Both wanted to be sure that the President fully understood the implications of the order and that he would endorse it. Crowley predicted a sharp response from the Russians and "did not want them to be running all over town looking for help." Grew and Crowley had little difficulty getting the President's approval. Apparently believing that the memorandum merely restated the ideas Harriman and Stettinius had discussed with him the day before, Truman, by his own recollection, signed it without even reading it. At the same time, he approved a note to the Soviet embassy which advised simply that the end of the European war necessitated a readjustment of the lend-lease program and indicated the basic principles of that readjustment.

Early in the morning of May 12, the Subcommittee on Shipping of the President's Soviet Protocol Committee met to implement Truman's order. A heated debate ensued. The May 11 memorandum stated that supplies on order for the Soviets which were not required for Far Eastern operations or to complete industrial plants would be "cut off immediately as far as physically practicable." The Foreign Economic Administration representative on the subcommittee insisted on interpreting that phrase literally. Even ships at sea containing supplies for uses other than Far Eastern operations should be brought back, or the committee would have to explain why to Congress. The approach should be "when in doubt, hold," instead of "when in doubt, give."

Army officials disagreed and observed that this rigid approach would require calling back ships, unloading them and sorting supplies, then reloading only those supplies intended for the Far East. It was customary, they argued, that, once a shipment started, it continued to its destination, and deviation from this rule would cause chaos in the ports. But the Foreign Economic Administration stuck to its position and received the backing of General John York, acting chairman of the Soviet Protocol Committee, who contended that Congress felt that the drastic action should be taken. The army acquiesced, and the subcommittee immediately issued orders to stop loading supplies for the Soviet Union and to recall ships at sea en route to Russia.

The Foreign Economic Administration's zealous execution of the order caused consternation at San Francisco, in the state department, and in the Russian embassy. Stettinius later referred to the May 12 decision as an "untimely and incredible step." When Harriman and Assistant Secretary of State Will Clayton learned what had happened, they were shocked. Harriman said that he had intended to cut off production of new supplies for the Soviets, but not shipments of supplies already programmed and ready for loading. He immediately secured Truman's permission to countermand the order. The new orders allowed ships at sea to turn

around once more, sent ships that were loaded on their way, and
continued loadings of ships at berth. The Soviets protested
bitterly to the state department. Clayton attempted to explain
that the action had been a mistake and that it had been corrected,
but again he warned that the law required review and readjustment
of all lend-lease programs on V-E Day.

The May 12 decision had resulted in a serious diplomatic
blunder. The cutoff did exactly what Harriman had sought to avoid:
it gave the Soviets the impression that the United States was trying to force political concessions through economic pressure. Any
adjustment after months of preferential treatment was bound to
evoke loud protests from the Russians. But the rude, sudden, and
drastic stoppage of shipments needlessly antagonized the Soviets
at a critical period and gave them a splendid opportunity—which
they exploited to the fullest—to accuse the United States of acting in bad faith.

In his *Memoirs*, Truman blamed the blunder on his own inexperi-
ence and on Grew and Crowley, whom he accused of taking policy-
making into their own hands and of being motivated primarily by
their dislike for the Russians. Truman's charges are misleading
at best. His *Memoirs* give the impression that the May 11 decision
was made hastily and without much prior discussion. The evidence
shows, however, that the decision was considered at length within
the administration and that he was fully informed regarding these
discussions. There is no evidence that Grew and Crowley attempted
to undermine the policy agreed upon by Truman and Harriman. The
record suggests rather that the blunder resulted primarily from
the lack of a clear understanding among the President's advisers
on exactly what measures were to be taken and from the rigid interpretation given the President's order by the Foreign Economic Administration and the Soviet Protocol Committee.

The hard line on Soviet lend-lease taken by Crowley and the
Foreign Economic Administration seems to have stemmed more from a
rigid legalism than from Russophobia. During the congressional
hearings on the extension of lend-lease, Crowley had made unequivocal commitments that lend-lease was to be used only to prosecute
the war. Imbued with an extemely narrow concept of executive
authority and not concerned with the diplomatic impact of his actions, he waged an unrelenting battle to honor these commitments.
His crusade to limit post V-E Day lend-lease to the minimum, it
should be emphasized, was not restricted to Russia, but applied to
Britain and France as well.

Finally, in assessment of responsibility for the May 12 blunder, Roosevelt must assume a large share of the burden. His unwillingness to face squarely the problem of lend-lease after V-E
Day, his reluctance to present candidly to the American people and
Congress the tremendous postwar economic needs of the Allied nations, and his refusal to prepare the Soviets adequately for the

adjustments he knew would be necessary left his successor in a
difficult position. Roosevelt's postponement of planning on these
important issues had the effect of misleading the American people
and antagonizing the Allies.

In considering lend-lease to Russia after V-E Day, it should
be stressed that the United States fulfilled most of its commitments to support Russian Far Eastern operations and that it gave
Soviet requests at least equal consideration with those of other
nations. The question of future shipments was discussed in a series of meetings from May 12 to May 15. It was decided that no
additional ships would be loaded in Atlantic or Gulf ports until
cargo had been screened and items intended for Europe separated
from those intended for the Far East. Crowley attempted to apply
the same screening procedure in West Coast ports, but Harriman
insisted on a more flexible approach which would allow ships
scheduled for departure from West Coast ports during May and June
to sail as planned on the premise that the route was *prima facie*
evidence that the material was to be used in the Far East. Harriman won his point, although about 15 percent of these shipments
was not included in specific commitments for the Far East.

The cutback in aid to Russia which resulted from the new
policy was not immediately reflected in shipping. Shipments for
the Far East had played a major part in the programs scheduled for
May and June, and tonnage remained high during this period—May
was the peak month for shipments to Russia during the war. But
the statistics of procurement and production tell a different
story. In the week of May 19 to May 26 alone, 435 requisitions
with an estimated dollar value of $35,000,000 were cancelled by
the Foreign Economic Administration. In January 1945, by contrast, 478 requisitions had been forwarded for procurement, and
only seventy-five had been cancelled.

It is not correct to conclude from these figures, however,
that the Soviets were treated less favorably than the other Allies between V-E Day and V-J Day. In the second quarter of 1945,
on the contrary, the dollar value of aid to Russia surpassed for
the first time that of aid to the United Kingdom. In the third
quarter, dollar values were about equal. In late May, Churchill
strongly protested to Truman against the sharp cutback in American
aid to Britain, and in the same month the administration halted
all lend-lease shipments to France when General Charles DeGaulle
refused to evacuate a strip of Italian territory held by French
troops.

Further modifications were introduced in Russian aid policy
as a result of the Hopkins-Stalin conversations in late May. The
discussions ranged over a variety of issues, and Stalin made a
special point of complaining about the "unfortunate and even
brutal" manner in which lend-lease had been reduced. Hopkins
carefully explained that the drastic action of May 12 did not

represent a policy decision, but had been a "technical misunderstanding" by one government agency. He repeated that the law required a readjustment of the lend-lease program after V-E Day and
reaffirmed the American commitment to assist Soviet Far Eastern
operations.

Stalin seems to have accepted Hopkins' explanation, and on
the suggestion of Harriman, it was agreed that the ambassador
should discuss the lend-lease question with Soviet Foreign Minister Molotov and Commissar of Foreign Trade Anastas Mikoyan. On
May 28, the Soviets presented a detailed list of their supply requirements for the second half of 1945. Included in the list were
requests for 1,000,000 tons of supplies originally promised in the
Fourth Protocol, but not delivered before V-E Day, and requests
for 570,000 tons of new items.

Harriman and Deane viewed the requests sympathetically and
urged their superiors to provide "timely and effective" support to
Soviet Far Eastern operations, even at the risk of providing some
items which could not be fully justified. Deane selected a list
of items which he was certain were "vitally important" to the Soviets and recommended their prompt shipment, even though the Soviets had not provided adequate justification of need. Harriman
urged the state department to consider seriously Russian requests
for industrial equipment promised under the Fourth Protocol but
not shipped at V-E Day, since Annex III (a section of the Protocol
intended specifically to support Far Eastern operations) had not
been intended to fill all Soviet needs for the war against Japan,
but was a supplement to other requests. The ambassador also proposed that the state department reopen the 3(c) negotiations with
the Russians, provided they entered the war against Japan, so that
industrial equipment in the May 28 lists approved but unshipped at
V-J Day could be delivered later on credit.

The climate of opinion in Washington in May and June 1945,
however, was uncongenial to any new requests for foreign aid.
British supply officials reported to London that a "wave of economy" had swept over Washington after V-E Day. Supply shortages
were making it difficult to fill many requests for lend-lease.
Republicans in the House and Senate were charging the administration with a "breach of faith" by continuing shipments to Europe
and to nations which had not yet declared war on Japan. Crowley,
vigorously supported by the President's chief of staff, Admiral
William Leahy, was waging a veritable crusade to uphold to the letter his pledges to Congress by limiting shipments to those for specific use in the war against Japan. The Joint Chiefs of Staff,
who had greatly extended their control over lend-lease since Truman took office, were most concerned with accumulating supplies
for American operations against Japan and were increasingly unsym-
pathetic to Allied requests for assistance. Beset with a multi-
tude of domestic and foreign problems, and with his advisers

divided, Truman delayed for weeks before establishing a firm policy for post V-E Day lend-lease. His decision closely followed the Crowley-Leahy approach.

It is not surprising that the May 28 requests encountered extended delays. Harriman became so concerned that on June 21 he dispatched a personal message to Hopkins which urged him to secure "immediate action" on the Soviet requests. Finally, on June 27, the Joint Chiefs of Staff ruled that the United States would provide the Russians with items on the May 28 list which were approved by the Military mission in Moscow and which could be procured and loaded on ship before August 31, 1945. Several weeks later, the date was extended to September 30, after which a new statement of policy was to be issued.

The sudden advent of V-J Day rendered any new statement of policy unnecessary. As the first signs of Japanese capitulation reached Washington, the administration began planning the liquidation of the lend-lease program. On August 17, the President ordered the war and navy departments to end shipments of munitions to all lend-lease nations immediately; and three days later, he ordered all lend-lease operations terminated at once unless the recipient government agreed to purchase supplies for cash.

The sudden termination of the lend-lease program after V-J Day required little adjustment in the Soviet aid program, since operations had been scheduled only through September 30. Neither Annex III nor the approved items on the May 28 list had been completed when Truman ordered lend-lease stopped, but the American performance in Soviet supply from May to August was still creditable and compares favorably with performance on the British Phase II program during the same period. American shipments to Russia totalled more than 1,500,000 tons—over one fourth the volume shipped between July 1, 1944, and May 12, 1945, the peak period in Soviet supply. The United States shipped most of Annex III and the undelivered Fourth Protocol items requested on May 28. Only on the new requests of May 28 did shipments fall far short. Of the 570,000 tons requested, the war department approved for procurement only 185,000 tons, and about half of this was made available for shipment before V-J Day. The Soviets agreed to pay cash for some of the remaining supplies and on October 15, 1945, concluded with the United States a "pipeline agreement" which allowed them to purchase on credit the bulk of supplies undelivered at V-J Day.

The question of lend-lease forms an important chapter in the history of Soviet-American relations during the critical period from April to August 1945. After V-E Day, the Truman administration introduced a drastic change in Russian lend-lease policy which terminated Roosevelt's unconditional aid policy and placed the Soviet aid program on an equal basis with other programs. It cannot be implied from this, however, that the change resulted

simply from Truman's accession to the presidency or entirely from
the rising tension in Russian-American relations. On the contrary,
the exigencies of domestic politics and Congress' determination
that lend-lease should be used only to prosecute the war would
have necessitated a major change in the Russian aid program once
the war in Europe ended. Roosevelt might have made the adjustment
more smoothly, and he would probably have sent a personal explanation to Stalin, but the change would have been made.

Truman's decision to reduce lend-lease after V-E Day did not
discriminate against the Soviets. It did not mark an abandonment
of American attempts to cooperate with Russia, nor was it intended
to coerce the Soviets. The lend-lease cutback was general; it applied to all nations. The reason the Russian aid program required
separate handling before V-E Day was the unique status it had been
given at the beginning of the war. The V-E Day decision hit the
Soviets harder because aid to Russia had not, like aid to Britain,
been gradually reduced after the summer of 1944. The termination
of the unconditional aid policy did not mean that Truman had ended
Roosevelt's policy of attempting to cooperate with the Russians.
Harriman and Truman believed, on the contrary, that the unconditional aid policy had jeopardized that objective. Only if the
United States demonstrated a determination to defend its own interests could a sound basis for postwar cooperation be constructed.

There is no evidence whatever that the May 11 decision was
designed to drive the Russians from Eastern Europe. From time to
time some of Truman's advisers had suggested such a course. But
after V-E Day, Harriman had underscored the need for caution in
handling lend-lease to avoid any break during the San Francisco
Conference. The use of economic pressure was left open after the
conference ended, but in the case of lend-lease aid it was not
reconsidered. No attempt was made during the period from V-E Day
to V-J Day to extort concessions, large or small, in return for
American material.

Neither Harriman nor Truman intended the V-E Day slashes to
be so drastic. This resulted from a misinterpretation of the May
11 directive by the Foreign Economic Administration and the Soviet
Protocol Committee. The mistake was quickly corrected, however,
and after V-E Day the United States did provide substantial aid
for Soviet Far Eastern operations.

There can be no doubt that the May 12 reduction hurt the Russians economically. As Stalin admitted to Hopkins in May, however,
the Soviets were aware that the end of war in Europe would force a
substantial reduction in American assistance. The impact of the
cutback could have been lessened by Soviet acceptance of the proposed 3(c) agreement, but the Russians lost this opportunity by
trying to drive a hard bargain. In any event, the point of
Stalin's protest to Hopkins was not the reduction of lend-lease,
but the abrupt manner in which the reduction had been effected.

Stalin had ample ground for complaint, but his talks with Hopkins, and Harriman's subsequent discussions with Molotov and Mikoyan, seem to have repaired at least some of the damage. On June 11, 1945, Stalin wired Truman a personal expression of gratitude for American aid, a move he had earlier told Hopkins would be impossible in view of the rude termination of lend-lease.

The lend-lease question was an irritant in Soviet-American relations during 1945, but not a decisive issue in the origins of the Cold War. The conflict that developed over lend-lease aid was essentially a reflection of the deeper controversy over political issues. There is no evidence to suggest that a continuation of Roosevelt's lend-lease policy, had that been possible, would have made any substantial difference in the course of Soviet-American relations. It would certainly not have resolved the fundamental conflict over Eastern Europe. From the American point of view, however, the post V-E Day reduction was unavoidable. From the Russian point of view, the manner in which the reduction was handled was provocative. But it would be some years later, after Cold War divisions had hardened, before Soviet propagandists would turn on lend-lease as a "weapon of aggressive American imperialism."

SUGGESTED ADDITIONAL READINGS

Dawson, Raymond H. *The Decision to Aid Russia, 1941: Foreign Policy and Domestic Politics.* Chapel Hill, N.C., 1959. A detailed investigation of the extensive debate over extending Lend-Lease aid to Russia.

Deane, John R. *The Strange Alliance: The Story of Our Efforts at Wartime Co-operation with Russia.* New York, 1947, esp. pp. 87-103. The wartime head of the American military mission in Moscow, an advocate of toughness in dealing with the Soviets, discusses the Lend-Lease program.

Feis, Herbert. *Between War and Peace: The Potsdam Conference.* Princeton, N.J., 1961, esp. pp. 27-28 and 329-330, for a discussion of Lend-Lease aid.

Herz, Martin F. *Beginnings of the Cold War.* Bloomington, Ind., 1966, esp. pp. 153-174. A thorough study of American-Soviet relations from the Yalta to the Potsdam Conferences. Based on published records, made more lucid by Herz's former service in the Department of State.

Jones, Robert Huhn. *The Roads to Russia: United States Lend-Lease to the Soviet Union.* Norman, Okla., 1969. A general survey aimed at refuting claims that Lend-Lease was imperialistic and of little help to Russia.

Kimball, Warren F. *The Most Unsordid Act: Lend-Lease, 1939-1941.* Baltimore, 1969. Excellent for understanding the origins and enactment of Lend-Lease legislation in 1941.

Stettinius, Edward R., Jr. *Lend-Lease, Weapon for Victory.* New York, 1944, esp. pp. 119-131 and 203-229. A participant's uncritical, but very readable, account of the early Lend-Lease program.

WHY WE DROPPED THE BOMB*

Gar Alperovitz

*Gar Alperovitz obtained a doctorate in political economy at
Cambridge University, England. He served as a legislative assistant in Congress and as a special assistant in the State Department
in the mid-1960s. Since 1968 he has been co-director of the Cambridge Institute in Cambridge, Massachusetts.* His works include
Atomic Diplomacy: Hiroshima and Potsdam, The Use of the Atomic
Bomb and the American Confrontation with Soviet Power *(New York,
1965), from which the article reprinted below is adapted, and* Cold
War Essays *(New York, 1970).*

*No single book in the decade of the 1960s did more to sharpen
the debate over cold war origins than did* Atomic Diplomacy. *Although Alperovitz was not the first to suggest that America's possession and use of the atomic bomb was a key factor in understanding U.S.-Soviet relations in 1945, his book appeared at a time
(1965) when the revisionist critique of traditional interpretations of cold war origins was gaining a wide audience.* Atomic
Diplomacy *seemed to offer further proof that the United States
shared a large measure of responsibility for the collapse of the
Allied wartime coalition.*

*Alperovitz maintains that "shortly after taking office Presi-
dent Truman launched a powerful foreign policy initiative aimed at
reducing or eliminating Soviet influence in Europe." As Truman
and his advisers saw it, America's monopoly of the atomic bomb
would make it possible to accomplish that objective. But possession of the bomb was not enough; its awesome capability had to be
demonstrated so that Soviet leaders would realize the superior
power upon which American policy initiatives were based. Thus Truman's abiding claim that the bomb was used only to end Japanese resistance and save millions of lives is misleading. It ignored and
clouded the extent to which a desire to contain Soviet influence
guided American statesmen in the fateful decision that destroyed
Hiroshima and Nagasaki.*

*Alperovitz argues that post-Yalta disagreements between the
Soviet Union and the United States over eastern Europe strengthened the position in Washington of those who advocated a get-tough-*

----

*From The Progressive, 29 (August 1965), 11-14. Reprinted by per-
mission of The Progressive, Inc. and Simon and Schuster, Inc.
Copyright © 1965 by Gar Alperovitz.

with-Russia line. The opinions of prominent American military advisers to the effect that Japan would surrender without use of the bomb or an invasion were ignored. Truman failed to solicit the views of General Douglas MacArthur on the advisability of using the bomb, and he exhibited little interest in negotiations with Japan to end the war. He listened, instead, to his hard-line advisers and used the bomb, not so much to defeat Japan as to intimidate Russia.

> Dear Mr. President,
>   I think it is very important that I should have a talk with you as soon as possible on a highly secret matter. I mentioned it to you shortly after you took office, but have not urged it since on account of the pressure you have been under. It, however, has such a bearing on our present foreign relations and has such an important effect upon all my thinking in this field that I think you ought to know about it without much further delay.
>   —Secretary of War Henry L. Stimson to
>   President Truman, April 24, 1945

This note was written twelve days after Franklin Delano Roosevelt's death and two weeks before World War II ended in Europe. The following day Secretary Stimson advised President Truman that the "highly secret matter" would have a "decisive" effect upon America's postwar foreign policy. Stimson then outlined the role the atomic bomb would play in America's relations with other countries. In diplomacy, he confided to his diary, the weapon would be a "master card."

In the spring of 1945, postwar problems unfolded as rapidly as the Allied armies converged in Central Europe. During the fighting which preceded Nazi surrender the Red Army conquered a great belt of territory bordering the Soviet Union. Debating the consequences of this fact, American policy-makers defined a series of interrelated problems: What political and economic pattern was likely to emerge in Eastern and Central Europe? Would Soviet influence predominate? Most important, what power—if any—did the United States have to effect the ultimate settlement on the very borders of Russia?

Roosevelt, Churchill, and Stalin had attempted to resolve these issues of East-West influence at the February, 1945, Yalta Conference. With the Red Army clearly in control of Eastern Europe, the West was in a weak bargaining position. It was important to reach an understanding with Stalin before American troops began their planned withdrawal from the European continent.

Poland, the first major country intensely discussed by the Big
Three, took on unusual significance; the balance of influence
struck between Soviet-oriented and Western-oriented politicians in
the government of this one country could set a pattern for big-
power relationships in the rest of Eastern Europe.
     Although the Yalta Conference ended with a signed accord cov-
ering Poland, within a few weeks it was clear that Allied understanding was more apparent than real. None of the heads of government interpreted the somewhat vague agreement in the same way.
Churchill began to press for more Western influence; Stalin urged
less. True to his well-known policy of cooperation and conciliation, Roosevelt attempted to achieve a more definite understanding for Poland and a pattern for East-West relations in Europe.
Caught for much of the last of his life between the determination
of Churchill and the stubbornness of Stalin, Roosevelt at times
fired off angry cables to Moscow, and at others warned London
against an "attempt to evade the fact that we placed, as clearly
shown in the agreement, somewhat more emphasis . . . [on Soviet-
oriented Polish politicians in the government]."
     President Roosevelt died on April 12, 1945, only two months
after Yalta. When President Truman met with Secretary Stimson to
discuss the "bearing" of the atomic bomb upon foreign relations,
the powers were deeply ensnarled in a tense public struggle over
the meaning of the Yalta agreement. Poland had come to symbolize
all East-West relations. Truman was forced to pick up the tangled
threads of policy with little knowledge of the broader, more complex issues involved.
     Herbert Feis, a noted expert on the period, has written that
"Truman made up his mind that he would not depart from Roosevelt's
course or renounce his ways." Others have argued that "we tried
to work out the problems of the peace in close cooperation with
the Russians." It is often believed that American policy followed
a conciliatory course, changing—in reaction to Soviet intransigence—only in 1947 with the Truman Doctrine and the Marshall Plan.
My own belief is somewhat different. It derives from the comment
of Mr. Truman's Secretary of State, James F. Byrnes, that by early
autumn of 1945 it was "understandable" that Soviet leaders should
feel American policy had shifted radically after Roosevelt's death:
It is now evident that, far from following his predecessor's policy of cooperation, shortly after taking office President Truman
launched a powerful foreign policy initiative aimed at reducing or
eliminating Soviet influence in Europe.

     The ultimate point of this study is not, however, that Ameri-
ca's approach to Russia changed after Roosevelt. Rather it is
that the atomic bomb played a role in the formulation of policy,
particularly in connection with President Truman's only meeting
with Stalin, the Potsdam Conference of late July and early August,

1945. Again, my judgment differs from Feis's conclusion that "the
light of the explosion 'brighter than a thousand suns' filtered
into the conference rooms at Potsdam only as a distant gleam." I
believe new evidence proves not only that the atomic bomb influenced diplomacy, but that it determined much of Mr. Truman's shift
to a tough policy aimed at forcing Soviet acquiescence to American
plans for Eastern and Central Europe.

The weapon "gave him an entirely new feeling of confidence,"
the President told his Secretary of War, Henry L. Stimson. By the
time of Potsdam, Mr. Truman had been advised on the role of the
atomic bomb by both Secretary Stimson and Secretary of State
Byrnes. Though the two men differed as to tactics, each urged a
tough line. Part of my study attempts to define how closely Truman followed a subtle policy outlined by Stimson, and to what extent he followed the straightforward advice of Byrnes that the
bomb (in Mr. Truman's words) "put us in a position to dictate our
own terms at the end of the war."

Stalin's approach seems to have been cautiously moderate during the brief few months here described. It is perhaps symbolized
by the Soviet-sponsored free elections which routed the Communist
Party in Hungary in the autumn of 1945. I do not attempt to inter
pret this moderation, nor to explain how or why Soviet policy
changed to the harsh totalitarian controls characteristic of the
period after 1946.

The judgment that Truman radically altered Roosevelt's policy
in mid-1945 nevertheless obviously suggests a new point of departure for interpretations of the cold war. In late 1945, General
Dwight D. Eisenhower observed in Moscow that "before the atom bomb
was used, I would have said, yes, I was sure we could keep the
peace with Russia. Now I don't know. . . . People are frightened
and disturbed all over. Everyone feels insecure again." To what
extent did postwar Soviet policies derive from insecurity based
upon a fear of America's atom bomb and changed policy? I stop
short of this fundamental question, concluding that further research is needed to test Secretary Stimson's judgment that "the
problem of our satisfactory relations with Russia [was] not merely
connected with but [was] virtually dominated by the problem of
the atomic bomb."

Similarly, I believe more research and more information are
needed to reach a conclusive understanding of why the atomic bomb
was used. The common belief is that the question is closed, and
that President Truman's explanation is correct: "The dropping of
the bombs stopped the war, saved millions of lives." My own view
is that available evidence shows the atomic bomb was not needed to
end the war or to save lives—and that this was understood by
American leaders at the time.

General Eisenhower recently recalled that in mid-1945 he expressed a similar opinion to the Secretary of War: "I told him I

was against it on two counts. First, the Japanese were ready to surrender and it wasn't necessary to hit them with that awful thing. Second, I hated to see our country be the first to use such a weapon. . . ." To go beyond the limited conclusion that the bomb was unnecessary is not possible at present.

Perhaps the most remarkable aspect of the decision to use the atomic bomb is that the President and his senior political advisers do not seem ever to have shared Eisenhower's "grave misgivings." They simply assumed that they would use the bomb, never really giving serious consideration to not using it. Hence, to state in a precise way the question "Why was the atomic bomb used?" is to ask why senior political officials did *not* seriously question its use, as General Eisenhower did.

The first point to note is that the decision to use the weapon did not derive from overriding military considerations. Despite Mr. Truman's subsequent statement that the weapon "saved millions of lives," Eisenhower's judgment that it was "completely unnecessary" as a measure to save lives was almost certainly correct. This is not a matter of hindsight; *before the atomic bomb was dropped each of the Joint Chiefs of Staff advised that it was highly likely that Japan could be forced to surrender "unconditionally," without use of the bomb and without an invasion.* Indeed, this characterization of the position taken by the senior military advisers is a conservative one.

General George C. Marshall's June 18 appraisal was the most cautiously phrased advice offered by any of the Joint Chiefs: "The impact of Russian entry on the already hopeless Japanese may well be the decisive action levering them into capitulation. . . ." Admiral William D. Leahy was absolutely certain there was no need for the bombing to obviate the necessity of an invasion. His judgment after the fact was the same as his view before the bombing: "It is my opinion that the use of this barbarous weapon at Hiroshima and Nagasaki was of no material assistance in our war against Japan. The Japanese were already defeated and ready to surrender. . . ." Similarly, through most of 1945, Admiral Ernest J. King believed the bomb unnecessary, and Generals Henry H. Arnold and Curtis E. LeMay defined the official Air Force position in this way: Whether or not the atomic bomb should be dropped was not for the Air Force to decide, but explosion of the bomb was not necessary to win the war or make an invasion unnecessary.

Similar views prevailed in Britain long before the bombs were used. General Hastings Ismay recalls that by the time of Potsdam, "for some time past it had been firmly fixed in my mind that the Japanese were tottering." Ismay's reaction to the suggestion of the bombing was, like Eisenhower's and Leahy's, one of "revulsion." And Churchill, who as early as September, 1944, felt that Russian entry into the war with Japan was likely to force capitulation, has written: "It would be a mistake to suppose that the fate of

Japan was settled by the atomic bomb. Her defeat was certain before the first bomb fell. . . ."

The military appraisals made before the weapons were used
have been confirmed by numerous post-surrender studies. The best
known is that of the United States Strategic Bombing Survey. The
Survey's conclusion is unequivocal: "Japan would have surrendered
even if the atomic bombs had not been dropped, even if Russia had
not entered the war, and even if no invasion had been planned or
contemplated."

That military considerations were not decisive is confirmed—
and illuminated—by the fact that the President did not even ask
the opinion of the military adviser most directly concerned. General Douglas MacArthur, Supreme Commander of Allied Forces in the
Pacific, was simply informed of the weapon shortly before it was
used at Hiroshima. Before his death he stated on numerous occasions that, like Eisenhower, he believed the atomic bomb was completely unnecessary from a military point of view.

Although military considerations were not primary, unquestionably political considerations related to Russia played a major
role in the decision; from at least mid-May in 1945, American policy-makers hoped to end the hostilities before the Red Army entered
Manchuria. For this reason they had no wish to test whether Russian entry into the war would force capitulation—as most thought
likely—long before the scheduled November Allied invasion of
Japan. Indeed, they actively attempted to delay Stalin's declaration of war.

Nevertheless, it would be wrong to conclude that the atomic
bomb was used simply to keep the Red Army out of Manchuria. Given
the desperate efforts of the Japanese to surrender, and President
Truman's willingness to offer assurances to the Emperor, it is
entirely possible that the war could have been ended by negotiation before the Red Army had begun its attack. But after history's first atomic explosion at Alamogordo neither the President
nor his senior political advisers were interested in exploring
this possibility.

One reason may have been their fear that if time-consuming
negotiations were once initiated, the Red Army might attack in
order to seize Manchurian objectives. But, if this explanation is
accepted, once more one must conclude that the bomb was used primarily because it was felt to be politically important to prevent
Soviet domination of the area.

Such a conclusion is difficult to accept, for American interests in Manchuria, although historically important to the State
Department, were not of great significance. The further question
therefore arises: Were there other political reasons for using
the atomic bomb? In approaching this question, it is important
to note that most of the men involved at the time who since have
made their views public always mention *two* considerations which

dominated discussions. The first was the desire to end the Japanese war quickly, which was not primarily a military consideration, but a political one. The second is always referred to indirectly.

In June, for example, a leading member of President Truman's Advisory Interim Committee's scientific panel, A. H. Compton, advised against the Franck report's suggestion of a technical demonstration of the new weapon: Not only was there a possibility that this might not end the war promptly, but failure to make a combat demonstration would mean the "loss of the opportunity to impress the world with the national sacrifices that enduring security demanded." The general phrasing that the bomb was needed "to impress the world" has been made more specific by J. Robert Oppenheimer. Testifying on this matter some years later, he stated that the second of the two "overriding considerations" in discussions regarding the bomb was "the effect of our actions on the stability, on our strength, and the stability of the postwar world." And the problem of postwar stability was inevitably the problem of Russia. Oppenheimer has put it this way: "Much of the discussion revolved around the question raised by Secretary Stimson as to whether there was any hope at all of using this development to get less barbarous relations with the Russians."

Vannevar Bush, Stimson's Chief aide for atomic matters, has been quite explicit: "The bomb was developed on time. . . ." Not only did it mean a quick end to the Japanese war, but "it was also delivered on time so that there was no necessity for any concessions to Russia at the end of the war."

In essence, the second of the two overriding considerations seems to have been that a combat demonstration was needed to convince the Russians to accept the American plan for a stable peace. And the crucial point of this effort was the need to force agreement on the main questions in dispute: the American proposals for Central and Eastern Europe. President Truman may well have expressed the key consideration in October, 1945; publicly urging the necessity of a more conventional form of military power (his proposal for universal military training), in a personal appearance before Congress, the President declared: "It is only by strength that we can impress the fact upon possible future aggressors that we will tolerate no threat to peace. . . ."

If indeed the "second consideration" involved in the bombing of Hiroshima and Nagasaki was the desire to impress the Russians, it might explain the strangely ambiguous statement by Mr. Truman that not only did the bomb end the war, but it gave the world "a chance to face the facts." It would also accord with Stimson's private advice to Assistant Secretary of War John J. McCloy: "We have got to regain the lead and perhaps do it in a pretty rough and realistic way. . . . We have coming into action a weapon which will be unique. Now the thing [to do is] . . . let our actions speak for themselves."

Again, it would accord with Stimson's statement to Mr. Truman that the "greatest complication" would occur if the President negotiated with Stalin before the bomb had been "laid on Japan." It would tie in with the fact that from mid-May, strategy toward all major diplomatic problems was based upon the assumption the bomb would be demonstrated. Finally, it might explain why none of the highest civilian officials seriously questioned the use of the bomb as Eisenhower did; for, having reversed the basic direction of diplomatic strategy *because* of the atomic bomb, it would have been difficult indeed for anyone subsequently to challenge an idea which had come to dominate all calculations of high policy.

It might also explain why the sober and self-controlled Stimson reacted so strongly when General Eisenhower objected to the bombing: "The Secretary was deeply perturbed by my attitude, almost angrily refuting the reasons I gave. . . ." Stimson's post-Hiroshima reversal, and his repeated references to the gravity of the moral issues raised by the new weapon, are evidence of his own doubts. General Eisenhower's searching criticism may well have touched upon a tender point—namely, Stimson's undoubted awareness that Hiroshima and Nagasaki were to be sacrificed primarily for political, not military, reasons.

At present no final conclusion can be reached on this question. But the problem can be defined with some precision: Why did the American government refuse to attempt to exploit Japanese efforts to surrender? Or, alternatively, why did it refuse to test whether a Russian declaration of war would force capitulation? Were Hiroshima and Nagasaki bombed primarily to impress the world with the need to accept America's plan for a stable and lasting peace—that is, primarily America's plan for Europe? The evidence strongly suggests that the view which the President's personal representative offered to one of the atomic scientists in May, 1945, was an accurate statement of policy: "Mr. Byrnes did not argue that it was necessary to use the bomb against the cities of Japan in order to win the war. . . . Mr. Byrnes's . . . view [was] that our possessing and demonstrating the bomb would make Russia more manageable in Europe. . . ."

SUGGESTED ADDITIONAL READINGS

Blackett, P.M.S. *Fear, War, and the Bomb: Military and Political Consequences of Atomic Energy*. New York, 1949, esp. Ch. 10, for the argument that there were clear diplomatic reasons for the use of the bomb.

Feis, Herbert. *The Atomic Bomb and the End of World War II*, rev. ed., Princeton, N.J., 1966, esp. pp. 190-201. A thorough review of the decision to drop the bomb. Differs in emphasis and interpretation from that of Alperovitz.

Kawai, Kazuo. "Mokusatsu, Japan's Response to the Potsdam Declaration," *Pacific Historical Review*, XIX (November 1950), 409-414. The wartime editor of the Tokyo *Nippon Times* argues that Japan did not reject the Potsdam declaration, which traditionalists claim triggered American use of the atomic bomb against Japan.

Morton, Louis. "The Decision to Use the Atomic Bomb," *Foreign Affairs*, 35 (January 1957), 334-353. A defense of the decision, by a Department of the Army historian.

Schoenberger, Walter Smith. *Decision of Destiny*. Athens, Ohio, c. 1969, esp. pp. 285-307. One of the best studies available on the development of the bomb and the decision to use it.

Stimson, Henry L. "The Decision to Use the Atomic Bomb," *Harper's Magazine*, 194 (February 1947), 97-107. The Secretary of War gives a participant's account of how the decision was arrived at.

THE ABORTIVE AMERICAN LOAN TO RUSSIA
AND THE ORIGINS OF THE COLD WAR, 1943-1946*

Thomas G. Paterson

*Thomas G. Paterson is associate professor of history at the
University of Connecticut. In the course of research on the article reprinted below, he was allowed access to some of the personal
papers of W. Averell Harriman.* Professor Paterson has edited Cold
War Critics: Alternatives to American Foreign Policy in the Truman Years *(Chicago, 1971), and* The Origins of the Cold War *(Lexing
ton, Mass., 1970). He is the author of "Eastern Europe and the
Early Cold War: The Danube Controversy,"* The Historian, *XXXIII,
No. 2 (February 1971), 237-247, and a forthcoming study on American economic foreign policy and the origins of the cold war.*

*Paterson's findings on the issue of postwar American credits
to the Soviet Union strengthen the conclusion that economic objectives were important determinants of U.S. policies toward Russia
as the war drew to a close.*

*As early as 1943, Soviet leaders had expressed interest in
receiving American postwar aid to assist in reconstructing their
devastated economy. Those Americans who seemed to favor such aid
saw expanded trade with Russia as one way to cushion the American
transition from a wartime to a peacetime economy. But when the
Russians submitted a formal request for a $6 billion postwar loan
in January 1945, W. Averell Harriman, American Ambassador to Moscow, wrote that any loan "should be dependent upon Russian behavior in overall international relations—that is, the Russians must
conduct their diplomatic affairs according to American wishes and
standards." Throughout 1945 and into 1946 the subject was discussed frequently in Washington and with Moscow, but Harriman's
view continued to reflect the U.S. attitude toward the loan.*

*To receive an American credit, Russia was asked to accept the
principles of multilateral trade and the "open door" in eastern Eu
rope. She was also asked to join the International Bank and the
International Monetary Fund, both of which were dominated by Ameri
can money and votes. The Russians showed little inclination to
abandon the state-trading practices they had used for 25 years,
and Washington equivocated on the credits. The question of the*

----
*Reprinted, without footnotes, from *The Journal of American His-
tory*, LVI (June 1969), 70-92, by permission of the Organization
of American Historians and the author.

loan fell into abeyance. But at what cost? Paterson notes that reparations demands and an American credit "were closely linked in Soviet political thinking," and he implies that a more enlightened handling of the loan issue by the United States might well have tempered the severity of Russia's reparations policies.

The American ambassador to Moscow, W. Averell Harriman, called the Department of State in January 1945 that the Soviet Union placed "high importance on a large postwar credit as a basis for the development of 'Soviet-American relations.' From his [V. M. Molotov's] statement I sensed an implication that the development of our friendly relations would depend upon a generous credit." In October 1945, a diplomat at the Foreign Ministers Council meeting in London noted the issues which he thought were impeding amicable Russian-American relations—the atomic bomb and an American loan to Russia. A few years later, an associate of Donald M. Nelson, War Production Board chairman, wrote: "Although little publicized, the possibility of this loan for a time almost certainly influenced Soviet policy toward the United States, and its refusal coincided significantly with the increasing aggressiveness of the Kremlin."

In the 1943-1945 period, a postwar American loan to the Soviet Union might have served as peacemaker; but by the early part of 1946 both nations had become increasingly uncompromising on the major international issues, and the usefulness of a loan to the United States, to Russia, and to amicable and productive relations had been called into serious doubt. "Whether such a loan," Secretary of State Edward R. Stettinius, Jr., later wrote, "would have made the Soviet Union a more reasonable and cooperative nation in the postwar world will be one of the great 'if' questions of history." The recent availability of historical sources provides material for a suggestive answer to Stettinius' question. The evidence suggests that America's refusal to aid Russia through a loan similar to that granted to the British in early 1946, perhaps contributed to a continuation of a low standard of living for the Russian people with detrimental international effects, to a less conciliatory and harsher Russian policy toward Germany and Eastern Europe, and to unsettled and inimical postwar Soviet-American relations.

World War II had been cruel to the Soviet Union. Coupled with the deaths of millions was the devastation of most of Western Russia. Over 30,000 industrial factories and 40,000 miles of railroad line had been destroyed. In 1945, Soviet agricultural output was about half the 1940 level. One state department study reported that the Soviet Union had lost sixteen billion dollars in fixed capital, or one quarter of the prewar total. Secretary of War

Henry L. Stimson recorded that the "completeness of the destruction was absolute" in the Ukraine. To help repair the massive war
damage, the Russians looked eagerly to the United States.

   Shortly after his arrival in Moscow in October 1943, Harriman
asked to meet with A. I. Mikoyan, the commissar for foreign trade,
to discuss postwar American aid for Russian reconstruction. Harri
man found the Russians "intensely interested." He indicated to
Mikoyan that healthy postwar Russian-American trade financed by
credits "would be in the self-interest of the United States to be
able to afford full employment during the period of transition
from war-time to peace-time economy." About the same time, Nelson
visiting with Premier Joseph Stalin in Moscow, told the Russian
dictator that the United States had a "great surplus capacity for
producing the goods that you need. We can find a way to do business together." When Nelson proposed that a group of American
businessmen meet with Russian leaders to map plans for postwar
trade and reconstruction, Stalin replied enthusiastically; but
Harriman dissented and wanted the question to be "initiated
through Government channels. . . ." Harriman informed the secretary of state in November 1943 that "this question of reconstruction is considered by the Soviet Government as, next to the war,
the most important political as well as economic problem that con-
fronts them."

   At the Teheran Conference in 1943, Franklin D. Roosevelt, Har
ry Hopkins, and Harriman discussed a postwar loan to Russia, but
the issue was not taken up with Stalin. The Russian leader, however, welcomed Roosevelt's suggestion that the British and Americans donate ships to the Russian merchant fleet. Such aid would
help expand Russian-American trade, and Stalin indicated that Russia could exchange raw materials for American equipment. At the
close of the meeting, Roosevelt was sorry he had not talked with
the Soviets "about the whole question of reconstruction in Russia.

   Immediately after Teheran, at Molotov's initiative, Harriman
and Molotov examined the question. Harriman suggested that the
Soviets tell the United States "the specific type and quantity of
equipment which were most urgently needed and over what period."
He also broached the "possibility" of a credit from the United
States. "Molotov showed the keenest interest. . . ." But there
was no definite loan policy, and Harriman cabled Washington for
preliminary instructions. Meanwhile, in early 1944, he more
closely formulated his own position.

   Harriman proposed that the "first credit might be relatively
small, to be expanded at a later date if desirable, and that the
specific projects under this credit would be approved in Washington item by item, with such recommendations from us here as may be
required." The United States should exert firm control over the
Russian allocation of any credit. Indeed, the United States
should determine "item by item" what projects the Russians could

undertake. In the light of Russia's sensitivities about its sovereign relations with capitalist nations, and Russian reluctance
to divulge the uses of lend-lease goods during the war, this approach would have seemed to be impracticable. Hopkins apparently
opposed Harriman's recommendation. But Harriman, realizing the
"anxious" Soviet interest in postwar aid, desired to use "American
aid as a tool of diplomacy." He was also aware that a credit
would stimulate Russian orders in the United States, which could
"be of considerable value in easing dislocations to our employment
problems. . . ." He repeated his observation that Russia "places
the utmost importance on our cooperation in this field. . . ."

In late January 1944, Mikoyan asked Harriman how large a
postwar loan the Soviet Union could expect from the United States.
Harriman, lacking specific instructions, could not answer. On
February 1, Mikoyan suggested a figure of one billion dollars to
run for twenty-five years with .5 percent interest. Harriman de-
murred; he found the amount too large, the repayment schedule too
liberal, and the interest rate too low. The state department
still had no clear policy on a Russian loan and urged Harriman to
"limit yourself to generalities" because Washington was worried
about "certain legal limitations."

Harriman, eager to proceed in order to exercise diplomatic
leverage on the Russians, was unhappy with American lethargy in
early 1944:

> If we don't become involved now in discussions with the
> Soviets over this program and obtain an understanding
> of it we will lose a competitive advantage to which we
> are entitled and information of value in other directions.
> In addition *the Soviets place great importance on know-
> ing now our general attitude toward their reconstruction
> problems and if we push aside the consideration of their
> whole program doubts may be aroused as to our serious
> intents.*

The United States should move with haste to secure an agreement
with Russia on reconstruction assistance for three reasons. First,
he noted its value to the American economy "in cushioning the
shock from war to peace if we are prepared to put into production
Russian orders immediately upon cessation of hostilities." Second,
an agreement would spur the Russian war effort. And, finally (Harriman revealed the uses to which the United States would put its
postwar economic power):

> . . . if aid for reconstruction is to be of real value
> in our over-all relations with the Soviets as a benefit
> which can be obtained from us if they work cooperative-
> ly with us on international problems *in accordance with
> our standards*, we must have a well forged instrument to
> offer them. Vague promises excite Soviet suspicions
> whereas a precise program offered to them (but always
> kept within our control thru the approval of each trans-
> action) will, in my judgement, be of definite value.

Some business and government leaders studied the loan question in 1944. Eric Johnston, president of the Chamber of Commerce
visited with Stalin in June to discuss postwar trade. Johnston
speculated that "Russia is going to turn to the United States for
. . . things she will need not only to rebuild her war-worn economy but to give her people the higher standard of living she has
been promising them for 20 years." He believed that a loan would
be "the nub of our trade with the Soviet," and he told Stalin that
he would do everything possible to promote a postwar loan from the
United States. Harriman welcomed Johnston's trip, but earlier had
insisted that Johnston "discuss postwar trade matters only in the
most general way and after consultation with me."
        In Washington, some treasury department officials, at the re-
quest of Secretary Henry Morgenthau, prepared a report which
matched Johnston's enthusiasm for trade and credits. Harry D.
White sent a detailed memorandum which stated that he found a post
war loan both feasible and desirable. The key argument in favor
of a loan, White pointed out, was that America's stock of raw materials had seriously diminished because of war demands, and the
United States was now dependent upon foreign supplies. The nation's dire need for manganese, tungsten, graphite, zinc, lead,
chrome, mercury, petroleum, platinum, vanadium, and mica could be
met in substantial part by Russian production of these materials.
He stated bluntly that "the necessity of growing U.S. dependence
on foreign sources of supply in order to satisfy anticipated postwar industrial requirements and to maintain security reserves, is
inescapable." Russia could export these items to America only if
it were provided with developmental funds. Therefore, White proposed a loan of five billion dollars to be repaid in full over a
thirty year period in the form of raw materials. He brushed aside
the notion that postwar trade with Russia would return to the low
prewar levels and argued that both economies "have been fundamentally restructured by the war," which indicated to him "the new
and larger dimensions which foreign trade can assume in both economies in the postwar period." Repeating what Nelson and Harriman
had said before, White believed that Russia "could make an important contribution to the maintenance of full employment during our

transition to a peace economy." White concluded that a loan
'would provide a sound basis for continued collaboration between
the two governments in the postwar period." Morgenthau endorsed
the White study and later urged the President to extend an even
larger loan.

On January 3, 1945, Molotov handed Harriman the first formal
Russian request for a postwar loan. Harriman considered the Russian proposal a "curiously worded document." Three days later he
reported: "I have recovered from my surprise at Molotov's strange
procedure in initiating discussions regarding a post-war credit in
such a detailed *aide-mémoire*. . . ." What surprised and obviously
upset Harriman was the nature of Molotov's proposal:

> The Soviet Government accordingly wishes to state the
> following: Having in mind the repeated statements of
> American public figures concerning the desirability of
> receiving extensive large Soviet orders for the postwar
> and transition period, the Soviet Government considers
> it possible to place orders on the basis of long-term
> credits to the amount of 6 billion dollars. Such orders
> would be for manufactured goods (oil pipes, rails, rail-
> road cars, locomotives and other products) and indus-
> trial equipment. The credit would also cover orders for
> locomotives, railroad cars, rails and trucks and indus-
> trial equipment placed under Lend-Lease but not delivered
> to the Soviet Union before the end of the war. The cred-
> its should run for 30 years, amortization to begin on
> the last day of the 9th year and to end on the last day
> of the 30th year. Amortization should take place in the
> following annual payments reckoned from end of 9th year:
> First 4 years 2½% of principal; second 4 years 3½%; third
> 4 years 4½%; fourth 4 years 5½%; last 6 years 6%. Soviet
> Government will be entitled to pay up principal premature-
> ly either in full or in part. If the two Governments de-
> cide that because of unusual and unfavorable economic
> conditions payment of current installments at any time
> might not be to mutual interest, payment may be postponed
> for an agreed period. Annual interest to be fixed at 2½
> [2¼%].
> The United States Government should grant to Soviet
> Union a discount of 20% off the Government contracts with
> firms, of [*on*] all orders placed before end of war and
> falling under this credit. Prices for orders placed
> after the end of the war should be left to agreement be-
> tween the American firms in question and Soviet represent-
> atives.

Harriman urged Washington officials to "disregard the uncon-
ventional character of the document and the unreasonableness of
its terms and chalk it up to ignorance of normal business procedures and the strange ideas of the Russians on how to get the best
trade." He chided the Russians for starting "negotiations on the
basis of 'twice as much for half the price'. . . ." Any loan, he
argued, should be dependent upon Russian behavior in overall inter
national relations—that is, the Russians must conduct their diplomatic affairs according to American wishes and standards. "I
feel strongly," he added, "that the sooner the Soviet Union can
develop a decent life for its people the more tolerant they will
become." But such a concern was secondary, and he demanded complete American control of the funds "in order that the political
advantages may be retained and that we may be satisfied that the
equipment purchased is for purposes that meet our general approval."

Harriman's response was curious and, certainly from the Russians' point of view, unreasonable. Certainly, the United States
had been approached before by foreign governments with detailed
requests for aid. Later, the United States was to insist that the
Marshall Plan recipients do the same. Indeed, Harriman had earlier asked the Russians to be precise. And it is diplomatic practice to ask for more than one expects to get. Harriman should not
have been surprised that Russia was aware of the repeated statements of American public figures concerning the desirability of
receiving extensive, large Soviet orders. What perhaps disturbed
him most was the boldness, thoroughness, and the attitude of independence expressed in the Russian request. He seemed fearful
that the United States would fail to make political gain from the
loan—that diplomatic leverage would be lost.

Assistant Secretary of State William Clayton staunchly agreed
with Harriman: "From a tactical point of view, it would seem harm
ful to us to offer such a large credit at this time and thus lose
what appears to be the only concrete bargaining lever for use in
connection with the many other political and economic problems
which will arise between our two countries." The Department of
State soon lined up behind Harriman. A department study, probably based upon a report by the Office of Strategic Services, concluded that Russia could recover without American aid. Without
foreign assistance, but with the help of reparations, Russia could
regain her prewar level of capital investment by 1948; and a loan
of two billion dollars would only speed up reconstruction by three
to four months. The study went on to deemphasize American-Russian
trade potential by citing comparatively low prewar figures and
argued cynically that "she will repay unless she feels it politically desirable not to do so." Again conscious of bargaining
power, the state department memorandum stated what both Harriman
and Clayton feared—that "the U.S.S.R. will be in a position to

take a highly independent position in negotiations regarding
foreign credits." Joseph C. Grew and Clayton insisted that the
time was "harmful" to offer such a large credit to Russia because
the United States would lose a "bargaining" position. They pointed to the need for congressional approval, complications arising
from international transactions such as those of the Bretton
Woods institutions, and

> the suggested [by the treasury department] commodity ar-
> rangement would probably not be as strong an argument with
> the Congress as the Treasury believes, would arouse the
> opposition of petroleum and mineral interests, would not
> provide a fully distinctive basis for offering special
> credit terms to the U.S.S.R., and might raise questions
> of general commercial and commodity policy.

Morgenthau had in early January, dissented vociferously from
the state department's conclusions. He opposed the use of America's massive economic power as a political weapon and urged Roosevelt to present the Russians with a "concrete plan to aid them in
the reconstruction period. . . ." Morgenthau offered his own program: a ten billion dollar loan at 2 percent interest amortized
over a period of thirty-five years. He saw no problems of repayment. Repeating White's warning of raw materials shortages, he
concluded that Russia could sell the United States strategic materials. And he reminded the President: "This credit to Russia
would be a major step in your program to provide 60 million jobs
in the post-war period." But at a January 10, 1945, meeting with
Stettinius and Roosevelt, Morgenthau encountered the repeated opposition of the state department, which persuaded the President
that the loan issue should not be raised at the forthcoming Yalta
Conference. Morgenthau openly protested and later told Admiral
William Leahy "that both the President and Stettinius were wrong
and that if they wanted to get the Russians to do something they
should . . . do it nice. . . . Don't drive such a hard bargain
that when you come through it does not taste good." Morgenthau,
unwilling to use the loan to coerce, found the American position
too uncompromising and too demanding, and he thought that a generous loan would facilitate the solution of political and economic questions, including those growing out of Russian troop movement through Eastern Europe to Germany.

A week before the Yalta Conference, Grew informed Harriman
that the loan matter "has been discussed with the President who
has displayed a keen interest and believes that it should not be
pressed further pending actual discussions between himself and
Stalin and other Soviet officials." Yet at Yalta in February

1945, there was virtual silence on the subject. The failure of
the Roosevelt administration to discuss the loan question at
length doomed postwar American reconstruction assistance to the
Soviet Union, for President Harry S. Truman adopted Harriman's
view after Roosevelt's death.

In an important message to the state department, in April,
Harriman was pessimistic about any postwar economic cooperation
with Russia. Although the Russians were "keen" to obtain a six
billion dollar credit, he believed that "It certainly should be
borne in mind that our basic interests might better be served by
increasing our trade with other parts of the world rather than
giving preference to the Soviet Union as a source of supply." The
United States should undertake a domestic conservation program and
end its dependence upon Soviet imports by seeking supplies in Bra-
zil, Africa, and India. He also suggested that the President ask
Congress for a blanket foreign loan program which would leave the
administration the flexibility to name the recipient countries,
including the Soviet Union, if agreement were possible on American
terms. No credits should be extended to Russia unless the United
States retained "the power to restrict or reduce them as we may
see fit," he wrote, because "it is not possible to bank general
goodwill in Moscow. . . ." But he cautioned: "It would be inad-
visable to give the Soviets the idea that we were cooling off on
our desire to help, although we should at all times make it plain
that our cooperation is dependent upon a reciprocal cooperative
attitude of the Soviet Government on other matters." Indeed, Harriman and Clayton both argued that the postwar loan to Russia "was
the greatest element in our leverage" in Soviet-American diplomatic questions which centered on Eastern Europe, China, and Turkey.
The "other matters" referred to by Harriman dealt largely with
Eastern European countries, especially Poland, which were entering
a Russian sphere of influence.

President Truman, generally unprepared to handle the difficult and growing foreign policy problems facing the country,
relied heavily upon subordinates. On the subject of the Russian
loan, the state department (Grew and Clayton in particular) and
Harriman were ready to advise the President. On April 23, Truman
met with Molotov in Washington to discuss the Polish question.
The exchange was acrimonious, and Truman addressed Molotov as if
he were a rebellious Missouri ward politician. He warned Molotov
that the Russian government's international behavior would affect
American decisions; "legislative appropriations were required for
any economic measures in the foreign field, and I had no hope of
getting such measures through Congress unless there was public support for them."

Truman's scruples about congressional impediments are not
convincing. The new administration and the state department had
not prepared either the public or Congress for a loan to Russia.

In fact, public discussion had been discouraged. The administration had neither sought to inform public opinion nor demonstrate to the Soviet Union that the United States was willing to undertake serious negotiations on the loan question. And the state department was lethargic in recommending that the Johnson Act be repealed and that the funds of the Export-Import Bank be expanded. Over a year and a half after the Russians first approached the United States for postwar help, the state department had still not acted effectively to remove legislative impediments. Not until July 1945 did Truman ask Congress to increase the lending authority of the Export-Import Bank from 700 million dollars to three and one half billion dollars with the idea that one billion of it would be earmarked for Russia, should a loan agreement be worked out. The administration did not have to apologize for suggesting that funds might go to Russia, a full-scale public congressional debate never occurred, and Truman got the increase as well as repeal of the Johnson Act insofar as it related to the Export-Import Bank. The legislative considerations that state department officials and Truman thought so imposing were quickly and painlessly swept away.

Just before Truman left for the Potsdam Conference in July 1945, the head of the Office of War Mobilization and Reconversion, Fred Vinson, advised him that "A sound and adequate program of credits for foreign reconstruction would directly and immediately benefit the United States in both its domestic economy and its foreign policy." Vinson like many Americans feared a postwar economic slump, looked to foreign markets to take up the slack, and included the Russians in his plan for both economic and diplomatic reasons. He noted that the "Soviet Union desperately needs aid," a fact which would give Truman leverage at Potsdam. He suggested that Soviet control of Eastern Europe could be loosened by financial aid, "Our ace in the hole."

One of the items the Americans intended to discuss bilaterally with the Russians at Potsdam was "Credits to the USSR." But the subject did not come up, even though Truman later contended that he had gone there planning to offer help for Russian reconstruction. Truman said that all Stalin wanted to talk about was the ending of lend-lease. The Potsdam records do not reveal that Stalin pushed the lend-lease issue. But why did the United States fail to push the Russian loan if Truman was as prepared as he said he was to do so?

When Truman was at Potsdam, Nelson sent the President a memorandum which encouraged him to foster Russian-American trade relations. He explained that Roosevelt had wanted to reach agreement on a trade program, that Stalin had shown considerable interest in the establishment of a business delegation to handle economic relations between the two countries, and that Harriman had insisted that the question be placed in the hands of the state

department, in conjunction with other agencies. Nelson summed up
his frustration: "I could find no way to get the proposal out of
the State Department pigeonhole." He went on to observe: "Postwar trade relations between America and Russia still remain unsettled—a factor which I am convinced militates against satisfactory
political relations between the two countries."

With the legislative hurdles overcome and with hope that some
bargaining power still rested in a loan to Russia, Harriman informed the Russians on August 9, 1945, that the Export-Import Bank
was prepared to consider in Washington Soviet proposals for a credit. On August 28, the Russians presented the Bank with a request
for a one billion dollar credit at two and three-eighths-percent
interest. The drop from a six billion dollar figure to one billion was necessitated by the limited lending power of the Export-
Import Bank, and the Administration chose not to seek larger funds
for the Bank or to approach Congress for a special appropriation,
as it did later for the British loan. But the Bank rejected the
Russian-proposed interest rate as too low. The Bank's comparatively high and inflexible interest rate of three percent thus impeded
negotiations.

When a group of congressmen met with Stalin in Moscow in September, the Russian remarked that the United States had not initiated discussions on the Soviet request for a postwar loan and
curiously mentioned the six billion dollar figure rather than the
smaller request. But Stalin was optimistic that "there are possibilities for the trade between the United States and Russia to
increase." He told Senator Claude Pepper of Florida, who also
made the trip, that it would be "suicide" for Russia to use any
loan funds for military purposes. Stalin told the congressmen
that war damages in railroads and plant equipment had been especially heavy and that Russia would need 5,000,000 tons of rails,
10,000 locomotives, 100,000 to 150,000 railroad cars, rolling and
furnace equipment, and machine tools for rail construction and for
metallurgical plants. Russia also needed grain, meat, and cotton.
In short, he added, ". . . our internal market is bottomless and
we can swallow God knows how much." The Soviet Union could offer
the United States manganese, timber, chrome, and gold.

A National Association of Manufacturers report in October,
which stated that the United States had blocked all credits to the
Soviets until diplomatic relations improved, was denied by an un-
identified government official as "not wholly true." This individual did say that there were good diplomatic reasons to "make
haste slowly." Secretary of State James F. Byrnes, in rejecting
publicly the charge that he had put aside the Russian loan, stated
that the United States would treat a Soviet request on the same
basis as that from any other country. He was deceptive here, for,
at that very same time, the United States was offering the British
a three and three quarter billion dollar loan with an interest

rate of only two percent. He also expressed hope that the Soviets
would send a mission to the United States to discuss their needs.
But there is no evidence that he ever invited the Russians to Washington. On the contrary, he wrote Harriman in late November that
the Department of State "has been pursuing policy of not encouraging active discussions and at present matter is dormant."

In November the administration received some support from the
Colmer congressional committee in its policy of using the loan as
a diplomatic weapon. Its eighth report on *Economic Reconstruction
in Europe* acknowledged that the Russian economy was in massive dis-
array and that the German "scorched earth" policy had left much of
Russia in ruins. Economic cooperation with Russia should be effected, but certain points, the committee argued, should be clarified
before a "sound relationship" could develop. First, the United
States must be assured that any aid would not go into armaments
buildup. Second, the Russians should make "a full and frank dis-
closure" of their production statistics. Third, Russia must withdraw its occupation forces from Eastern Europe; and, fourth, the
Soviets must disclose the terms of their trade treaties with Eastern Europe. Fifth, relief should be administered on nonpolitical
grounds, with no siphoning of relief supplies to Russia from Eastern Europe. And, last, before any loans were made to Eastern European countries, there must be protection for American property
there. Other items mentioned also centered on the "open door":
"free entry" of American planes flying ordinary Russian air routes;
willingness to protect American copyrights; and the granting of
visas in "adequate quantities."

Shortly after the Colmer committee report, Harriman assessed
the status of the loan question. He wrote significantly and in-
quisitively that American economic policy toward the U.S.S.R. had
"so far added to our misunderstanding and increased the Soviets
[sic] recent tendency to take unilateral action." Moreover, the
American loan policy "has no doubt caused them to tighten their
belts as regards improvement of the living conditions of their
people and *may have contributed to their avaricious policies in
the countries occupied or liberated by the Red Army*." He added
that Russia worked on long-range plans and by November had probably formulated its program leaving aside American credits. Hence,
any help the United States extends, he wrote, would be over and
above the Soviet program. He called for a review of Soviet-American economic relations, apparently with the idea of denying Russia
any further United Nations Relief and Rehabilitation Administration aid, which he thought did the United States little good, and
from lend-lease, and an Export-Import Bank loan. His assessment
indicated that the use of economic power as a diplomatic weapon
had failed. Russia had not been swayed by such power. But, more
importantly, Harriman's memorandum suggested that, had the United
States earlier granted a loan to Russia, tension between the two

nations might have been reduced. If he was right in his overall
assessment, the United States, in its desire to use its economic
power as a diplomatic weapon to gain American solutions to world
issues, rather than as a negotiating tool, contributed to the
schism in international relations. One correspondent from Moscow
noted in early December 1945 that observers there thought that
American leaders "are most interested in using that country's favorable economic position to promote United States political aims"
and that Moscow publications repeatedly criticized American "dollar diplomacy" and "atom diplomacy."

A conference of the United States Economic Counselors and Ad-
visors met in Paris from January 28 to February 2, 1946, on the
subject of American economic policy toward the Soviet Union. The
conference concluded that the United States should insist on full
reciprocity and should be ready to withhold benefits from the Soviet Union in order to obtain reciprocity. Reciprocity at this
point meant several things. Russia was supposed to open the allegedly closed trade and investment door in Eastern Europe, and it
was supposed to accept American principles of international trade
multilateralism as expressed in the Bretton Woods institutions,
the International Bank, and the International Monetary Fund. Apparently no mention was made of Russia's political activities in
Eastern Europe. Harriman's chief assistant, George F. Kennan,
concluded that no loan should be made "unless they show a recipro-
cally cooperative attitude and give some assurance that their international trading will proceed along lines consistent with our
overall approach to international economic collaboration."

On February 21, the Russian chargé in Washington was handed
a note drafted by Harriman which explained that the one billion
dollar credit was "one among a number of outstanding economic
questions" between the United States and the Soviet Union. The
note suggested negotiations and invited the Soviet Union to send
observers to the first meeting of the International Monetary Fund
and the International Bank scheduled for March 1946. In early
March 1946, the Department of State made the false and bizarre announcement that the Russian loan request had been "lost" since
August; it had been misplaced during the transference of the
papers of the Foreign Economic Administration (overseer of the Export-Import Bank during and shortly after the war) to the state
department. As Arthur Schlesinger, Jr., recently wrote, this
"only strengthened Soviet suspicions of American purposes." What
is the scholar to make of this strange announcement? The evidence
is clear that the loan question was not "lost." Did the United
States, because it needed a public excuse for not having pursued
the loan with the Soviet Union from August to February, feign administrative clumsiness and incompetence? This question raises an
even more crucial one: Why did not the Truman administration take
up the matter with the Soviet Union in that period? Did the

United States believe that the bargaining power of the loan was slipping and seek time to retrieve it? With the first meeting of the Bretton Woods institutions forthcoming, and with the necessity of deciding where the limited funds of the Export-Import Bank would be distributed, the administration may have considered late February the most propitious time for reviving the loan question.

The American conditions for a loan—multilateral trade policy, membership in the International Bank and the International Monetary Fund, and the open door in Eastern Europe—conflicted with Soviet policies. The Russians were not eager to assume American trade principles and to reject the state-trading practices that its economic and social system required that had been in use since the early years of the Soviet government. They were also wary of joining the International Bank and Fund, both dominated by American dollars, voting power, and leadership. Russia would have derived little economic benefit from membership and would have had to reverse a long-time reluctance to divulge details about its economy to the institutions. Nor were the Soviets willing to accept the American position that the open door—especially Russian trade treaties with the Eastern European countries—be discussed in the loan negotiations. Predictably, Russia replied to the February 21 note with a refusal to discuss her economic links with Eastern Europe; but, apparently, it left the question of Bretton Woods membership in abeyance.

A few days before the Russian reply, Secretary of Commerce Henry Wallace, an advocate of a loan, urged Truman to make "a new approach along economic and trade lines." Critical of the current American handling of economic relations with Russia and conscious of the state department's laxity in pursuing the loan question, he advised that a "new group" be appointed to undertake the discussions. And he summarized the issue:

> We know that much of the recent Soviet behavior which has caused us concern has been the result of their dire economic needs and their disturbed sense of security. The events of the past few months have thrown the Soviets back to their pre-1939 fears of 'capitalist encirclement' and to their erroneous belief that the western world, including the USA, is invariably and unanimously hostile.

Truman later wrote: "I ignored this letter of Wallace's."

In late April 1946, the United States sent Russia another note and offered to begin talks in May on a loan. This note was very similar to the first, but apparently milder in its demands on Eastern Europe. Yet, one news correspondent commented, ". . . the conditions laid down by the United States are still regarded as so

rugged from the Soviet point of view that there was little expectation among informed officials that the Russians would accept
them." The note raised the questions of trade policy, Bretton
Woods, and political and commercial policy in Eastern Europe.

At this point, American domestic politics influenced the status of the loan. A troublesome dilemma faced the administration.
If the Export-Import Bank earmarked one billion dollars for Russia,
the administration would have to go to Congress for an additional
one and one quarter billion dollars needed for France. If it did
not earmark the one billion, it would have to go to Congress specifically for a Russian loan. In either case, Truman would have
to face open debate on the Russian loan. Such a debate would in-
flame Russian-American relations and embarrass the administration.
First, since the administration had never prepared the public or
Congress for a Russian loan and Russian-American relations were
increasingly divisive, it seemed improbable that the loan could
pass (the vote on the British loan was very close). Second, Congress at that time was not in a spending mood. And third, the administration was reluctant to place another controversial issue
in the political arena on the eve of congressional elections.

The loan issue was not dead, however, for in May the Soviet
Union, in a note to Washington, again demonstrated its interest.
The American response firmly insisted that Eastern Europe be included on the agenda for negotiations and specifically protested
Russian five-year trade treaties with Hungary and Rumania. With
only 300 to 400 million dollars remaining in the Export-Import
Bank in July, and with Congress leaving Washington to prepare for
elections, there was little likelihood that the United States
would grant Russia's requested loan. Clayton confirmed that the
loan was virtually shelved when, a few days later, he told a Senate committee that discussions had never gone beyond "a preliminary stage." Indeed, "We've had an application but we have never
agreed even on an agenda for negotiations." By October, Harriman
could tell the National Press Club that the loan was no longer a
"current issue." Wallace, in November, continued to call for a
nonpolitical loan to Russia; and Stalin indicated in the fall of
1946 that he still hoped for economic aid from the United States.
But the general question of American assistance to Russian reconstruction was seldom heard again until June of 1947, when Secretary of State George C. Marshall offered American dollars to a
European recovery program. By that time the Cold War was tense,
and it was clear that the Marshall Plan was to be closely super-
vised by Americans. Russia at first considered membership, but
later summarily rejected the offer and began to tighten its grip
on Eastern Europe through new trade treaties, the Molotov Plan,
fixed elections, and political *coups*.

The abortive Russian loan question has received little attention from historians. Herbert Feis devotes a few pages to the

subject in *Churchill, Roosevelt, Stalin*, but he apparently considers the loan controversy to have been no significant stumbling
block to amicable relations with the Soviet Union. Martin F. Herz,
in a brief account of the loan issue, finds it a disruptive issue,
but erroneously concludes that the United States was "oblivious of
the leverage" that its economic power could exert as a diplomatic
weapon. Standard diplomatic texts do not discuss the topic, in
part because the *Foreign Relations* volumes relating to the question are only now in the process of publication. But some works,
using the Yalta and Potsdam papers and various manuscript collec-
tions, have placed the loan question in a more prominent role in
the coming of the Cold War and suggest that the reconstruction
loan issue exacerbated tension between the Soviet Union and the
United States and perhaps even blocked friendly relations. Indeed,
Harriman's cable to the state department in early 1945 should not
be ignored: "Molotov made it very plain that the Soviet Government placed high importance on a large post-war credit as a basis
for the development of 'Soviet-American relations.' From his
statement I sensed an implication that the development of our
friendly relations depends upon a generous credit."
   The history of the abortive Russian loan posits some provocative questions. Would the Soviet Union have sought such heavy
reparations from former Axis countries in Eastern Europe had a
loan been granted? Harriman suggested that the Russians would not
have been so "avaricious." Would there have been so much tension
arising from Eastern European issues? Harriman stated that the
Russians might not have followed a "unilateral" course had a loan
been granted. Morgenthau argued, according to biographer John
Blum, that a postwar credit to Russia would "soften the Soviet
mood on all outstanding political questions." And in June 1945,
Grenville Clark asked President Truman:

> Now that Russia has regained self-confidence and military
> strength, is it surprising that without firm promises of
> aid from the United States . . . she should seek other
> methods of self-protection? I do not think so. On the
> contrary, it is inevitable and natural. This might have
> been mitigated if months ago we had made a treaty with
> Russia. . . .

   Would the Soviets have been so demanding *vis-à-vis* Germany
had a loan been offered? Would they have eased up on reparation
demands and have agreed early to unite the German zones if the
United States had acted with speed to aid Russia, as it was later
to do for Britain? One scholar writes that a loan might have
taken "the acrimony out of the Russian attitude on reparations."

Albert Carr concludes that "It seems altogether probable that
these two matters, an American credit and German reparations, were
closely linked in Soviet political thinking, for our attitude toward both questions profoundly affected the rate of Russia's postwar recovery." Indeed, as early as 1944, the American ambassador
to Great Britain, John G. Winant, linked the two issues and urged
Washington to assist Russian recovery. According to one of his
former staff members, Winant argued "that the Russian need for material aid in repairing the vast destruction in the Soviet Union
was bound to make the Soviet government particularly eager to
receive reparations deliveries from Germany on a large scale."
American leaders did not doubt that there was a direct connection
between Russia's reparation demands and her postwar reconstruction
crisis. Edwin Pauley, American reparations ambassador, wrote in
1947 that "It can be assumed . . . that Russia's intransigent position on unification and reparations is due to a desire to obtain
the maximum amount of industrial and consumer goods from Germany,
to meet internal political prestige needs and to help rebuild the
Soviet industrial machine." Reporter Edgar Snow noted in the same
year that "Ivan" was asking: "Did America offer Russia a serious
alternative to reparations?" Finally, what effect would a loan
have had upon the internal severities of the Russian nation? Recent indications suggest, as did Harriman earlier, that the more
prosperous Russia becomes, the more attention Russian officials
give to popular preferences.

At the close of World War II, Stalin told Harriman: "I will
not tolerate a new *cordon sanitaire*." The American use of the
loan as a diplomatic weapon, at the same time that Great Britain
was granted a handsome loan at below two percent interest, fed exaggerated Soviet fears, but fears nevertheless, that the United
States was creating an international bloc and repeating post-World
War I experience. As Wallace put it in a July 1946 letter to
Truman: "From the Russian point of view, also, the granting of a
loan to Britain and the lack of tangible results on their request
to borrow for rehabilitation purposes may be regarded as another
evidence of strengthening of an anti-Soviet bloc."

The proposed American loan to Russia was never given the opportunity to demonstrate if it could serve as a peace potion for
easing increasingly bitter Soviet-American relations in the 1945-
1946 period. From the Soviet point of view, the American insist-
ent requests for both a politically and economically "open door"
in Eastern Europe, for Soviet acceptance of American multilateral
most-favored-nation trade principles, and for Soviet membership in
the Bretton Woods institutions, seemed to require capitulation of
national interest and security concerns. From the American point
of view, Soviet failure to concede these issues endangered the
American conception of postwar peace and prosperity. In order to
fulfill that conception, the Truman administration—over the objections of Morgenthau, Nelson, White, and Wallace, among others—

decided to employ the loan as a diplomatic *weapon before* negotiations began rather than as a diplomatic *tool at* the conference table. Few nations or individuals are eager to enter negotiations when the attitude of the other party is simplistically "Our way or not at all." The diplomatic use of economic power by any nation possessing it is to be expected and can conceivably be helpful in achieving fruitful and mutually beneficial negotiations. But if that power thwarts negotiations or is employed to buttress demands which alone are held to be the *sine quo non* for peaceful settlement, the result is schism and conflict.

SUGGESTED ADDITIONAL DOCUMENTATION AND READINGS

Carr, Albert Z. *Truman, Stalin, and Peace*. Garden City, N.Y.,
     1950, esp. pp. 13-42. An expert on German reparations on why
     Stalin started the cold war, the fall of China, Truman's
     peaceful intentions, and how Germany benefited economically
     from the cold war.

Feis, Herbert. *Churchill, Roosevelt, Stalin: The War They Waged
     and the Peace They Sought*. Princeton, N.J., 1957, esp. pp.
     641-648. A study of the wartime meetings and negotiations
     of the Big Three.

Feis, Herbert. "Political Aspects of Foreign Loans," *Foreign
     Affairs*, 23 (July 1945), 609-619. An examination of alterna-
     tive ways to use American economic power. Feis urges that
     foreign loans not be extended to wring concessions from
     debtors, thus avoiding charges of imperialism.

Herz, Martin F. *Beginnings of the Cold War*. Bloomington, Ind.,
     1966, esp. pp. 153-169. A thorough study of American-Soviet
     relations from the Yalta to the Potsdam Conferences. Based
     on published records, made more lucid by Herz's former serv-
     ice in the Department of State.

Marzani, Carl. *We Can Be Friends*. New York, 1952, esp. pp. 245-
     261. An angry book by a victim of postwar Red hunters. The
     cold war is an American conspiracy concocted by Truman, Harri-
     man, Leahy, Forrestal, Byrnes, Vandenberg, and others to
     frighten the American people into believing Russia wanted war.

U.S. Department of State. *Foreign Relations of the United States,
     Diplomatic Papers: The Conferences at Malta and Yalta, 1945*.
     Washington, D.C., 1955, pp. 309-324, for documentation on the
     loan.

COLD WAR: GERMAN FRONT*

John Gimbel

John Gimbel is professor of history at Humboldt State College, Arcata, California. His book A German Community under American Occupation: Marburg, 1945-1952 *(Stanford, Calif., 1961) received the Pacific Coast Branch, American Historical Association annual book prize in 1962. He has also published* The American Occupation of Germany: Politics and the Military, 1945-1949 *(Stanford, Calif. 1968), and is currently working on a study of Germany and the Marshall Plan.*

Traditionalist and revisionist interpreters of cold war origins are often less concerned with the complexities of historical causation than they are with advancing "single-minded theories." They frequently call attention to neglected aspects of a controversial issue, but their work often suffers from distortions occasioned by "chronological leaps, sequential inversions, blind spots, and weighted quotations." That is the thrust of the argument in the following selection.

Gimbel's review of two recent articles on American occupation policies in Germany challenges the thesis that American officials maneuvered to increase German industrial production in 1945 and 1946 to protect American economic interests and inhibit the spread of Communism. Wolfgang Schlauch and Lloyd C. Gardner, authors of the articles under review, support the revisionist claim that Truman's elevation to the presidency signaled adoption by American officials of a hard-line policy toward Russia. Gimbel's point is that the documents on the early years of the occupation do not support the contention that American policies in Germany validate the revisionist interpretation.

At root, however, Gimbel's article is concerned less with urging a particular interpretation of cold war origins than it is with exposing what he considers to be the superficiality of much allegedly sound research on the subject. He observes that "if judgments, conclusions, or generalizations are a function of the elements that led to them, neither Schlauch nor Gardner have much— if anything—to contribute to our understanding of American occupation policies in Germany."

----

*Reprinted, without footnotes, from *The Maryland Historian*, II (Spring 1971), 41-55, by permission.

The revisionist critics of American foreign policy have concentrated mainly on the politics and diplomacy of war, on eastern
Europe, on the decision to use the bomb, and on the general "American search for a world capitalist hegemony" (via the open door and
other means). Two recent studies of American occupation policies
in Germany have now also cast that subject into the mold of the
revisionist version of cold-war history. Given Germany's long
recognition as "the chief prize to be won in Europe," it is both
unusual and surprising that this did not occur before. The cold
war—whatever its ultimate origins—developed in 1946 and crystal-
lized in 1947 on issues involving central Europe and Germany.
Coupled with that, United States participation in the German occupation created records that provide one of the richest veins in
that gold mine of revisionist historians: *Foreign Relations of
the United States*. Finally, many of the elements so important to
the revisionist version of cold-war history have long since been
available in the works of Wilfred Burchett, James F. Byrnes, Lucius Clay, James Martin, Robert Murphy, George Wheeler; in the
works of the East German writers; and in the public records of the
continuing discussion of German policy after 1945, especially
those created during the review and consideration of the Marshall
Plan. Be that as it may, we now have two studies that merit attention.

Lloyd C. Gardner and Wolfgang Schlauch have published two
somewhat different studies of how United States policy in Germany
fits into the larger revisionist analysis of American foreign policy. It is natural and appropriate to review such studies. Since
both contribute so measurably to cold-war revisionism, it is also
appropriate to use the two studies as a means to illustrate and
comment on the kind of hocus-pocus that is often passed off as historical research by those who write cold-war history. I carry no
brief for the traditional interpretation of the cold war, and some
of my criticisms of the revisionists would apply to the traditionalists as well. I do maintain, however, that the historian's most
effective response to simple and single-minded theories of cold-
war responsibilities—either traditionalist or revisionist—is research into the complexities of historical development and causation. That is what this essay is all about.

Wolfgang Schlauch, in his article "American Policy toward
Germany, 1945," says, in a footnote, that it is not his object "to
go into the debate on the origins of the Cold War." But he does
say his purpose is "to show how major forces and individuals in
American government and Congress, and American officials in Germany, demanded and partly achieved [a] change of American foreign
policy towards Germany in 1945." He concludes that this revision
"must be regarded as inaugurating further policy adjustments as
reflected in the Stuttgart speech of Byrnes in September 1946, the
Truman Doctrine and Marshall Plan of 1947, and the evolution of

the containment policy which dominated American foreign policy for
twenty years to come." Schlauch thus contributes to an essential
revisionist view of the Truman administration: the early change
in German policy is but another example to be added to what is
known about eastern Europe, the decision to use the bomb as a political weapon, the cancellation of lend-lease, the Russian loan,
and so on.

Schlauch's contribution to revisionism seems, at times, to be
almost inadvertent. He thinks the change in American policy was
fully justified by Russian actions. He says that "one of the
major reasons requiring a revision of American foreign policy towards Europe was the rise of Soviet imperialism," and he talks
about "Moscow's unbending attitude at Allied conferences, its
determination to prevent Germany from being treated as a genuine
economic unit, and to bring the Soviet zone within its satellite
system." Truman, Marshall, and Kennan said it no more precisely
in 1947.

Although he says Soviet actions necessitated policy revision
in 1945, Schlauch's major discussion of how this came to pass is
characteristic of revisionism. He concentrates on the economics
of the occupation, on the level-of-industry plans, on reparations
and dismantling, and on the relationship of Germany to European
rehabilitation. He describes the Joint Chiefs of Staff (JCS) directive 1067 and the hard-line school of Henry Morgenthau, Bernard Baruch, Senator Kilgore, and Senator Pepper only to conclude
that "the attitude of these Senators and of advisers like Morgenthau and Baruch ran counter to the policy of the American Military
Government." He tells us that General William A. Draper and Calvin Hoover, in the Economics Division of the Office of Military
Government for Germany (OMGUS), tried to modify JCS 1067 before
the Potsdam Conference, and that they questioned the practicality
of the Potsdam agreement in September. Members of Congress joined
in. The so-called Colmer committee warned against excessive industrial disarmament in Germany and it was generally critical of
the hard-line policy. Senator James Eastland of Mississippi "attacked it in a monumental speech before the Senate on 4 December
1945."

In the meantime, the Truman administration—moved by the
Byron Price report to the President on November 9, 1945—began to
talk about policy revision. James Riddleberger, the chief of the
State Department's Division of Central European Affairs, made a
speech in Kansas City to that effect on November 24, 1945. All
of this leads to a document released by the State Department on
December 12, 1945, which Schlauch regards as conclusive evidence
that policy had changed in 1945. Significantly, in regard to
Shlauch's major concern, the document is entitled "The Reparations
Settlement and the Peacetime Economy of Germany," and it is restricted to an interpretation of the economic policies agreed

at Potsdam. Thus, whether Schlauch intended it that way or not,
his analysis adds force to two major elements of the revisionist
school of cold-war history: (1) the Truman administration's early
reversal of Franklin Roosevelt's stance toward Russia, its anti-
Communism, its rigidity toward the Soviet Union, and (2) the dominant influence of United States economic interests in foreign policy (a feature of the "American search for a world capitalist
hegemony").

Whereas Schlauch detects a revision in American policy toward
Germany by the end of 1945, Lloyd Gardner believes the major turning points to be in three related decisions taken in 1946: (1)
Clay's reparations stop of May 3, 1946, (2) Byrnes' 25-year treaty
of guarantees, and (3) the Byrnes-Clay economic, political, and
ideological offensive, which is marked by Byrnes' Stuttgart speech
of September 6, 1946.

For reasons that may become clear later, I find Gardner's
article "America and the German Problem" very difficult to summarize and condense. Nevertheless, I submit the following: Roosevelt's plans for United States policy toward Germany remained in-
explicit when he died. The Byrnes-Clay partnership "clarified the
conception of German policy, so that imperfect plans could be
brought into line with overall American policy." Byrnes' proposal
at Potsdam took care of the Russian reparations demands of $10
billion, and it also provided a basis for much future disagreement.
The United States redefined its reparations policies late in 1945
and applied certain pressures on France early in 1946 to follow
United States leadership in Germany. But the growing Soviet-American split eclipsed that effort for the time being. Clay suspended
reparations shipments to the East in May, 1946, and Byrnes used
this "momentous decision" to set the stage for a two-phase policy
revision. First, he renewed his proposal for a 25-year treaty of
guarantees, assuming Soviet disagreement and hoping to gain needed
"leverage against Britain and France." Second, Byrnes delivered a
speech in Stuttgart that "would embarrass the Russians," and "somehow finesse the French." In the speech, he also endorsed the earlier British-American decisions to merge their zones, and he promised early German political development in the future. Gardner
maintained that to achieve the economic aims of Bizonia, Americans
believed the free enterprise system must prevail at all costs.
Social democrats and trade unionists therefore suffered at the
hands of Clay's superior power. Having revised their own policy
in 1946, and having locked the British in via Bizonia, Americans
(Dulles and Marshall) resisted Molotov's proposals at Moscow in
1947 for German unification, Ruhr control, and reparations to a
total of $10 billion. The conference ended in disagreement. "In
Bizonia," Gardner wrote, "it was full speed ahead after Moscow,"
a program he sees marked by continuing American antisocialist decisions, a new level-of-industry plan, American demands that the

Soviet Union account for its reparations removals, American-British-French trizonal discussions, Western currency reform, the Berlin crisis, and finally the formation of the Bonn government. The result, according to Gardner, was the "forced harmony in the West under United States leadership," which was made possible by the Russian blockade of Berlin and ensured by having Marshall Plan aid channeled to Germany through American Military Government. Gardner's own concluding statement reads: "What actually took place in Western Germany . . . was an American counterrevolution—against the policy of postponement, then against French obstructionism, German social democracy, and, finally, European radicalism."

The evidence is in, the conclusions are unequivocal, and the theses are apparently appealing and satisfying. But if conclusions are a function of the elements that led to them, both Schlauch's and Gardner's are less than convincing. In the language of the marketplace, the product is developed, the packaging is neat and attractive, and it all seems merchantable. But what of the ingredients?

Schlauch says, for example, that the hard-line views on German policy ran counter to the policy of American Military Government. His evidence for this is drawn from the activities of William Draper, Clay's economics adviser, and from the content and impact of the report of the German Standard of Living Board (the Calvin Hoover Report). It is quite true that both Draper and Hoover were unhappy with JCS 1067, and they thought the Potsdam agreement was too restrictive on the German economy. But the unhappiness and the thoughts of second-level administrators in the field do not necessarily translate into policy. Furthermore, it is simply not true that they were expressing military government policy in 1945. Clay wrote John J. McCloy in June, 1945, that JCS 1067 "requires what is manifestly necessary, a realistic and firm attitude toward Germany." After seeing a draft of the Calvin Hoover Report in mid-September, Clay penciled a note to Draper that Potsdam will be adhered to until changed. Further, on learning that Hoover was discussing his report back in Washington, Clay cabled from Berlin on September 26, 1945, saying the report was not policy, but a document for use in discussing the level-of-industry plan within the military government and the Allied Control Council. He added, "Hoover abhors destruction and his personal views are toward leniency." A short time later—but still *before* the Hoover Report was partially published in the *New York Times*—Clay wrote McCloy that Hoover "was greatly distressed over the reparations program in Germany and I fear basically at heart not in sympathy with the policies agreed upon at Potsdam. The result was that he was not happy in his work."

I am aware that Clay and Murphy wrote in their memoirs that they were dissatisfied with JCS 1067, and that they tried to get a policy revision in 1945. The variance between the documents I have used and the memoirs is, perhaps, understandable. Clay— fresh from the "Battle of Berlin," identified with the creation of the Bonn government, and familiar with the Marshall Plan debates of 1947 and 1948—was apparently unable to recreate his perspectives of 1945 when he wrote in 1949. Murphy relied on Clay's previous publication, and on his own memory.

The Hoover Report made no more of an impact in Washington than it did in Berlin. The War Department accepted Clay's assessment of the report, and it added some criticisms of its own. It was especially concerned about the Hoover Report's failure to distinguish between the short run (when German deficits would undoubtedly have to be made up by relief from outside to avoid disease, starvation, and threats to the occupation) and the long run (when Germany would have to subsist on its own, in accord with the Potsdam agreement). Schlauch notes the State Department's October 12 rejection of the Hoover Report. He attributes the rejection to the "result of the general criticism provoked by its partial publication," which occurred four days earlier. Are we to assume, from this, that the State Department had been ignoring Murphy's inquiry and "warning" of September 30 until the *New York Times* prompted it? As a matter of fact, State had been preparing its reply to Murphy by checking Hoover's findings against its own previous studies on the German economy, and by coordinating with the War Department, whose views we have already noted. It seems reasonably clear, from these few examples, that neither in Germany nor in Washington was there any inclination whatsoever—*at the policy level*—to abandon the Potsdam agreement on the basis of the recommendations of the Hoover Report. Schlauch: "It should be emphasized that it was the Hoover Report which, by criticizing the Potsdam Agreement and stressing the impossibility of carrying out the severe programme of industrial disarmament, had induced a change in policy."

Schlauch believes that Calvin Hoover *et al.* were assisted in their efforts to achieve change by pressures from members of Congress, and by the impact on the Truman administration of the Byron Price report to the President. He assigns significance to the so-called Colmer congressional committee report, which was indeed critical of the hard line. In the context of 1945, however, its influence is probably best described as a very weak antidote to the public response to the Patton incident in Germany, to the publication of Morgenthau's book in New York, and to the press coverage given to Russell Nixon's criticisms before the Kilgore Committee of the military government's soft-line course in Germany. I shall leave my readers to judge for themselves whether Senator

James Eastland's "monumental speech" in the Senate on December 4,
1945, was either an enunciation of administration policy or representative of those who influenced it. It might be noted in passing, however, that even Senator William Knowland seemed skeptical,
and that Eastland was angry with the State Department for having
temporarily obstructed a program developed by Southern Senators to
"unload" American surplus cotton in Germany. The State Department's action was an application of stated policy against using
the occupation to further special interest groups in the United
States. Eastland charged: "With Germany deindustrialized so that
she produces only a limited domestic consumer supply of peacetime
industrial products, the producers of the United States are deprived of one of their greatest foreign markets. . . . If the
American farmer is permanently to lose this market . . . then
American agriculture will not and cannot be prosperous. . . .
This is a terrible price . . . which the American farmer must pay
if we continue the policies generated by Mr. Morgenthau's hatred
of the German people."

   The Byron Price report, as Schlauch says, recommended a reappraisal and a revision of policy, food shipments to Germany to
prevent starvation, and other specifics. But Schlauch fails to
note that Price also reported that France was defeating "the underlying purposes of Allied policy," and that he apparently considered that problem important enough to become the basis of his
first formal recommendation to the President:

>   The necessity for breaking the present deadlock
>   in the Control Council in Berlin is so important that
>   use of the full force and prestige of American diplo-
>   matic power to that end is fully warranted. . . . As a
>   result of the French attitude, Germany is not being
>   treated as an economic unit. . . . If France is really
>   bent on the dismemberment of Germany, as her acts indi-
>   cate, she should be made to acknowledge that policy be-
>   fore the world and not permitted to hide behind the
>   opposite pronouncements of the Potsdam Declaration.
>   Our own policies should then be reexamined accordingly.

   On November 23, 1945, McCloy wrote Clay that Byron Price had
been pushing for a revised directive for the occupation. On December 1, 1945, the War Department cabled Clay that Truman had circulated the Price report to the Secretaries of War, State, and Navy.
The message "imperatively requested" Clay's views on revision.
Clay's answer:

. . . do not understand what Byron Price had in mind.
On the whole, JCS 1067 as modified by Potsdam has proved
workable. . . . Here any changes would be confusing. . . .
It would be helpful probably to delete from JCS 1067 those
matters covered by Potsdam and Allied Control Authority
actions. . . . I don't know how we could have effectively
set up our military government without JCS 1067.

Clay's answer, plus a general reluctance in Washington to repeat the wrangling that occurred in drafting JCS 1067, seems to
have ended Price's effort at revision. But what about the December 12, 1945, State Department statement, which Schlauch regards
as the culmination of the drive for policy revision that occurred
in 1945?

The origins of the December 12 statement are to be found in
the internal relations between the War Department and the State
Department in the last months of 1945, rather than in the influence of Calvin Hoover, James Eastland, Byron Price, *et al.* The
Army had only reluctantly assumed responsibility for civil func-
tions in Germany in the first place. Truman finally directed it
to do so in July. Byrnes continued to turn a deaf ear to Eisenhower's recommendations for an early State Department takeover,
and he apparently convinced Truman that it was impossible. The
Allied Control Council was in stalemate, and the State Department
—for its own reasons—would not accept the Army's recommendation
that France be pressed harder on the matter of establishing central economic administrations in Germany. Both the State Department and the War Department had rejected Calvin Hoover's alternatives to Potsdam as a basis for policy, and it seemed clear in
Germany and in Washington that the Army faced the unpopular alternatives of presiding over a starving, restless, and depressed
population or asking Congress for "disease and unrest" appropriations to feed the recently defeated enemy. The Army, in its role
as the occupation force in Germany, wanted to accept neither of
the alternatives unless doing so was clearly in accord with stated
government policy. Since Truman's directive of July, 1945, had
assigned policy determination to the Department of State, the Army
used the leverage it derived from the impact of the Byron Price
report and asked the State Department to clarify and restate the
policies the Army was to follow in Germany. Clarification was
urgent at the time, because—according to the Potsdam agreement—
the plan for reparations and the postwar level of the German economy was to be agreed in the Allied Control Council by February 2,
1946. In the end, the Civil Affairs Division of the War Department prepared the draft of the statement released by Byrnes on
December 12, 1945. The Army thus got, for planning purposes, an

interpretation of Potsdam, including such things as what Germany's
boundaries should be, and other things.

One may forgive a researcher for being unaware of complex internal and interdepartmental relations and developments such as
those just noted. It is, however, another matter to find that the
overall meaning of a document has been distorted by selective quo-
tation and strategic deletions. Schlauch, for example, quotes
from the December 12 statement to show how policy had changed in
favor of "a determination to reconstruct postwar Germany" since
the State Department's rejection of the Hoover Report on October
12: the "United States and other occupying powers must finance
minimum essential imports into Germany to the extent that exports
from stocks and current production do not suffice to cover the
cost of such imports." His deletion of the opening words, "During
the next two years," and his failure to summarize the remainder of
the paragraph leave the reader without the slightest inkling that
this statement had nothing to do with a policy of general industrial rehabilitation in Germany. It was a short-term policy (two
years), and it applied to prevention of "disease and unrest," and
to exports to pay for previous outlays for that purpose.

One last comment on Schlauch's major thesis, which is perhaps
best stated in his own version:

>   Moscows's unbending attitude at Allied conferences,
> its determination to prevent Germany from being treated
> as a genuine economic unit, and to bring the Soviet zone
> within its satellite system, above all, the realization
> by the United States that a restored Germany was essen-
> tial not only for the economic restoration of Western
> Europe but also for inhibiting the spread of communism,
> necessitated a policy revision.

If that be so, and if the policy revision occurred sometime
between October 12 and December 12, what should we make of Clay's
cable to the War Department on September 24, asking for permission
to join with his British and Russian colleagues in establishing
trizonal central administrations? What should we make of the approval he got on October 21 from the War Department and the State
Department to do just that? Lastly, what should we make of Acheson's advice to the Secretary of War, on January 12, 1946, that
current policy authorized the establishment of central administrations in Germany by the three powers that signed the Potsdam Protocol, that is, the Americans, the British, and the Russians?

More so than Schlauch, Lloyd Gardner recognizes and discusses
the enormous complexities involved in the making of foreign-policy
decisions. He is, for example, extremely cautious about fixing a

precise date for the turning point of American policy in Germany.
He sees the change occurring in a series of decisions and actions
by the Byrnes-Clay partnership in 1946. Gardner's main theme
seems clear enough, however: American policies in Germany are
part of the larger American foreign policy of the Truman administration as it is understood by the revisionist school of the cold
war. He opens the article by stating that the German problem had
been turned upside down by 1947 ("Germany must be revived instead
of repressed"), and closes with the statement about the American
counterrevolution, quoted above.

If it is true that "the German 'problem' had been turned upside down" in 1947, it might also be suggested that Gardner interprets American policy in Germany while standing on his head. Even
more than Schlauch's, Gardner's entire analysis works backwards.
He has selected a point in time when he judges the German problem
to have been upside down, and he leads the reader back over the
preceding events to show why that happened. Decisions and actions
are seen as though they were moving toward the conditions characterizing the chosen point in time. For purposes of analysis, the
reference point provides rigid, fixed, and absolute criteria for
judging what went on before. The things that are important are
those that explain how, when, and why the German problem came to
be turned upside down. Except as they explain the inevitable development toward the defined goal, there is little room in the
analysis for missed alternatives, for the chances that failed, or
for the kind of muddling that characterizes decision-making by
committee or interdepartmental coordination.

Two examples from Gardner may be illustrative.

First, the possibility that Americans may have tried to live
within the terms of the Potsdam agreement—one might argue, until
September, 1946, or even until April, 1947—is dismissed out of
hand. It is just too preposterous to be true, in terms of what
we know about 1949. Official United States claims to the contrary
are apparently dishonest. According to Gardner, American reparations proposals at Potsdam were influenced by things like Clay's
desire to "integrate Germany into American policy," and the general American desire to leave "options for using economic levers
against the Soviets in Eastern Europe." Byrnes' reparations formula, which was finally accepted at Potsdam, is "understandable only
as a quest for an agreement which would require the least cooperation between East and West." Besides giving the United States
clear advantages over the Yalta reparations scheme, the Byrnes
formula at Potsdam "forced the Russians to continue looting East
Germany if they expected to get anything like $10 billion in repa-
rations," and it thus bought insurance against a possible Russian-
German rapprochement in the future. Potsdam, in this view, is
hardly an agreement to be implemented. It is, rather, one of the
episodes in time on the way to 1949, and it is an interesting

example of how Byrnes "dished" the Russians. ("There was no denying that was the way the Potsdam protocol read—just as Byrnes had
wanted it to.")

Second, the possibility that Americans seriously pursued a
policy of four-power cooperation in Germany, and that France—
rather than Russia—blocked that alternative, does not enter
Gardner's analysis. Such an omission is particularly interesting
because Gardner's discussion shows that he is fully aware of the
problems France caused in the Allied Control Council and in Germany. Yet, he never quite applied that knowledge to his larger
thesis that Germany is an area of dispute in the cold war, and
that the issues are between the East and the West. He talks, instead, about Clay and Byrnes needing "leverage against Britain and
France" early in 1946, apparently to force them into an anti-
Soviet coalition with the United States. He claims that in the
Stuttgart speech on September 6, 1946, "Byrnes wanted to deliver a
speech that would embarrass the Russians . . . and somehow finesse
the French all at once." His discussion of the State Department's
statement of December 12, 1945, leaves the impression that he apparently regards its repeated references to the implementation of
the Potsdam agreement as unimportant, mere window dressing. He
neglected to mention the sections dealing with the Potsdam agreement's restrictive measures, which the statement endorsed, and
zeroed in, instead, upon the section about Germany producing for
"world markets." He did not bother to note, however, that his
quoted material referred specifically to "industries of a peaceful
character" in the period *after* the four powers had already accomplished Germany's demilitarization and industrial disarmament
under the plan for reparations and postwar level of industry yet
to be developed. Gardner's implication that this recommendation
pre-empted the German level-of-industry plan and Soviet reparations receipts is nonsense.

Though he has obviously read sources where its existence is
manifest, Gardner omits reference to what is, perhaps, the most
convincing evidence that the United States was not on an anti-
Soviet policy course in Germany in 1945 and early 1946, but was in
fact on a cooperative policy course based on the implementation of
the Potsdam agreement. It would be interesting, indeed, to know
what he judges to be the significance of Clay's request of September 24, 1945, to join the United States zone with those of the
British and the Russians, of the State and War Departments' approval of the recommendation at the policy level on October 21,
1945, and of Acheson's prod in the same direction on January 12,
1946. Instead, after the discussion of the December 12 statement—
and in explanation of his interpretation thereof—Gardner observes
that: "Among American policy-makers the predominant view was that
the Soviet reaction had to be risked: Germany was the 'spark plug'
of the whole European economy. If there was to be an East-West

struggle, it was imperative that the West integrate Germany into the American-led political-economic system." I leave to my readers to judge whether references to and quotations from Alfred P. Sloan's letters to Bernard Baruch are sufficient evidence to substantiate the conclusions immediately preceding.

Gardner's stance gives rise to a myriad of other peculiarities and difficulties that affect his interpretation of America and the German problem. He does not focus clearly on historical facts, he is careless about chronology and sequential relationships, and he is sometimes simply wrong. A few examples are particularly noteworthy.

In contrast to Gardner's analysis, Clay was not "responsible for most American decisions in Germany from the beginning of the occupation through the Berlin blockade of 1948." Clay maintained constant and continuous communication with Washington. He did not get his way, for example, on currency reform and equalization of burdens in 1946. Neither did he get his way on equalization of burdens in 1948. Further, he did not get his way on de-Nazification in 1947 and 1948. He did not get his way on reparations and industrial dismantling in 1947 and thereafter. He did not get his way on decartelization in 1946 and 1947. Neither did he get his way on the revised level-of-industry plan in 1947. Gardner's conclusion that the Clay-Byrnes "partnership clarified the conception of German policy, so that imperfect plans could be brought into line with overall American policy" apparently takes no account of these things.

Also in contrast to Gardner's position is the fact that United States officials in Germany did not charge the Russians with breaking their promise to ship raw materials as reciprocal deliveries for reparations by May of 1946. Gardner suggests that the Russian failure to deliver was one of the bases for Clay's reparations stop in May, 1946. That would be convincing if it were not wrong. The Russians had not received any reparations from the West by May, 1946 (the first ships were just being loaded), and there was nothing owing in reciprocal deliveries. The Russians had five years (until 1950, if Potsdam is the base; until 1951, if the level-of-industry plan is the base) to make good on reciprocal deliveries for reparations that were scheduled for completion in two years.

Partly for reasons just noted, Gardner's discussion of Clay's suspension of reparations is out of focus. Clay did not suspend reparations to the East only. He suspended *all* reparations from the American zone on May 3, 1946, except for those already assigned and committed. The effect of the stop was greater on the other Allies than it was on Russia, and Clay was aware of that fact. To regard it as an action against Russia only, as Gardner does, is to ignore the reparations formula of Potsdam, which Gardner discussed elsewhere. To regard it as an anti-Russian measure

also questions the credibility of Clay's remarks in a press conference on May 27, 1946, and his predictions about Russian cooperation in his long cable of May 26, 1946, to the War Department.
Clay was not above misleading the press, but are we to believe
that he would try to deceive the War Department and the State Department in a message not for public distribution?

In the French and Russian plans for the future of the Ruhr,
Gardner sees the basis for an "uneasy alliance" between France and
Russia on Germany. He regards the alliance as "a wedge against
American efforts to establish a unified policy in the West." But
a close look at French and Russian plans and proposals will show
Gardner's view of the "uneasy alliance" to be an illusion. In contrast to the Russians, France did not want four-power control of
the Ruhr. The French consistently (and persistently) demanded
separation of the Ruhr from Germany and its removal from four-power control in Berlin. The French wanted independence for the Ruhr
under international supervision. They were always *officially*
vague on whether they assumed Russia would participate on the international control boards. Nevertheless, Georges Bidault made it
clear to Byrnes as early as August 23, 1945, that France feared
the consequences of Soviet influence—even on a four-power committee in Germany—so near the French border. In November French diplomats were reported to be talking with the British about a small
international administrative staff (without Russian representation
for the Ruhr. At about the same time, Charles de Gaulle was issu-
ing warnings to United States Ambassador Jefferson Caffery in
Paris about Russia's use of the control agencies in Germany to en-
croach into central Europe.

Gardner's argument that Byrnes' Stuttgart speech of September
6, 1946, was at least partly motivated by the Clay-Byrnes desire
to "smite the socialist bogeyman directly" disregards chronology
and sequential relationships entirely. He sees Article 41 of the
Hessian state constitution as the immediate impetus. But Article
41 of the Hessian constitution, which provided for socialization
of basic industries and banks in Hesse, was not ready when Byrnes
spoke at Stuttgart in September. Even if it had been ready then,
Byrnes' speech was almost an exact replication of a paper Clay had
prepared and sent to Washington in the middle of July, 1946. In
any case, for Gardner to read an antisocialist message into Byrnes
Stuttgart speech is not only inaccurate, but it is ridiculous as
well. Clay's, Byrnes', Murphy's, Draper's, Forrestal's, Howard
Petersen's, Kenneth Royall's, and the United States government's
antisocialism is so obvious in so many things that it should hardly be necessary to grab for straws that do not exist.

Gardner's assertion that a draft constitution for Germany,
based on the American plan for a national council of minister
presidents, would have been approved by three votes to one is
simply wrong. The French, late in 1946 and early in 1947, would

not have approved the American plan for unification by having the minister presidents form a national council, and neither would the British. The results of the Moscow conference should be evidence enough. If they are not, the reasons for the breakup of the Munich minister-presidents' conference in June, 1947, make it abundantly clear. Three votes to one, indeed, but right side up, if you please.

The article under review is marked by other faults. Bevin did not announce British approval to form Bizonia on July 12, 1946, as Gardner believes. Molotov's statement on the Polish boundary in mid-September, 1946, may have been "forced" by the Byrnes speech, as Gardner asserts, but it also solved a dispute that was splitting the Socialist Unity Party wide open in the Soviet-zone election campaign taking place at the time. Gardner's statement that the French agreed to German discussions at London, during the foreign ministers' conference late in 1947, is doubtful. His statement that trizonal meetings had gone on for two months when Sokolovsky left the Control Council meeting in Berlin on March 20, 1948, is inaccurate. Besides, they were six-power talks.

Returning to my reasons for such a detailed commentary on specifics, I repeat that if judgments, conclusions, or generalizations are a function of the elements that led to them, neither Schlauch nor Gardner have much—if anything—to contribute to our understanding of American occupation policies in Germany. The examples of factual errors, chronological leaps, sequential inversions, blind spots, and weighted quotations from documents seem to establish that. But I have also said that Schlauch and Gardner contribute measurably to cold-war revisionism. These two apparently contradictory statements are not, in fact, contradictory. They show, however, that the two articles under review illustrate with considerable clarity a feature of cold-war historiography that Charles S. Maier has recently discussed more ably than I can. In a review of the conceptual bases of revisionist history, Maier observed that "revisionists are asking what the meaning of policies is in terms of values imposed from outside the historical narrative." Their values, he continues, are not "derived from the mere amassment of historical data nor do they follow from strictly historical judgments." In conclusion, Maier observes that "much Cold War historiography has become a confrontation *manqué*—debatable philosophy taught by dismaying example." Schlauch and Gardner can, according to this view, contribute measurably to the subject of the cold war on the German front (which they do) without writing history at all.

SUGGESTED ADDITIONAL READINGS

Backer, John H. *Priming the German Economy: American Occupational Policies, 1945-1948.* Durham, N. C., 1971. A thorough study of American economic policies and practices in Germany. Based on original sources and enriched by personal experience

Cecil, Robert. "Potsdam and Its Legends," *International Affairs.* London, 46 (July 1970), 455-465. A commentary on the legends current in the literature regarding the Potsdam Conference, especially the myths that the conference could have done something about the areas east of the Oder-Neisse boundary (already in Polish possession), that it was Russia (rather than France) who blocked four-power control in Germany, and others.

Clay, Lucius D. *Decision in Germany.* Garden City, N.Y., 1950. A history of the American occupation and four-power control in Germany, by the American military governor. Based on materials and sources still unavailable to private researchers. Candid and valuable, though not uninfluenced by Clay's position and views.

Epstein, Klaus. "The German Problem, 1945-1950," *World Politics,* XX (January 1968), 279-300. A review article of Hans-Peter Schwarz, *Vom Reich zur Bundesrepublik,* and a general summary of German history during the occupation. Breaks it down into periods corresponding to the periodization of the cold war and sees the division of Germany in 1947 as an important aspect of the cold war between the United States and the Soviet Union.

Gardner, Lloyd C. "America and the German 'Problem,' 1945-1949," *Politics and Policies of the Truman Administration,* ed. Barton J. Bernstein. Chicago, 1970, pp. 113-148.

Gareau, Frederick H. "Morgenthau's Plan for Industrial Disarmament in Germany," *The Western Political Quarterly,* XIV (June 1961), 517-534. A study of American economic policies in the occupation of Germany, emphasizing the policy of industrial disarmament, American disenchantment with the policies of Morgenthau, and the reversal of American policy from industrial disarmament to industrial recovery.

Schlauch, Wolfgang. "American Policy toward Germany, 1945," *Journal of Contemporary History,* V, No. 7 (1970), 113-128.

PART 3

THE ISSUES IN SELECTED DOCUMENTS, 1945-1947

The documents reprinted in this section were selected by the editors to focus on three important periods or phases in the developing Soviet-American confrontation in the postwar period. The first selection, on Hopkins' mission to Moscow, depicts the ruptures and frictions between the wartime allies as the war came to an end in 1945. The next two selections, Stalin's speech and Kennan's report, are reasonably clear expressions of the belief that the wartime coalition had come to an end early in 1946. The last two selections, Marshall's report on the Moscow Conference and Zhdanov's speech to Communist party leaders in Poland, are typical of many other documents that reveal the open break that occurred in 1947.

THE HOPKINS MISSION TO MOSCOW,
MAY-JUNE, 1945*

At the suggestion of W. Averell Harriman, American Ambassador
to the Soviet Union, and Charles E. Bohlen, Assistant to the Secre
tary of State, President Truman sent Harry L. Hopkins to Moscow in
May 1945 to assure Stalin that American policies had not changed
as a result of the death of President Roosevelt. Hopkins had been
the first influential American or British representative to visit
Moscow after the German attack on Russia in 1941, and Stalin gave
a cordial reception to the man who had been F.D.R.'s closest adviser. The two men held six conversations between May 26 and June
6, 1945.
   Hopkins and Stalin candidly reviewed the points of friction
between the wartime allies at the end of the European war. Hopkins said his purpose in coming to Moscow was to discuss the deterioration that had occurred in the relations between the two nations, and he emphasized the Polish problem as one of the factors
that had caused the deterioration. As the published correspond-
ence between the heads of state clearly shows, a British-American-
Russian impasse on the future of Poland had, in fact, been the immediate reason for Truman's decision to send Hopkins to Moscow.
The Polish question became the major topic of the talks, but
Stalin also outlined the Russian explanations for the strain in
Soviet-American relations. He said the American stance on the
formation of the United Nations, on reparations from Germany and
the role of France, on Poland's future, on Lend-Lease shipments
and their termination, and on the disposition of the German navy
and merchant fleet reflected the apparent American decision that
Russia was no longer needed now that the European war had ended.
The theme that Stalin expressed is apparently as persistent in
Russia as its counterpart is among traditionalists in the United
States. It undergirds Stalin's election speech of 1946, and it i
the basis for Zhdanov's speech of 1947. It is also a fundamental
thesis in Marushkin's article, printed in Part 1, above.

----

*Reprinted, with deletions, from U.S. Department of State, Foreig
Relations of the United States, Diplomatic Papers: The Conferenc
of Berlin (the Potsdam Conference), 1945, Vol. 1 (Washington, D.C
1960), pp. 21-62.

After an exchange of amenities during which Marshal Stalin expressed his great pleasure on seeing Mr. Hopkins again, there was a brief conversation concerning Mr. Hopkins's flight in over Germany. . . .

Mr. Hopkins then said that a few days ago President Truman had sent for him and had asked him to come to Moscow to have a talk with Marshal Stalin. There were a number of things that he and Mr. Harriman hoped to discuss with Marshal Stalin and Mr. Molotov while he was in Moscow, but before going into those specific questions he wished to tell the Marshal of the real reason why the President had asked him to come, and that was the question of the fundamental relationship between the United States and the Soviet Union. Two months ago there had been overwhelming sympathy among the American people for the Soviet Union and complete support for President Roosevelt's policies which the Marshal knew so well. This sympathy and support came primarily because of the brilliant achievements of the Soviet Union in the war and partly from President Roosevelt's leadership and the magnificent way in which our two countries had worked together to bring about the defeat of Germany. The American people at that time hoped and confidently believed that the two countries could work together in peace as well as they had in war. Mr. Hopkins said there had always been a small minority, the Hearsts and the McCormicks, who had been against the policy of cooperation with the Soviet Union. These men had also been bitter political enemies of President Roosevelt but had never had any backing from the American people as was shown by the fact that against their bitter opposition President Roosevelt had been four times elected President. He said he did not intend to discuss this small minority but to discuss the general state of American opinion and particularly the present attitude of the millions of Americans who had supported President Roosevelt's policy in regard to the Soviet Union and who believed that despite the different political and economic ideology of the two countries, the United States and the Soviet Union could work together after the war in order to bring about a secure peace for humanity. He said he wished to assure the Marshal with all the earnestness at his command that this body of American public opinion who had been the constant support of the Roosevelt policies were seriously disturbed about their relations with Russia. In fact, in the last six weeks deterioration of public opinion had been so serious as to affect adversely the relations between our two countries. He said he wished to emphasize that this change had occurred in the very people who had supported to the hilt Roosevelt's policy of cooperation with the Soviet Union. He said that for the moment he was not going into the reasons why this had occurred, or the merits of the case, but merely wished to emphasize that it was a fact. The friends of Roosevelt's policy and of the Soviet Union were alarmed and

worried at the present trend of events and did not quite understand why, but it was obvious to them that if present trends continued unchecked the entire structure of world cooperation and relations with the Soviet Union which President Roosevelt and the
Marshal had labored so hard to build would be destroyed. Prior to
his departure President Truman had expressed to him his great anxiety at the present situation and also his desire to continue
President Roosevelt's policy of working with the Soviet Union and
his intention to carry out in fact as well as in spirit all the
arrangements, both formal and informal, which President Roosevelt
and Marshal Stalin had worked out together. Mr. Hopkins added
that, as the Marshal knew, he had not been well and he would not
be in Moscow unless he had felt the situation was serious. He
also said he would not have come had he not believed that the
present trend could be halted and a common basis found to go forward in the future.

Mr. Hopkins said that it was not simple or easy to put a
finger on the precise reasons for this deterioration but he must
emphasize that without the support of public opinion and particularly of the supporters of President Roosevelt it would be very
difficult for President Truman to carry forward President Roosevelt's policy. He said that, as the Marshal was aware, the cardinal basis of President Roosevelt's policy which the American people had fully supported had been the concept that the interests of
the United States were world wide and not confined to North and
South America and the Pacific Ocean and it was this concept that
had led to the many conferences concerning the peace of the world
which President Roosevelt had had with Marshal Stalin. President
Roosevelt had believed that the Soviet Union had likewise world-
wide interests and that the two countries could work out together
any political or economic considerations at issue between them.
After the Yalta Conference it looked as though we were well on the
way to reaching a basic understanding on all questions of foreign
affairs of interest to our respective countries, in regard to the
treatment of Germany; Japan and the question of setting up a world
security organization, to say nothing of the long-term interests
between the United States and the U.S.S.R. He said in a country
like ours public opinion is affected by specific incidents and in
this case the deterioration in public opinion in regard to our relations with the Soviet Union had been centered in our inability
to carry into effect the Yalta Agreement on Poland. There were
also a train of events, each unimportant in themselves, which had
grown up around the Polish question, which contributed to the deterioration in public opinion. President Truman feels, and so
does the American public, although they are not familiar with all
the details, a sense of bewilderment at our inability to solve the
Polish question.

Marshal Stalin replied that the reason for the failure on the Polish question was that the Soviet Union desired to have a friendly Poland, but that Great Britain wanted to revive the system of *cordon sanitaire* on the Soviet borders.

Mr. Hopkins replied that neither the Government nor the people of the United States had any such intention.

Marshal Stalin replied he was speaking only of England and said that the British conservatives did not desire to see a Poland friendly to the Soviet Union.

Mr. Hopkins stated that the United States would desire a Poland friendly to the Soviet Union and in fact desired to see friendly countries all along the Soviet borders.

Marshal Stalin replied if that be so we can easily come to terms in regard to Poland.

Mr. Hopkins said that during his visit here there were a number of specific questions that he and Mr. Harriman hoped to discuss with Marshal Stalin and Mr. Molotov but that the general statement he had just made concerning public opinion in the United States was the principal reason for his coming and the principal cause of anxiety at the present time. He said he had wished to state frankly and as forcibly as he knew how to Marshal Stalin the importance that he, personally, attached to the present trend of events and that he felt that the situation would get rapidly worse unless we could clear up the Polish matter. He had therefore been glad to hear the Marshal say that he thought the question could be settled. . . .

Marshal Stalin said he would not attempt to use Soviet public opinion as a screen but would speak of the feeling that had been created in Soviet governmental circles as a result of recent moves on the part of the United States Government. He said these circles felt a certain alarm in regard to the attitude of the United States Government. It was their impression that the American attitude towards the Soviet Union had perceptibly cooled once it became obvious that Germany was defeated, and that it was as though the Americans were saying that the Russians were no longer needed. He said he would give the following examples:

1. The case of Argentina and the invitation to the San Francisco Conference. At Yalta it had been agreed that only those states which had declared war on Germany before the first of March would be invited but at San Francisco this decision had been overturned. He said it was not understood in the Soviet Union why Argentina could not have been asked to wait three months or so before joining the world organization. He added that the action of the Conference and the attitude of the United States had raised the question of the value of agreements

between the three major powers if their decisions could
be overturned by the votes of such countries as Honduras
and Puerto Rico.

2. The question of the Reparations Commission. At
Yalta it had been agreed that the three powers would sit
on this Commission in Moscow and subsequently the United
States Government had insisted that France should be
represented on the same basis as the Soviet Union. This
he felt was an insult to the Soviet Union in view of the
fact that France had concluded a separate peace with Germany and had opened the frontier to the Germans. It was
true that this had been done by Pétain's Government but
nevertheless it was an action of France. To attempt to
place France on the same footing as the Soviet Union
looked like an attempt to humiliate the Russians.

3. The attitude of the United States Government towards the Polish question. He said that at Yalta it had
been agreed that the existing government was to be recon-
structed and that anyone with common sense could see that
this meant that the present government was to form the
basis of the new. He said no other understanding of the
Yalta Agreement was possible. Despite the fact that they
were simple people the Russians should not be regarded as
fools, which was a mistake the West frequently made, nor
were they blind and could quite well see what was going
on before their eyes. It is true that the Russians are
patient in the interests of a common cause but that their
patience has its limits.

4. The manner in which Lend Lease had been curtailed.
He said that if the United States was unable to supply
the Soviet Union further under Lend Lease that was one
thing but that the manner in which it had been done had
been unfortunate and even brutal. For example, certain
ships had been unloaded and while it was true that this
order had been cancelled the whole manner in which it
had been done had caused concern to the Soviet Government.
If the refusal to continue Lend Lease was designed as
pressure on the Russians in order to soften them up then
it was a fundamental mistake. He said he must tell Mr.
Hopkins frankly that [if] the Russians were approached
frankly on a friendly basis much could be done but that
reprisals in any form would bring about the exact opposite effect.

5. The disposition of the German Navy and merchant
fleet which surrendered to the Allies. Stalin said that
as we knew certain units of the German Army who had been
fighting against the Russians had been anxious to surrender to the western allies but not to the Russians,

but under the surrender terms German troops were supposed to surrender to the army against which they had
fought. He said, for example, General Eisenhower as an
honest man had correctly turned over to the Soviet Command in Czechoslovakia some 135,000 German troops who
had tried to surrender to the American Army. This was
an example of fair and honest behavior. However, as regards to the German fleet which had caused so much damage to Leningrad and other Soviet ports not one had
been turned over to the Russians despite the fact the
fleet had surrendered. He added that he had sent a message to the President and Prime Minister suggesting that
at least one-third of the German Navy and merchant ma-
rine thus surrendered be turned over to the Soviet Union.
The rest could be disposed of by Great Britain and the
United States as they saw fit. He added that if the Soviet Union had been entitled to a part of the Italian
fleet they certainly had more right to their fair share
of the German fleet, since they had suffered five million
casualties in this war. He said that the Soviet Government had certain information leading it to believe that
both the United States and England intended to reject the
Soviet request and he must say that if this turned out to
be true it would be very unpleasant. The Marshal concluded by saying that he had completed the range of his
account. . . .

Mr. Hopkins then said on the subject of Lend Lease he thought
it had been clear to the Soviet Union that the end of the war with
Germany would necessitate a reconsideration of the old program of
Lend Lease to the Soviet Union.
Marshal Stalin said that was entirely understandable.
Mr. Hopkins continued that the history of Lend Lease showed
that although in certain cases we had not always been able to meet
every Soviet request we had nonetheless freely accepted commitments which we had done our best to carry out in spirit as well as
in fact.
Marshal Stalin said that was undoubtedly true.
Mr. Hopkins stated that even prior to the end of the war in
Europe we had made an agreement with the Soviet Union known as
Annex 3 to Protocol I [*IV*], which involved delivery of supplies
which might be of use in the Far East. He said that this grew
out of recent conferences in which Far Eastern matters had been
discussed. He emphasized that this commitment was accepted in
full by the United States and we were in the process of carrying
it out. In regard to the unloading of the ships he said that
that was a technical misunderstanding and did not in any sense

represent a decision of policy on the part of the United States. That it had been the action of one government agency involved in Lend Lease and that it had been countermanded promptly within twenty-four hours. He said no one who was responsible for Lend Lease policy or American Government policy had had anything to do with that mistaken order. The only question which had to be reconsidered was the program of deliveries to the Soviet Union which had been based on the needs of the war against Germany and that it had been made clear that on the basis of this reconsideration we would be glad to reconsider any Soviet requests and that he thought some were now being considered. He said he wished to emphasize that he had seen no tendency on the part of those responsible for American policy to handle the question of future Lend Lease to the Soviet Union in an arbitrary fashion. It was in fact a question of law, since the basic Lend Lease Act made it clear that materials could only be delivered which would be useful in the process of the war. The United States Government, however, had interpreted this in its broadest sense and had included in addition to munitions of war foodstuffs and other non-military items.

Marshal Stalin said this was true.

Mr. Hopkins concluded by saying that there had naturally been considerable confusion in the United States Government as to the status of Lend Lease towards Russia at the end of the war and that there had been varying legal interpretations but that he wished to emphasize that the incident to which Marshal Stalin referred did not have any fundamental policy significance.

Marshal Stalin said he wished to make it clear that he fully understood the right of the United States to curtail Lend Lease shipments to the Soviet Union under present conditions since our commitments in this respect had been freely entered into. Even two months ago it would have been quite correct for the United States to have begun to curtail shipments but what he had in mind was the manner and form in which it was done. He felt that what was after all an agreement between the two Governments had been ended in a scornful and abrupt manner. He said that if proper warning had been given to the Soviet Government there would have been no feeling of the kind he had spoken of; that this warning was important to them since their economy was based on plans. He added that they had intended to make a suitable expression of gratitude to the United States for the Lend Lease assistance during the war but the way in which this program had been halted now made that impossible to do.

Mr. Hopkins replied that what disturbed him most about the Marshal's statement was the revelation that he believed that the United States would use Lend Lease as a means of showing our displeasure with the Soviet Union. He wished to assure the Marshal that however unfortunate an impression this question had caused in

the mind of the Soviet Government he must believe that there was
no attempt or desire on the part of the United States to use it as
a pressure weapon. He said the United States is a strong power
and does not go in for those methods. Furthermore, we have no conflict of immediate interests with the Soviet Union and would have
no reason to adopt such practices.

Marshal Stalin said he believed Mr. Hopkins and was fully satisfied with his statement in regard to Lend Lease but said he
hoped Mr. Hopkins would consider how it had looked from their side.
. . .

Mr. Hopkins then said with the Marshal's permission he would
like to review the position of the United States in regard to Poland. He said first of all he wished to assure the Marshal that
he had no thought or indeed any right to attempt to settle the Polish problem during his visit here in Moscow, nor was he intending
to hide behind American public opinion in presenting the position
of the United States.

Marshal Stalin said he was afraid that his remark concerning
Soviet public opinion had cut Mr. Hopkins to the quick and that he
had not meant to imply that Mr. Hopkins was hiding behind the
screen of American public opinion. In fact he knew Mr. Hopkins to
be an honest and frank man.

Mr. Hopkins said that he wished to state his position as
clearly and as forcibly as he knew how. He said the question of
Poland per se was not so important as the fact that it had become
a symbol of our ability to work out problems with the Soviet Union.
He said that we had no special interests in Poland and no special
desire to see any particular kind of government. That we would accept any government in Poland which was desired by the Polish people and was at the same time friendly to the Soviet Government.
He said that the people and Government of the United States felt
that this was a problem which should be worked out jointly between
the United States, the Soviet Union and Great Britain and that we
felt that the Polish people should be given the right to free elections to choose their own government and their own system and that
Poland should genuinely be independent. The Government and people
of the United States were disturbed because the preliminary steps
towards the reestablishment of Poland appeared to have been taken
unilaterally by the Soviet Union together with the present Warsaw
Government and that in fact the United States was completely ex-
cluded. He said he hoped that Stalin would believe him when he
said that this feeling was a fact. Mr. Hopkins said he urged that
Marshal Stalin would judge American policy by the actions of the
United States Government itself and not by the attitudes and public expressions of the Hearst newspapers and the *Chicago Tribune*.
He hoped that the Marshal would put his mind to the task of thinking up what diplomatic methods could be used to settle this question, keeping in mind the feeling of the American people. He said

he himself was not prepared to say how it could be done but that
he felt it must be done. Poland had become a symbol in the sense
that it bore a direct relation to the willingness of the United
States to participate in international affairs on a world-wide
basis and that our people must believe that they are joining their
power with that of the Soviet Union and Great Britain in the promotion of international peace and the well-being of humanity. Mr.
Hopkins went on to say that he felt the overwhelming majority of
the people of the United States felt that the relations between
the United States and the U.S.S.R. could be worked out in a spirit
of cooperation despite the differences in ideology and that with
all these factors in its favor he wished to appeal to the Marshal
to help find a way to the solution of the Polish problem.

Marshal Stalin replied that he wished Mr. Hopkins would take
into consideration the following factors: He said it may seem
strange, although it appeared to be recognized in United States
circles and Churchill in his speeches also recognized it, that the
Soviet Government should wish for a friendly Poland. In the
course of twenty-five years the Germans had twice invaded Russia
via Poland. Neither the British nor American people had experienced such German invasions, which were a horrible thing to endure
and the results of which were not easily forgotten. He said these
German invasions were not warfare but were like the incursions of
the Huns. He said that Germany had been able to do this because
Poland had been regarded as part of the *cordon sanitaire* around
the Soviet Union and that previous European policy had been that
Polish Governments must be hostile to Russia. In these circumstances either Poland had been too weak to oppose Germany or had
let the Germans come through. Thus Poland had served as a corri-
dor for the German attacks on Russia. He said Poland's weakness
and hostility had been a great source of weakness to the Soviet
Union and had permitted the Germans to do what they wished in the
East and also in the West since the two were mixed together. It
is therefore in Russia's vital interest that Poland should be both
strong and friendly. He said there was no intention on the part
of the Soviet Union to interfere in Poland's internal affairs,
that Poland would live under the parliamentary system which is
like Czechoslovakia, Belgium and Holland and that any talk of an
intention to Sovietize Poland was stupid. He said even the Polish
leaders, some of whom were communists, were against the Soviet system since the Polish people did not desire collective farms or
other aspects of the Soviet system. In this the Polish leaders
were right since the Soviet system was not exportable—it must
develop from within on the basis of a set of conditions which were
not present in Poland. He said all the Soviet Union wanted was
that Poland should not be in a position to open the gates to Germany and in order to prevent this Poland must be strong and democratic. Stalin then said that before he came to his suggestion as

to the practical solution of the question he would like to comment
on Mr. Hopkins's remarks concerning future United States interests
in the world. He said that whether the United States wished it or
not it was a world power and would have to accept world-wide interests. Not only this war but the previous war had shown that without United States intervention Germany could not have been defeated and that all the events and developments of the last thirty
years had confirmed this. In fact the United States had more reason to be a world power than any other state. For this reason he
fully recognized the right of the United States as a world power
to participate in the Polish question and that the Soviet interest
in Poland does not in any way exclude those of England and the
United States. Mr. Hopkins had spoken of Russian unilateral action in Poland and United States public opinion concerning it. It
was true that Russia had taken such unilateral action but they had
been compelled to. He said the Soviet Government had recognized
the Warsaw Government and concluded a treaty with it at a time
when their Allies did not recognize this government. These were
admittedly unilateral acts which would have been much better left
undone but the fact was they had not met with any understanding on
the part of their Allies. The need for these actions had arisen
out of the presence of Soviet troops in Poland and it would have
been impossible to have waited until such time as the Allies had
come to an agreement on Poland. The logic of the war against Germany demanded that the Soviet rear be assured and the Lublin Committee had been of great assistance to the Red Army at all times
and it was for this reason that these actions had been taken by
the Soviet Government. He said it was contrary to the Soviet policy to set up [a] Soviet administration on foreign soil since this
would look like occupation and be resented by the local inhabitants. It was for this reason that some Polish administration had
to be established in Poland and this could be done only with those
who had helped the Red Army. He said he wished to emphasize that
these steps had not been taken with any desire to eliminate or exclude Russia's Allies. He must point out however that Soviet action in Poland had been more successful than British action in
Greece and at no time had they been compelled to undertake the
measures which they had done in Greece. Stalin then turned to his
suggestion for the solution of the Polish problem.

Marshal Stalin said that he felt that we should examine the
composition of the future Government of National Unity. He said
there were eighteen or twenty ministries in the present Polish Government and that four or five of these portfolios could be given
representatives of other Polish groups taken from the list submitted by Great Britain and the United States (Molotov whispered to
Stalin who then said he meant four and not five posts in the government). He said he thought the Warsaw Poles would not accept
more than four ministers from other democratic groups. He added

that if this appears a suitable basis we could then proceed to consider what persons should be selected for these posts. He said of
course that they would have to be friendly to the U.S.S.R. and to
the Allies. . . .

Mr. Hopkins inquired if the Marshal believed it would be a
fact that the United States and British participation would be
helpful.

Marshal Stalin said that undoubtedly the solution would carry
more weight if it was tripartite.

Mr. Hopkins said he would like to accent once again the reasons for our concern in regard to Poland, and indeed, in regard to
other countries which were geographically far from our borders.
He said there were certain fundamental rights which, when impinged
[*infringed?*] upon or denied caused concern in the United States.
These were cardinal elements which must be present if a parliamentary system is to be established and maintained. He said for example:

> 1. There must be the right of freedom of speech so
> that people could say what they wanted to, right of as-
> sembly, right of movement and the right to worship at
> any church that they desired.
> 2. All political parties[,] except the fascist party
> and fascist elements[,] who represented or could repre-
> sent democratic governments should be permitted the free
> use, without distinction, of the press, radio, meetings
> and other facilities of political expression.
> 3. All citizens should have the right of public trial,
> defense by council [*counsel*] of their own choosing, and
> the right of habeas corpus.

He concluded that if we could find a meeting of minds in regard to these general principles which would be the basis for future free elections then he was sure we could find ways and means
to agree on procedures to carry them into effect. He then asked
the Marshal if he would care to comment in a general sense or more
specifically in regard to the general observations he had made concerning the fundamentals of a new Polish state.

Marshal Stalin replied that these principles of democracy are
well known and would find no objection on the part of the Soviet
Government. He was sure that the Polish Government, which in its
declaration had outlined just such principles, would not only not
oppose them but would welcome them. He said, however, that in
regard to the specific freedoms mentioned by Mr. Hopkins, they
could only be applied in full in peace time, and even then with
certain limitations. He said for example the fascist party, whose

intention it was to overthrow democratic governments, could not be
permitted to enjoy to the full extent these freedoms. He said sec-
ondly there were the limitations imposed by war. All states when
they were threatened by war on [*or*] their frontiers were not secure had found it necessary to introduce certain restrictions.
This had been done in England, France, the Soviet Union and elsewhere and perhaps to a lesser extent in the United States, which
was protected by wide oceans. It is for these reasons that only
in time of peace could considerations be given to the full application of these freedoms. For example he said that in time of war
no state will allow the free unrestricted use of radio transmit-
ters which could be used to convey information to the enemy. With
reference to freedom of speech certain restictions had to be imposed for military security. As to arrest, in England during the
war individuals dangerous to the state had been arrested and tried
in secret; these restrictions had been somewhat released [*relaxed?*]
but not entirely repealed in England since the war in the Pacific
was still going on.

He said, therefore, to sum up: (1) during time of war these
political freedoms could not be enjoyed to the full extent, and (2)
nor could they apply without reservations to fascist parties trying to overthrow the government. . . .

SUGGESTED ADDITIONAL DOCUMENTATION AND READINGS

Churchill, Winston S. *Triumph and Tragedy*. Boston, 1953, esp.
    Ch. 6, pp. 418-439; Ch. 10, pp. 486-503; and Ch. 20, pp. 647-
    667, for the British Prime Minister's discussion of the Pol-
    ish issue and its ramifications.

Clemens, Diane Shaver. *Yalta*. New York, 1970. Outstanding study
    of the Yalta Conference and its immediate aftermath. Uses
    Russian sources and materials. See esp. pp. 8-28 and 173-215
    for the Polish question and the Hopkins mission.

Lippmann, Walter. "A Year of Peacemaking," *The Atlantic Monthly*,
    178 (December 1946), 35-40. Analysis of the Byrnes-Bevin
    concentration on eastern Europe and its effects. Critical of
    the failure to concentrate on Germany and Japan, where they
    had the most power.

Rozek, Edward J. *Allied Wartime Diplomacy: A Pattern in Poland*.
    New York, 1958. The Polish issue in full review. A study of
    differences and suspicions among the wartime allies.

Sherwood, Robert E. *Roosevelt and Hopkins: An Intimate History*.
    New York, 1948, esp. Ch. 35, "The Last Mission," for Hopkins'
    visit to Moscow for Truman. Based on Hopkins' papers.

Smith, Gaddis. *American Diplomacy during the Second World War,
    1941-1945*. New York, 1965. A general survey. See esp.
    Ch. 8, "The Fate of Poland."

Truman, Harry S. *Memoirs*, Vol. 1, *Year of Decisions*. New York,
    1955, esp. pp. 110, 229, 257-259, 262-265, and 287, on the
    Polish issue.

U.S. Department of State. *Foreign Relations of the United States,
    Diplomatic Papers: The Conferences at Malta and Yalta, 1945*.
    Washington, D.C., 1955, pp. 202-236, for American documenta-
    tion.

U.S. Department of State. *Foreign Relations of the United States,
    1945*, Vol. 5. Washington, D.C., 1967, pp. 110-436, for de-
    tailed documentation on the Polish issue.

AN ELECTION SPEECH IN MOSCOW, FEBRUARY 9, 1946*

J. V. Stalin

*Stalin's election speech of February 9, 1946, is an argument
that World War II was an imperialist war in which the Soviet system and the Communist Party defeated their enemies and in which
the Soviet system and the Communist Party proved beyond question
their vitality and viability for the future. The speech is full
of detail, tedious repetitions, and praise for the Soviet system,
the Red Army, and the Russian people. It is designed to refute
the foreign press and other critics of the Soviet Union, who had
predicted—before and during the war—Soviet military, social, and
economic collapse.*

*Stalin's speech has been widely regarded as an expression of
the Soviet Union's postwar policies and programs. It received a
great deal of attention in the United States, and a State Department request for his comments on the speech led George F. Kennan,
the U.S. Charge d'Affaires in Moscow at the time, to prepare the
long telegram of February 22, 1946. The telegram was circulated
widely within the government, and Kennan drew heavily on its content and analysis in preparing his famous article in the July 1947
issue of* Foreign Affairs.

Eight years have elapsed since the last election to the Supreme Soviet. This was a period abounding in events of decisive
moment. The first four years passed in intensive effort on the
part of Soviet men and women to fulfill the Third Five-Year Plan.
The second four years embrace the events of the war against the
German and Japanese aggressors, the events of the Second World War.
Undoubtedly, the war was the principal event in the past period.

It would be wrong to think that the Second World War was a
casual occurrence or the result of mistakes of any particular
statesmen, though mistakes undoubtedly were made. Actually, the
war was the inevitable result of the development of world economic
and political forces on the basis of modern monopoly capitalism.

----

*Reprinted, with minor deletions, from Embassy of the Union of So-
viet Socialist Republics, *Information Bulletin* (Washington, D.C.,
1946).

Marxists have declared more than once that the capitalist system
of world economy harbors elements of general crises and armed conflicts and that, hence, the development of world capitalism in our
time proceeds not in the form of smooth and even progress but
through crises and military catastrophes.

The fact is that the unevenness of development of the capitalist countries usually leads in time to violent disturbance of equilibrium in the world system of capitalism, that group of capitalist countries which considers itself worse provided than others
with raw materials and markets usually making attempts to alter
the situation and repartition the "spheres of influence" in its
favor by armed force. The result is a splitting of the capitalist
world into two hostile camps and war between them.

Perhaps military catastrophes might be avoided if it were possible for raw materials and markets to be periodically redistrib-
uted among the various countries in accordance with their economic
importance, by agreement and peaceable settlement. But that is impossible to do under present capitalist conditions of the development of world economy.

Thus the First World War was the result of the first crisis
of the capitalist system of world economy, and the Second World
War was the result of a second crisis.

That does not mean of course that the Second World War is a
copy of the first. On the contrary, the Second World War differs
materially from the first in nature. It must be borne in mind
that before attacking the Allied countries the principal fascist
states—Germany, Japan and Italy—destroyed the last vestiges of
bourgeois democratic liberties at home, established a brutal ter-
orist regime in their own countries, rode roughshod over the principles of sovereignty and free development of small countries, proclaimed a policy of seizure of alien territories as their own
policy and declared for all to hear that they were out for world
domination and the establishment of a fascist regime throughout
the world.

Moreover, by the seizure of Czechoslovakia and of the central
areas of China, the Axis states showed that they were prepared to
carry out their threat of enslaving all freedom-loving nations.
In view of this, unlike the First World War, the Second World War
against the Axis states from the very outset assumed the character
of an anti-fascist war, a war of liberation, one the aim of which
was also the restoration of democratic liberties. The entry of
the Soviet Union into the war against the Axis states could only
enhance, and indeed did enhance, the anti-fascist and liberation
character of the Second World War.

It was on this basis that the anti-fascist coalition of the
Soviet Union, the United States of America, Great Britain and
other freedom-loving states came into being—a coalition which
subsequently played a decisive part in defeating the armed forces
of the Axis states.

That is how matters stand as regards the origin and character of the Second World War.

By now I should think everyone admits that the war really was not and could not have been an accident in the life of nations, that actually this war became the war of nations for their existence, and that for this reason it could not be a quick lightning affair.

As regards our country, for it this war was the most bitter and arduous of all wars in the history of our Motherland.

But the war was not only a curse. It was at the same time a great school in which all the forces of the people were tried and tested. The war laid bare all facts and events in the rear and at the front, it tore off relentlessly all veils and coverings which had concealed the true faces of the states, governments and parties and exposed them to view without a mask or embellishment, with all their shortcomings and merits.

The war was something like an examination for our Soviet system, for our State, for our Government, for our Communist Party, and it summed up the results of their work, saying to us as it were: "Here they are, your people and organizations, their deeds and their lives. Look at them well and reward them according to their deeds."

This was one of the positive aspects of the war. . . .

We concluded the war with complete victory over the enemies. That is the chief result of war. But that result is too general and we cannot stop at that. . . . In order to grasp the great historic importance of our victory we must examine the thing more concretely. . . .

Our victory means, first of all, that our Soviet social order has triumphed, that the Soviet social order has successfully passed the ordeal in the fire of war and has proved its unquestionable vitality.

As you know, it was claimed more than once in the foreign press that the Soviet social order was a "risky experiment" doomed to failure, that the Soviet order was a "house of cards" which had no roots in real life and had been imposed upon the people by the Cheka, and that a slight push from without was enough for this "house of cards" to collapse.

Now we can say that the war refuted all these claims of the foreign press as groundless. The war showed that the Soviet social order is a truly popular order springing from the depths of the people and enjoying their mighty support, that the Soviet social order is a form of organization of society which is perfectly stable and capable of enduring.

More than that, there is no longer any question today whether the Soviet social order is or is not capable of enduring, for after the object lessons of war none of the skeptics ventures any longer to voice doubts as to the vitality of the Soviet social

order. The point now is that the Soviet social order has shown itself more stable and capable of enduring than a non-Soviet social
order, that the Soviet social order is a form of organization, a
society superior to any non-Soviet social order.

Second, our victory means that our Soviet state system has
triumphed, that our multinational Soviet State has stood all the
trials of war and has proved its vitality.

As you know, prominent foreign press men have more than once
gone on record to the effect that the Soviet multinational State
was an "artificial, non-viable structure," that in event of any
complications, the disintegration of the Soviet Union would be
inevitable, that the fate of Austria-Hungary awaited the Soviet
Union.

Today we can say that the war refuted these claims of the
foreign press as totally unfounded. The war showed that the Soviet multinational state system passed the test successfully, that
it grew even stronger during the war and proved the state system
perfectly capable of enduring.

These gentlemen did not understand that the parallel with
Austria-Hungary did not apply, for our multinational State has not
grown up on a bourgeois foundation which stimulates sentiments of
national distrust and national animosity, but on the Soviet foundation which on the contrary cultivates the sentiments of friendship and fraternal collaboration among the peoples of our State.

As a matter of fact, after the lessons of the war these
gentlemen no longer venture to deny that the Soviet state system
is capable of enduring. Today it is no longer a question of the
vitality of the Soviet state system, for that vitality can no
longer be doubted; the point now is that the Soviet state system
has proved itself a model for a multinational state, has proved
that the Soviet state system is a system of state organization in
which the national question and the problem of collaboration among
nations has been settled better than in any other multinational
state.

Third, our victory means that the Soviet armed forces have
triumphed, that our Red Army has triumphed, that the Red Army bore
up heroically under all the trials of war, utterly routed the armies of our enemies and came out of the war as a victor.

Now everyone, friend as well as foe, admits that the Red Army
proved equal to its great tasks. But this was not the case some
six years ago during the prewar period. As you know, prominent
men from the foreign press and many recognized military authorities abroad declared more than once that the condition of the Red
Army gave rise to grave doubts, that the Red Army was poorly armed
and had no proper commanding personnel, that its morale was beneath all criticism, that while it might be of some use in defense
it was useless for an offensive, and that if the German forces
should strike, the Red Army was bound to crumble like a "colossus

with feet of clay." Statements like these were made not only in Germany, but in France, Great Britain and the United States as well.

Today we can say that the war has refuted all such statements as unfounded and absurd. The war showed that the Red Army is not a "colossus with feet of clay," but a first-class contemporary army with fully modern armaments, highly experienced commanding personnel and high moral and fighting qualities. It must not be forgotten that the Red Army is the army that utterly routed the German army which but yesterday was striking terror into the armies of the European states.

It should be noted that the "critics" of the Red Army are growing fewer and fewer. What is more, the foreign press now more and more frequently contains items which note the fine qualities of the Red Army, the skill of its fighting men and commanders and the flawlessness of its strategy and tactics. That is but natural. After the brilliant Red Army victories at Moscow and Stalingrad, at Kursk and at Belgorod, at Kiev and Kirovograd, at Minsk and Bobruisk, at Leningrad and Tallinn, at Jassy and Lvov, on the Vistula and the Niemen, on the Danube and the Oder, at Vienna and Berlin, it cannot but be admitted that the Red Army is a first-class army from which much could be learned.

Such is our concrete understanding of our country's victory over its foes.

Such in the main are the results of the war.

It would be a mistake to think that such a historic victory could have been won if the whole country had not prepared beforehand for active defense. It would be no less mistaken to imagine that such preparations could be carried through in a short time— in the space of some three or four years. It would be a still greater mistake to say that we won only owing to the gallantry of our troops.

Of course, victory cannot be achieved without gallantry. But gallantry alone is not enough to vanquish an enemy who has a large army, first-class armaments, well-trained officer cadres, and a fairly good organization of supplies. To meet the blow of such an enemy, to repulse him and then to inflict utter defeat upon him required, in addition to the matchless gallantry of our troops, fully up-to-date armaments and adequate quantities of them as well as well-organized supplies in sufficient quantities.

But that, in turn, necessitated having—and in adequate amounts—such elementary things as metal for the manufacture of armaments, equipment and machinery for factories, fuel to keep the factories and transport going, cotton for the manufacture of uniforms, and grain for supplying the Army.

Can it be claimed that before entering the Second World War our country already commanded the necessary minimum material potentialities for satisfying all these requirements in the main? I

think it can. In order to prepare for this tremendous job we had
to carry out three Five-Year Plans of national economic development. It was precisely these three Five-Year Plans that helped
us to create these material potentialities. At any rate, our country's position in this respect before the Second World War, in
1940, was several times better than it was before the First World
War, in 1913.

What material potentialities did our country command before
the Second World War? . . . [Here follow statistics on production.
Eds.]

Such an unprecedented increase in production cannot be regarded as the simple and usual development of a country from backwardness to progress. It was a leap by which our Motherland was
transformed from a backward into an advanced country, from an
agrarian into an industrial country.

This historic transformation was accomplished in the course
of three Five-Year Plan periods, beginning with 1928, the first
year of the First Five-Year Plan. Up to that time we had to concern ourselves with rehabilitating our ravaged industry and heal-
ing the wounds received in the First World War and the Civil War.
Moreover, if we bear in mind that the First Five-Year Plan was
fulfilled in four years, and that the fulfillment of the Third
Five-Year Plan was interrupted by war in its fourth year, we find
that it took only about 13 years to transform our country from an
agrarian into an industrial one.

It cannot but be admitted that 13 years is an incredibly
short period for the accomplishment of such an immense task.

This it is that explains the storm of conflicting comment
which the publication of these figures produced at the time in the
foreign press. Our friends decided that a "miracle" had taken
place, while our ill-wishers declared that the Five-Year Plans
were "Bolshevik propaganda" and the "tricks of the Cheka." But
since miracles do not happen, and the Cheka is not so powerful as
to abolish the laws of social development, "public opinion" abroad
had to accept facts.

By what policy did the Communist Party succeed in providing
these material potentialities in the country in such a short time?

First of all, by the Soviet policy of industrializing the
country.

The Soviet method of industrializing the country differs radically from the capitalist method of industrialization. In capitalist countries industrialization usually begins with light industry. Since in light industry smaller investments are required
and there is more rapid turnover of capital and since, furthermore
it is easier to make a profit there than in heavy industry, light
industry serves as the first object of industrialization in these
countries.

Only after a lapse of much time, in the course of which light industry accumulates profits and concentrates them in banks, does the turn of heavy industry arrive and accumulated capital begin to be transferred gradually to heavy industry in order to create conditions for its development.

But that is a lengthy process requiring an extensive period of several decades, in the course of which these countries have to wait until light industry has developed and must make shift without heavy industry. Naturally, the Communist Party could not take this course. The Party knew that a war was looming, that the country could not be defended without heavy industry, that the development of heavy industry must be undertaken as soon as possible, that to be behind with this would mean to lose out. The Party remembered Lenin's words to the effect that without heavy industry it would be impossible to uphold the country's independence, that without it the Soviet order might perish.

Accordingly, the Communist Party of our country rejected the "usual" course of industrialization and began the work of industrializing the country by developing heavy industry. It was very difficult, but not impossible. A valuable aid in this work was the nationalization of industry, and banking, which made possible the rapid accumulation and transfer of funds to heavy industry.

There can be no doubt that without this it would have been impossible to secure our country's transformation into an industrial country in such a short time.

Second, by a policy of collectivization of agriculture.

In order to do away with our backwardness in agriculture and to provide the country with greater quantities of marketable grain, cotton, and so forth, it was essential to pass from small-scale peasant farming to large-scale farming, for only large-scale farming can make use of new machinery, apply all the achievements of agronomical science and yield greater quantities of marketable produce.

There are, however, two kinds of large farms—capitalist and collective. The Communist Party could not adopt the capitalist path of development of agriculture, and not as a matter of principle alone but also because it implies too prolonged a development and involves preliminary ruination of the peasants and their transformation into farm hands. Therefore, the Communist Party took the path of the collectivization of agriculture, the path of creating large-scale farming by uniting peasant farms into collective farms.

The method of collectivization proved a highly progressive method not only because it did not involve the ruination of the peasants but especially because it permitted, within a few years, the covering of the entire country with large collective farms which are able to use new machinery, take advantage of all the achievements of agronomic science and give the country greater quantities of marketable produce.

There is no doubt that without a collectivization policy we could not in such a short time have done away with the age-old backwardness of our agriculture.

It cannot be said that the Party's policy encountered no resistance. Not only backward people, such as always decry everything new, but many prominent members of the Party as well, systematically dragged the Party backward and tried by hook or by crook to divert it to the "usual" capitalist path of development. All the anti-Party machinations of the Trotskyites and the Rightists, all their "activities" in sabotaging the measures of our Government, pursued the single aim of frustrating the Party's policy and obstructing the work of industrialization and collectivization. But the Party did not yield either to the threats from one side or to the wails from the other and advanced confidently regardless of everything.

It is to the Party's credit that it did not pander to the backward, was not afraid to go against the tide and always retained its position as the leading force. There can be no doubt that without such firmness and tenacity the Communist Party could not have upheld the policy of industrializing the country and collectivizing agriculture.

Was the Communist Party able to make proper use of the material potentialities thus created in order to develop war production and provide the Red Army with the weapons it needed?

I think that it was able to do so and with maximum success.
. . . [Here follow statistics on wartime production. Eds.]

That is how matters stand with regard to the work of the Communist Party of our country in the period up to the outbreak of war and during the war itself.

Now a few words about the Communist Party's plans of work for the immediate future. As is known these plans are set forth in the new Five-Year Plan which is shortly to be endorsed. The principal aims of the new Five-Year Plan are to rehabilitate the ravaged areas of the country, to restore the prewar level in industry and agriculture, and then to surpass this level in more or less substantial measure. To say nothing of the fact that the rationing system will shortly be abolished, special attention will be devoted to extending the production of consumer goods, to raising the living standard of the working people by steadily lowering the prices of all goods, and to the widespread construction of all manner of scientific research institutions that can give science the opportunity to develop its potentialities.

I have no doubt that if we give our scientists proper assistance they will be able in the near future not only to overtake but to surpass the achievements of science beyond the boundaries of our country.

As regards the plans for a longer period ahead, the Party means to organize a new mighty upsurge in the national economy, which would allow us to increase our industrial production, for example, three times over as compared with the prewar period. We must achieve a situation where our industry can produce annually up to 50 million tons of pig iron, up to 60 million tons of steel, up to 500 million tons of coal and up to 60 million tons of oil. Only under such conditions can we consider that our homeland will be guaranteed against all possible accidents. That will take three more Five-Year Plans, I should think, if not more. But it can be done and we must do it.

Such is my brief report on the Communist Party's work in the recent past and its plans of work for the future.

It is for you to judge how correctly the Party has been working and whether it could not have worked better.

There is a saying that victors are not judged, that they should not be criticized, should not be checked on. That is not so. Victors can and should be judged, they can and should be criticized and checked upon. That is good not only for work, but for the victors themselves; there will be less conceitedness and more modesty. I consider that in an election campaign the electors are sitting in judgment on the Communist Party as the ruling party. And the election returns will constitute the electors' verdict. The Communist Party of our country would not be worth much if it feared to be criticized and checked upon. The Communist Party is prepared to accept the electors' verdict.

In the election struggle the Communist Party is not alone. It goes to the polls in a bloc with non-Party people. In bygone days the Communists treated non-Party people and non-Party status with some mistrust. This was due to the fact that the non-Party flag was not infrequently used as a camouflage by various bourgeois groups for whom it was not advantageous to face the electorate without a mask.

That was the case in the past. But now we have different times. Our non-Party people are now divided from the bourgeoisie by a barrier known as the Soviet social order. This same barrier unites non-Party people with the Communists in a single community of Soviet men and women. Living in this single community they struggled together to build up the might of our country, fought and shed their blood together on the battle fronts for the sake of our country, and in greatness worked together to forge a victory over the enemies of our country and did forge that victory. The only difference between them is that some belong to the Party, others do not. But that is a formal difference. The important thing is that both are furthering the same common cause. Therefore, the bloc of Communists and non-Party people is a natural and vital thing.

In conclusion, allow me to thank you for the confidence you have shown me in nominating me to the Supreme Soviet. You need not doubt that I shall do my best to justify your trust.

SUGGESTED ADDITIONAL DOCUMENTATION AND READINGS

Fleming, Denna F. *The Cold War and Its Origins*. Garden City, N.Y
1961, esp. Vol. 1, Ch. 3, pp. 334-362. The pioneering revisionist study of the cold war's origins, which are dated from
1917. Based on published records and newspapers. Very criti
cal of U.S. policies.

Fleming, Denna F. "Who Won the Cold War?" *The Nation*, 206 (April
15, 1968), 508-510. A review of LaFeber's *America, Russia,
and the Cold War* and Seabury's *The Rise and Decline of the
Cold War*. Regards 1946 as the year when the cold war was declared.

Gardner, Lloyd C. *Architects of Illusion: Men and Ideas in Ameri
can Foreign Policy, 1941-1949*. Chicago, 1970, esp. Ch. 10,
pp. 270-300, "James V. Forrestal and George F. Kennan: Will
the Real 'Mr. X' Please Stand Up?"

Kennan, George F. *Memoirs, 1925-1950*. Boston, 1967, esp. Ch. 11,
pp. 271-297, for references to the Stalin speech and its implications, and Annex C, pp. 547-559, for the long telegram.

Niebuhr, Reinhold. "Europe, Russia, and America," *The Nation*, 163
(September 14, 1946), 288-289. An important liberal spokesman defends a policy of rebuilding Europe to make its people
less susceptible to Communist influence.

Ulam, Adam B. *Expansion and Coexistence: The History of Soviet
Foreign Policy, 1917-1967*. New York, 1968. A general survey
esp. Ch. 8, pp. 378-455, on the events of 1946.

U.S. Department of State. *Foreign Relations of the United States,
1946*, Vol. 6. Washington, D.C., 1969, esp. pp. 690-691 and
694-696, for documentation, and 696-709, for Kennan's long
telegram of February 22, 1946.

A REPORT FROM MOSCOW,
MARCH 20, 1946*

George F. Kennan

*George F. Kennan, the American Charge d'Affaires in Moscow,
responded to Stalin's speech of February 9, 1946, by preparing a
long telegram for the Department of State on February 22, 1946.
It analyzed the backgrounds and assumptions Kennan thought to be
the bases for Soviet policy. Kennan later drew heavily on the
long telegram to write his famous Mr. X article, "The Sources of
Soviet Conduct," for* Foreign Affairs. *Kennan's telegram of March
20, 1946, which is printed here, was a routine telegram from Moscow to the Secretary of State. It is significant, however, because it ties together two important elements of Kennan's reports
and advice: his assessment of the Soviet Union's postwar posture
and his judgment of an appropriate corresponding U.S. stance.*
*Kennan's March 20, 1946, telegram touches briefly on Kennan's
thoughts at the time, and it clearly reflects his interpretation
that the Soviet Union was—for domestic reasons—deliberately
building up the United States and Britain as enemies to replace
its former enemies, Germany and Japan. The telegram raises the
question of a Russian ruling-class psychosis, an idea that American cold-war traditionalists (see especially Arthur M. Schlesinger,
Jr.) later ascribed to Stalin personally. Kennan cautions against
further direct, three-power summit meetings, and he warns against
the most dangerous tendency of all: gestures of good will and conciliation toward a political entity constitutionally incapable of
being conciliated. The latter is Kennan's answer to Henry Wallace,
whom he mentions by name in the telegram.*

In recent days we have noted a number of statements made
either editorially in American papers or individually by prominent
Americans reflecting the view that Soviet "suspicions" could be assuaged if we on our part would make greater effort, by means of direct contact, persuasion or assurances, to convince Russians of
good faith of our aims and policies.

----

*Reprinted, with minor deletions, from U.S. Department of State,
Foreign Relations of the United States, 1946, Vol. 6 (Washington,
D.C., 1969), pp. 721-723.

I have in mind particularly numerous calls for a new three-power meeting, *Philadelphia Record's* proposal that U.S. give "assurances" to assuage Russia's fears, Lippmann's appeal for closer "diplomatic contact" and, above all, Henry Wallace's expressed belief (if BBC has quoted him correctly) that there is something our Government could and should do to persuade Stalin that we are not trying to form an anti-Soviet bloc. (We note many similar statements in British press.)

I am sending this message in order to tell Department of the concern and alarm with which we view line of thought behind these statements. Belief that Soviet "suspicions" are of such a nature that they could be altered or assuaged by personal contacts, rational arguments or official assurances reflects a serious misunderstanding about Soviet realities and constitutes, in our opinion, the most insidious and dangerous single error which Americans can make in their thinking about this country.

If we are to get any long-term clarity of thought and policy on Russian matters we must recognize this very simple and basic fact: official Soviet thesis that outside world is hostile and menacing to Soviet peoples is not a conclusion at which Soviet leaders have reluctantly arrived after honest and objective appraisal of facts available to them but an *a priori* tactical position deliberately taken and hotly advanced by dominant elements in Soviet political system for impelling selfish reasons of a domestic political nature. . . . A hostile international environment is the breath of life for prevailing internal system in this country. Without it there would be no justification for that tremendous and crushing bureaucracy of party, police and army which now lives off the labor and idealism of Russian people. Thus we are faced here with a tremendous vested interest dedicated to proposition that Russia is a country walking a dangerous path among implacable enemies. Disappearance of Germany and Japan (which were the only real dangers) from Soviet horizon left this vested interest no choice but to build up U.S. and United Kingdom to fill this gap. This process began even before termination of hostilities and has been assiduously and unscrupulously pursued ever since. Whether or not it has been successful with people as a whole, we are not sure. Although they are now, since publication of Stalin's interview, highly alarmed, we are not sure they are convinced of Anglo-American wickedness. But that this agitation has created a psychosis which permeates and determines behavior of entire Soviet ruling caste is clear.

We do not know where this effort has its origin. We do not know whether Stalin himself is an author or victim of it. Perhaps he is a little of both. But we think there is strong evidence that he does not by any means always receive objective and helpful information about international situation. And as far as we can see, the entire apparatus of diplomacy and propaganda under him

works not on basis of any objective analysis of world situation
but squarely on basis of the preconceived party line which we see
reflected in official propaganda.

I would be last person to deny that useful things have been
accomplished in past and can be accomplished in future by direct
contact with Stalin, especially where such contact makes it possible to correct his conceptions in matters of fact. But it would
be fair neither to past nor to future Ambassadors to expect too
much along this line. The cards are stacked against us. An Ambassador can, as a rule, see Stalin only relatively rarely, and
even then he has to overcome a heavy handicap of skepticism and
suspicion. Meanwhile Stalin is presumably constantly at disposal
of a set of inside advisers of whom we know little or nothing. As
far as I am aware, there is no limit to extent to which these people can fill his mind with misinformation and misinterpretations
about us and our policies, and all this without our knowledge.
Isolation of foreigners and (this is important to note) of high Soviet figures as well, both from each other and from rank and file
of Soviet population, makes it practically impossible for foreign
representatives to trace and combat the flow of deliberate misinformation and misinterpretation to which their countries are vic-
tims. Let no one think this system is fortuitous or merely traditional. Here again, we have a vested interest vitally concerned,
for excellent reasons, that things should be this way, that free
contact should not take place, that foreign representatives should
be kept in dark and that high Soviet figures should remain generally dependent on persons whose views are unknown, whose activities
unseen, whose influences unchallengeable because they cannot be
detected.

To all this there should be added fact that suspicion is basic in Soviet Government. It affects everything and everyone. It
is not confined to us. Foreign Communists in Moscow are subjected
to isolation and supervision more extreme, if anything, than those
surrounding foreign diplomats. They enjoy no more than we do any
individual confidence on part of Kremlin. Even Soviet internal
figures move in a world of elaborate security checks and balances
based on lack of confidence in their individual integrity. Moscow
does not believe in such things as good will or individual human
virtue.

When confidence is unknown even at home, how can it logically
be sought by outsiders? Some of us here have tried to conceive
the measures our country would have to take if it really wished to
pursue, at all costs, goal of disarming Soviet suspicions. We
have come to conclusion that nothing short of complete disarmament,
delivery of our air and naval forces to Russia and resigning of
powers of government to American Communists would even dent this
problem; and even then we believe—and this is not facetious—that
Moscow would smell a trap and would continue to harbor most bale-
ful misgivings.

We are thus up against fact that suspicion in one degree or another is an integral part of Soviet system, and will not yield entirely to any form of rational persuasion or assurance. It determines diplomatic climate in which, for better or for worse, our relations with Russia are going to have to grow. To this climate, and not to wishful preconceptions, we must adjust our diplomacy.

In these circumstances I think there can be no more dangerous tendency in American public opinion than one which places on our Government an obligation to accomplish the impossible by gestures of good will and conciliation toward a political entity constitutionally incapable of being conciliated. On other hand, there is no tendency more agreeable to purposes of Moscow diplomacy. Kremlin has no reason to discourage a delusion so useful to its purposes; and we may expect Moscow propaganda apparatus to cultivate it assiduously.

For these reasons, I wish to register the earnest hope that we will find means to bring about a better understanding on this particular point, particularly among people who bear public responsibility and influence public opinion in our country.

SUGGESTED ADDITIONAL READINGS

Acheson, Dean. *Present at the Creation: My Years in the State Department*. New York, 1969. A leading participant's memoirs. See pp. 150-151, on Stalin's speech of February 9, 1946, and Kennan's long telegram.

Hamby, Alonzo L. "Henry A. Wallace, the Liberals, and Soviet-American Relations," *The Review of Politics*, XXX (April 1968), 153-169. A study of the Truman administration's early foreign-policy critics.

Hertzberg, Sidney. "Can Old-Time Diplomacy Check Soviet Power? Mr. Kennan and the Politics of Containment," *Commentary*, XIII (April 1952), 336-343. A critique of Kennan's views. Focuses on the Mr. X article and on Kennan's book *American Diplomacy, 1900-1950*.

Kennan, George F. *Memoirs, 1925-1950*. Boston, 1967, esp. Chs. 10 and 11, pp. 252-297.

Kennan, George F. "The Sources of Soviet Conduct," *Foreign Affairs*, XXV (July 1947), 566-582. The famous Mr. X article, and the recognized standard statement of the policy of containment.

Wallace, Henry A. "The Path to Peace with Russia," *The New Republic*, 115 (September 30, 1946), 401-406. A plea for a continuation of Roosevelt's policy of understanding toward the Soviet Union.

Whelan, Joseph G. "George Kennan and His Influence on American Foreign Policy," *The Virginia Quarterly Review*, 35 (Spring 1959), 196-220. A general assessment of Kennan's role in developing the policy of containment.

THE MOSCOW MEETING OF THE COUNCIL OF FOREIGN MINISTERS,
MARCH 10, 1947, TO APRIL 24, 1947*

George C. Marshall

*Secretary of State George C. Marshall made his radio report
on the Moscow Conference to the American people on April 28, 1947.
On the following day he instructed George F. Kennan to activate
the Policy Planning Staff of the State Department. Kennan and his
staff subsequently prepared the studies that led to the Marshall
Plan speech at Harvard University on June 5, 1947. Coming after
the President's "Truman Doctrine" speech of March 12, 1947, Marshall's report identifies many of the issues—other than Greece
and Turkey—that were the basis for the Marshall Plan speech.*

*Marshall's radio report is a summary of the problems and is-
sues at the Moscow Conference. Both John Foster Dulles, who advised Marshall at Moscow, and Robert Murphy, the State Department's political adviser in Berlin, have stated that the Marshall
Plan was conceived in Moscow, during the foreign ministers' conference there. Marshall's emphasis on German recovery is particularly noteworthy as a clue to the nature of the European Recovery
Program. His apparent disillusionment with high-level talks (he
refers to his personal conversations with Stalin), and his decision to act on Europe and Germany without further delay, may be
reflections of Kennan's advice on these and other things. His
statement that Soviet recalcitrance was the sole cause for the
stalemate on German economic recovery and unity—though highly
questionable—is also in accord with Kennan's views on the sources
of Soviet conduct.*

Tonight I hope to make clearly understandable the fundamental
nature of the issues discussed at the Moscow Conference of Foreign
Ministers.

This Conference dealt with the very heart of the peace for
which we are struggling. It dealt with the vital center of Europe
—Germany and Austria—an area of large and skilled population, of
great resources and industrial plants, an area which has twice in
recent times brought the world to the brink of disaster. In the

----

*Reprinted from *The Department of State Bulletin*, XVI (May 11,
1947), 919-924.

Moscow negotiations all the disagreements which were so evident during the conferences regarding the Italian and Balkan treaties came into sharp focus and remained in effect unsolved.

Problems which bear directly on the future of our civilization cannot be disposed of by general talk or vague formulae—by what Lincoln called "pernicious abstractions." They require concrete solutions for definite and extremely complicated questions— questions which have to do with boundaries, with power to prevent military aggression, with people who have bitter memories, with the production and control of things which are essential to the lives of millions of people. You have been kept well informed by the press and radio of the daily activities of the Council, and much of what I have to say may seem repetitious. But the extremely complicated nature of the three major issues we considered makes it appear desirable for me to report in some detail the problems as I saw them in my meetings at the Conference table.

There was a reasonable possibility, we had hoped a probability, of completing in Moscow a peace treaty for Austria and a four-power pact to bind together our four governments to guarantee the demilitarization of Germany. As for the German peace treaty and related but more current German problems, we had hoped to reach agreement on a directive for the guidance of our deputies in their work preparatory to the next conference.

In a statement such as this, it is not practicable to discuss the numerous issues which continued in disagreement at the Conference. It will suffice, I think, to call attention to the fundamental problems whose solution would probably lead to the quick adjustment of many other differences.

It is important to an understanding of the Conference that the complex character of the problems should be understood, together with their immediate effect on the people of Europe in the coming months. To cite a single example, more coal is most urgently needed throughout Europe for factories, for utilities, for railroads, and for the people in their homes. More coal for Allied countries cannot be mined and delivered until the damaged mines, mine machinery, railroad communications and like facilities are rehabilitated. This rehabilitation, however, depends on more steel, and more steel depends in turn on more coal for steel making. Therefore, and this is the point to be kept in mind, while the necessary rehabilitation is in progress, less coal would be available in the immediate future for the neighboring Allied states.

But less coal means less employment for labor and a consequent delay in the production of goods for export to bring money for the purchase of food and necessities. Therefore, the delay necessary to permit rehabilitation of the mines so vitally affects France that the settlement of this matter has become for her a critical issue. All neighboring states and Great Britain and the

Soviet Union are directly affected in various ways since coal is required for German production of goods for export sufficient to enable her to buy the necessary imports of foods, et cetera, for much of which the United States is now providing the funds.

Moreover, in the background of this coal issue, which is directly related to steel production, is the important consideration of the buildup of heavy industry in Germany, which could later again become a threat to the peace of the world. I cite this single example to illustrate the complications which are involved in these negotiations.

The Allied Control Council in Berlin presented a detailed report of the many problems concerned with the political, military, economic, and financial situation under the present military government of Germany. In connection with these matters, the Ministers considered the form and scope of the provisional political organization for Germany and the procedure to be followed in the preparation of the German peace treaty.

The German negotiations involved not only the security of Europe and the world but the prosperity of all of Europe. While our mission was to consider the terms of a treaty to operate over a long term of years, we were faced with immediate issues which vitally concerned the impoverished and suffering people of Europe who are crying for help, for coal, for food, and for most of the necessities of life, and the majority of whom are bitterly disposed towards the Germany that brought about this disastrous situation. The issues also vitally concern the people of Britain and the United States who cannot continue to pour out hundreds of millions of dollars for Germany because current measures were not being taken to terminate expeditiously the necessity for such appropriations.

The critical and fundamental German problems to which I shall confine myself are: (a) the limits to the powers of the central government; (b) the character of the economic system and its relation to all of Europe; (c) the character and extent of reparations (d) the boundaries for the German state; and (e) the manner in which all Allied states at war with Germany are represented in the drafting and confirmation of the treaty.

All the members of the Council of Foreign Ministers are in apparent agreement as to the establishment of a German state on a self-supporting, democratic basis, with limitations imposed to prevent the reestablishment of military power.

This issue of the degree of centralization of the future German state is of greatest importance. Excessive concentration of power is peculiarly dangerous in a country like Germany which has no strong traditions regarding the rights of the individual and the rights of the community to control the exercise of governmental power. The Soviet Union appears to favor a strong central government. The United States and United Kingdom are opposed to such a government, because they think it could be too readily converted to the domination of a regime similar to the Nazis. They favor a central government of carefully limited powers, all other powers being reserved to the states, or *Länder* as they are called in Germany. The French are willing to agree only to very limited responsibilities for the central government. They fear a repetition of the seizure of power over the whole of Germany carried out by the Hitler regime in 1933.

Under ordinary circumstances there are always strong and differing points of view regarding the character of a governmental reorganization. In this case there are great and justifiable fears regarding the resurrection of German military power, and concern over expressed or concealed desires for quite other reasons.

Regarding the character of the German economic system and its relation to all of Europe, the disagreements are even more serious and difficult of adjustment. German economy at the present time is crippled by the fact that there is no unity of action, and the rehabilitation of Germany to the point where she is self-supporting demands immediate decision.

There is a declared agreement in the desire for economic unity in Germany, but when it comes to the actual terms to regulate such unity there are wide and critical differences. One of the most serious difficulties encountered in the effort to secure economic unity has been the fact that the Soviet-occupied zone has operated practically without regard to the other zones and has made few if any reports of what has been occurring in that zone. There has been little or no disposition to proceed on a basis of reciprocity, and there has been a refusal to disclose the availability of foodstuffs and the degree or character of reparations taken out of this zone.

This unwillingness of the Soviet authorities to cooperate in establishing a balanced economy for Germany as agreed upon at Potsdam has been the most serious check on the development of a self-supporting Germany and a Germany capable of providing coal and other necessities for the neighboring states who have always been dependent on Germany for these items. After long and futile efforts to secure a working accord in this matter, the British and American zones were combined for the improvement of the economic situation, meaning the free movement of excess supplies or produce available in one zone to another where there is a shortage. Our continuing invitation to the French and Soviets to join in the arrangement still exists. This merger is bitterly attacked by the Soviet authorities as a breach of the Potsdam Agreement and as a first step toward the dismemberment of Germany, ignoring the plain fact that their refusal to carry out that agreement was the sole cause of the merger. It is difficult to regard their attacks as anything but propaganda designed to divert attention from the Soviet failure to implement the economic unity agreed at Potsdam.

Certainly some progress towards economic unity in Germany is better than none.

The character of the control over the Ruhr industrial center,
the greatest concentration of coal and of heavy industries in Europe, continues a matter of debate. It cannot be decided merely
for the purpose of reaching an agreement. Vitally important considerations and future consequences are involved.

The question of reparations is of critical importance as it
affects almost every other question under discussion. This issue
naturally makes a tremendous appeal to the people of the Allied
states who suffered the terrors of German military occupation and
the destruction of their cities and villages.

The results of the Versailles Treaty of 1919 regarding payment of reparations on a basis of dollars, and the difficulties en
countered by the Reparations Commission appointed after Yalta in
agreeing upon the dollar evaluation of reparations in kind convinced President Truman and his advisers considering the question
at Potsdam that some other basis for determining reparations
should be adopted if endless friction and bitterness were to be
avoided in future years. They succeeded in getting agreement to
the principle of reparations to be rendered out of capital assets—
that is, the transfer of German plants, machinery, et cetera, to
the Allied power concerned.

It developed at the Moscow Conference that the Soviet officials flatly disagreed with President Truman's and Mr. Byrnes' understanding of the written terms of this agreement. The British
have much the same view of this matter as the United States.

We believe that no reparations from current production were
contemplated by the Potsdam Agreement. The Soviets strongly oppose this view. They hold that the previous discussions and agree
ments at Yalta authorize the taking of billions of dollars in repa
rations out of current production. This would mean that a substantial portion of the daily production of German factories would
be levied on for reparation payments, which in turn would mean
that the recovery of Germany sufficiently to be self-supporting
would be long delayed. It would also mean that the plan and the
hope of our Government, that Germany's economic recovery by the
end of three years would permit the termination of American appropriations for the support of the German inhabitants of our zone,
could not be realized.

The issue is one of great complications, for which agreement
must be found in order to administer Germany as an economic whole
as the four powers claim that they wish to do.

There is, however, general agreement among the Allies that
the matter of the factories and equipment to be removed from Germany as reparations should be reexamined. They recognize the fact
that a too drastic reduction in Germany's industrial setup will
not only make it difficult for Germany to become self-supporting

but will retard the economic recovery of Europe. The United States has indicated that it would be willing to study the possibility of a limited amount of reparations from current production to compensate for plants, previously scheduled to be removed as reparations to various Allied countries, which it now appears should be left in Germany; it being understood that deliveries from current production are not to increase the financial burden of the occupying powers or to retard the repayment to them of the advances they have made to keep the German economy from collapsing. The Soviet Government has made no response to this suggestion.

The issue regarding boundaries to be established for Germany presents a serious disagreement and another example of complete disagreement as to the meaning of the pronouncement on this subject by the heads of the three powers. In the rapid advance of the Soviet armies in the final phase of the war, millions of Germans in eastern Germany fled to the west of the Oder River. The Soviet armies, prior to Potsdam, had placed Poles in charge of this area largely evacuated by the German population. That was the situation that confronted President Truman at Potsdam. Under the existing circumstances, the President accepted the situation for the time being with the agreed three-power statement, "The three heads of government reaffirm their opinion that the final delimitation of the western frontier of Poland should await the peace settlement."

The Soviet Foreign Minister now states that a final agreement on the frontier between Germany and Poland was reached at Potsdam, and the expression I have just quoted merely referred to the formal confirmation of the already agreed upon frontier at the peace settlement, thus leaving only technical delimitation to be considered.

The United States Government recognized the commitment made at Yalta to give fair compensation to Poland in the west for the territory east of the Curzon Line incorporated into the Soviet Union. But the perpetuation of the present temporary line between Germany and Poland would deprive Germany of territory which before the war provided more than a fifth of the foodstuffs on which the German population depended. It is clear that in any event Germany will be obliged to support, within much restricted boundaries, not only her pre-war population but a considerable number of Germans from eastern Europe. To a certain extent this situation is unavoidable, but we must not agree to its aggravation. We do not want Poland to be left with less resources than she had before the war. She is entitled to *more*, but it will not help Poland to give her frontiers which will probably create difficulties for her in the future. Wherever the frontiers are drawn, they should not constitute barriers to trade and commerce upon which the well-being of Europe is dependent. We must look toward a future where a democratic Poland and a democratic Germany will be good neighbors.

There is disagreement regarding the manner in which the Allied powers at war with Germany are to participate in the drafting and confirmation of the German peace treaty. There are 51 states involved. Of these, in addition to the four principal Allied powers, 18 were directly engaged in the fighting, some of course to a much greater extent than others. It is the position of the United States that all Allied states at war with Germany should be given an opportunity to participate to some degree in the drafting and in the making of the peace treaty, but we recognize that there would be very practical difficulties if not impossibilities in attempting to draft a treaty with 51 nations participating equally at all stages. Therefore, the United States Government has endeavored to secure agreement on a method which involves two different procedures, depending on whether or not the state concerned actually participated in the fighting. But all would have an opportunity to present their views, and rebut other views, and all would sit in the peace conference to adopt a treaty.

It is difficult to get the agreement of the countries that have suffered the horrors of German occupation and were involved in heavy losses in hard fighting to accept participation in the determination of the treaty terms by countries who suffered no losses in men or material and were remote from the fighting. The United States, however, regards it as imperative that all the states who were at war with Germany should have some voice in the settlement imposed on Germany.

The proposal for the Four Power Pact was advanced by the United States Government a year ago. It was our hope that the prompt acceptance of this simple pact ensuring in advance of the detailed German peace settlement that the United States would actively cooperate to prevent the rearmament of Germany would eliminate fears as to the future and would facilitate the making of a peace suitable to Europe's present and future needs. It was our hope that such a commitment by the United States would relieve the fear of the other European powers that the United States would repeat its actions following the first World War, insisting on various terms for the peace settlement and then withdrawing from a position of any responsibility for their enforcement. It was thought that the compact of the four powers to guarantee the continued demilitarization of Germany would reassure the world that we were in complete accord in our intention to secure the peace of Europe.

However, the Soviet Government met our proposition with a series of amendments which would have completely changed the character of the pact, making it in effect a complicated peace treaty, and including in the amendments most of the points regarding the German problem, concerning which there was, as I have pointed out, serious disagreement. I was forced to the conclusion by this procedure that the Soviet Government either did not desire such a pact or was following a course calculated to delay any immediate prospect of its adoption. Whether or not an agreement can finally be reached remains to be seen, but the United States, I think, should adhere to its present position and insist that the pact be kept simple and confined to its one basic purpose—to keep Germany incapable of waging war.

The negotiations regarding the Austrian treaty resulted in agreement on all but a few points, but these were basic and of fundamental importance. The Soviet Union favors and the other governments oppose the payment of reparations and the cession of Carinthia to Yugoslavia.

But the Soviet Government attached much more importance to its demand that the German assets in Austria which are to be hers by the terms of the Potsdam Agreement should include those assets which the other three powers consider to have been taken from Austria and the citizens of the United Nations by force or duress by Hitler and his Nazi government following the taking over of Austria by military force in March 1938. The Soviet Government refused to consider the word *duress*, which in the opinion of the other three powers would be the critical basis for determining what property, that is, business, factories, land, forests, et cetera, was truly German property and not the result of seizures by terroristic procedure, intimidation, fake business acquisition, and so forth. The Soviet Union also refused to consider any process of mediation to settle the disputes that are bound to arise in such circumstances, nor would they clearly agree to have such property as they receive as German assets subject to Austrian law in the same manner as other foreign investments are subject to Austrian law.

The acceptance of the Soviet position would mean that such a large portion of the Austrian economy would be removed from her legal control that Austrian chances of surviving as an independent self-supporting state would be dubious. She would in effect be but a puppet state.

All efforts to find a compromise solution were unavailing. The United States, in my opinion, could not commit itself to a treaty which involved such manifest injustices and, what is equally important, would create an Austria so weak and helpless as to be the source of great danger in the future. In the final session of the Conference, it was agreed to appoint a Commission to meet in Vienna May 12th to reconsider our disagreements and to have a Committee of Experts examine the question of the German assets in Austria. Certainly prompt action on the Austrian treaty is necessary to fulfill our commitment to recognize Austria as a free and independent state and to relieve her from the burdens of occupation.

Complicated as these issues are, there runs through them a pattern as to the character and control of central Europe to be

established. The Foreign Ministers agreed that their task was to
lay the foundations of a central government for Germany, to bring
about the economic unity of Germany essential for its own existence as well as for European recovery, to establish workable bound
aries, and to set up a guaranteed control through a four-power
treaty. Austria was to be promptly relieved of occupation burdens
and treated as a liberated and independent country.

Agreement was made impossible at Moscow because, in our view,
the Soviet Union insisted upon proposals which would have established in Germany a centralized government, adapted to the seizure
of absolute control of a country which would be doomed economically through inadequate area and excessive population, and would be
mortgaged to turn over a large part of its production as reparations, principally to the Soviet Union. In another form the same
mortgage upon Austria was claimed by the Soviet Delegation.

Such a plan, in the opinion of the United States Delegation,
not only involved indefinite American subsidy, but could result
only in a deteriorating economic life in Germany and Europe and
the inevitable emergence of dictatorship and strife.

Freedom of information, for which our Government stands, inevitably involves appeals to public opinion. But at Moscow propaganda appeals to passion and prejudice appeared to take the place
of appeals to reason and understanding. Charges were made by the
Soviet Delegation, and interpretation given the Potsdam and other
agreements, which varied completely from the facts as understood
or as factually known by the American Delegation.

There was naturally much uncertainty regarding the real intention or motives of the various proposals submitted or of the
objections taken to the proposals. This is inevitable in any international negotiation.

However, despite the disagreements referred to and the difficulties encountered, possibly greater progress towards final settlement was made than is realized.

The critical differences were for the first time brought into
the light and now stand clearly defined so that future negotiations can start with a knowledge of exactly what the issues are
that must be settled. The Deputies now understand the precise
views of each government on the various issues discussed. With
that they can possibly resolve some differences and surely can fur
ther clarify the problems by a studied presentation of the state
of agreement and disagreement. That is the best that can be hope
for in the next few months. It marks some progress, however painfully slow. These issues are matters of vast importance to the
lives of the people of Europe and to the future course of world
history. We must not compromise on great principles in order to
achieve agreement for agreement's sake. Also, we must sincerely
try to understand the point of view of those with whom we differ.

In this connection, I think it proper to refer to a portion of a statement made to me by Generalissimo Stalin. He said with reference to the Conference, that these were only the first skirmishes and brushes of reconnaissance forces on this question. Differences had occurred in the past on other questions, and as a rule, after people had exhausted themselves in dispute, they then recognized the necessity of compromise. It was possible that no great success would be achieved at this session, but he thought that compromises were possible on all the main questions, including demilitarization, political structure of Germany, reparations and economic unity. It was necessary to have patience and not become pessimistic.

I sincerely hope that the Generalissimo is correct in the view he expressed and that it implies a greater spirit of cooperation by the Soviet Delegation in future conferences. But we cannot ignore the factor of time involved here. The recovery of Europe has been far slower than had been expected. Disintegrating forces are becoming evident. The patient is sinking while the doctors deliberate. So I believe that action cannot await compromise through exhaustion. New issues arise daily. Whatever action is possible to meet these pressing problems must be taken without delay.

Finally, I should comment on one aspect of the matter which is of transcendent importance to all our people. While I did not have the benefit, as did Mr. Byrnes, of the presence of the two leading members of the Senate Foreign Relations Committee, I did have the invaluable assistance of Mr. Dulles, a distinguished representative of the Republican party as well as a recognized specialist in foreign relations and in the processes of international negotiations and treaty making. As a matter of fact, the bipartisan character of the American attitude in the present conduct of foreign affairs was clearly indicated by the strong and successful leadership displayed in the Senate during the period of this Conference by Senators Vandenberg and Connally in the debate over a development of our foreign policy of momentous importance to the American people. The fact that there was such evident unity of purpose in Washington was of incalculable assistance to me in Moscow. The state of the world today and the position of the United States make mandatory, in my opinion, a unity of action on the part of the American people. It is for that reason that I have gone into such lengthy detail in reporting my views on the conference.

SUGGESTED ADDITIONAL READINGS

Clayton, William L. "GATT, the Marshall Plan, and OECD," *Politi-cal Science Quarterly*, 78 (December 1963), 493-503. The
    Assistant Secretary of State for Economic Affairs at the time
    on U.S. economic interests and negotiations and the origins
    of the Marshall Plan. Contains edited copy of Clayton's
    memorandum on the need for European recovery.

Dulles, John Foster. Report on Moscow CFM Meeting, April 30, 1947
    Vital Speeches of the Day, XIII (May 15, 1947), 450-453. A
    supplementary report to Secretary of State Marshall's. Re-
    views the conference and looks forward to European recovery
    and French reconstruction.

Jones, Joseph M. *The Fifteen Weeks (February 21-June 5, 1947)*.
    New York, 1955. The inside story of the origins of the Tru-
    man Doctrine and the Marshall Plan by a State Department
    participant. Readable and reflective.

Lippmann, Walter. *The Cold War: A Study in U.S. Foreign Policy*.
    New York, 1947. A collection of Lippmann's columns written
    in 1947. Critical of U.S. foreign policy, the Truman Doc-
    trine, and the policy of containment.

Mallalieu, William C. "The Origin of the Marshall Plan: A Study
    in Policy Formation and National Leadership," *Political Sci-
    ence Quarterly*, 73 (December 1958), 481-504. Based on unpub-
    lished State Department records.

Marshall, George C. Speech at Harvard University, June 5, 1947,
    The Department of State Bulletin, XVI (June 15, 1947), 1,159-
    1,160. The Marshall Plan speech.

Mason, Edward S. "Reflections on the Moscow Conference," *Inter-
    national Organization*, I (September 1947), 475-487. An ad-
    viser to Marshall at Moscow, commenting on the conference and
    the context out of which the Marshall Plan developed.

Thomas, G. B. "The Containment of Soviet Power," *Harper's Maga-
    zine*, 196 (January 1948), 10-18. U.S. policy toward the So-
    viet Union is changing from appeasement and accommodation to
    containment. The author finds this commendable and believes
    that the United States should give more attention to its
    friends, Britain and France.

THE INTERNATIONAL SITUATION, SEPTEMBER 1947*

Andrei A. Zhdanov

Andrei A. Zhdanov was secretary of the Central Committee of the Communist Party and a member of the Politburo. He was instrumental in the revival of the Cominform in the fall of 1947, and he helped to shape Soviet policies and programs in eastern Europe after the Russian decision not to participate in the Marshall Plan for European recovery. The selection printed below is from a speech Zhdanov delivered to a meeting of various European Communist Party representatives in Poland late in September 1947. Marshall's radio report to the American people in April 1947 and Zhdanov's speech to Communist Party leaders in September 1947 illuminate the final split between the two powers. The split is marked in Europe by the proclamation of the Truman Doctrine, the American-British decision to change the German level-of-industry and reparations plans, the adoption of the Marshall Plan, the establishment of the "Molotov Plan," and the formation of the Cominform.

Zhdanov analyzes the postwar world in the manner of Marxist dialecticians: The forces of imperialism (the United States and her allies) are opposed to the forces of anti-imperialism and democracy (the Soviet Union and her allies). The Soviet Union sought peace, disarmament, and good-neighbor relations after the war. But the United States became aggressive and expansionist, in the fashion of imperialist states. It supported reaction in Germany and Japan, and it sabotaged the Potsdam agreement on Germany. Furthermore, it accumulated atomic bombs. The more recent economic program, known as the Marshall Plan, is an aspect of the larger American strategic program of expansion, and it is designed to take advantage of the postwar economic difficulties in Europe to further American imperial interests. The plan will fail, however, as did the plan to use Fascism and World War II to weaken the Soviet system. The Soviet Union's exposure of the American plan to enthrall Europe, presumably by Soviet rejection of the Marshall Plan, is a great service to democratic countries everywhere.

----

*Reprinted, with deletions, from A. Zhdanov, *The International Situation* (Moscow, 1947).

*II.   The New Post-War Alignment of Political Forces and the Forma-
tion of Two Camps: Imperialist and Anti-democratic, and Anti-
imperialist and Democratic*

The fundamental changes caused by the war in the international scene and in the position of individual countries has entirely
changed the political landscape of the world. A new alignment of
political forces has arisen. The more the war recedes into the
past, the more distinct become two major trends in post-war international policy, corresponding to the division of the political
forces operating in the international arena into two major camps:
the imperialist and anti-democratic camp, on the one hand, and the
anti-imperialist and democratic camp, on the other. The principal
driving force of the imperialist camp is the U.S.A. Allied with
it are Great Britain and France. The existence of the Attlee-
Bevin Labour Government in Britain and the Ramadier Socialist Government in France does not hinder these countries from playing the
part of satellites of the United States and following the lead of
its imperialist policy on all major questions. The imperialist
camp is also supported by colony-owning countries, such as Belgium
and Holland, by countries with reactionary anti-democratic regimes
such as Turkey and Greece, and by countries politically and economically dependent on the United States, such as the Near Eastern
and South American countries and China.
    The cardinal purpose of the imperialist camp is to strengthen
imperialism, to hatch a new imperialist war, to combat Socialism
and democracy, and to support reactionary and anti-democratic pro-
fascist regimes and movements everywhere.
    In the pursuit of these ends the imperialist camp is prepared
to rely on reactionary and anti-democratic forces in all countries
and to support its former adversaries in the war against its wartime allies.
    The anti-imperialist and anti-fascist forces comprise the sec-
ond camp. This camp is based on the U.S.S.R. and the new democracies. It also includes countries that have broken with imperialism and have firmly set foot on the path of democratic development
such as Rumania, Hungary and Finland. Indonesia and Viet Nam are
associated with it; it has the sympathy of India, Egypt and Syria
The anti-imperialist camp is backed by the labour and democratic
movement and by the fraternal Communist parties in all countries,
by the fighters for national liberation in the colonies and depen-
encies, by all progressive and democratic forces in every country
The purpose of this camp is to resist the threat of new wars and
imperialist expansion, to strengthen democracy and to extirpate
the vestiges of fascism.
    The end of the Second World War confronted all the freedom-
loving nations with the cardinal task of securing a lasting
democratic peace sealing the victory over fascism. In the

ccomplishment of this fundamental task of the post-war period the
oviet Union and its foreign policy are playing a leading role.
*his follows from the very nature of the Soviet Socialist State,
o which motives of aggression and exploitation are utterly alien,
nd which is interested in creating the most favourable conditions
'or the building of a Communist society. One of these conditions
s external peace. As the embodiment of a new and superior social
ystem, the Soviet Union reflects in its foreign policy the aspira-
ions of progressive mankind, which desires enduring peace and has
othing to gain from a new war hatched by capitalism. The Soviet
nion is a staunch champion of the liberty and independence of all
ations, and a foe of national and racial oppression and colonial
xploitation in any shape or form. The change in the general
lignment of forces between the capitalist world and the Socialist
orld brought about by the war has still further enhanced the sig-
ificance of the foreign policy of the Soviet State and enlarged
he scope of its activity in the international arena.

All the forces of the anti-imperialist and anti-fascist camp
re united in the effort to secure a just and democratic peace.
t is this united effort that has brought about and strengthened
'riendly co-operation between the U.S.S.R. and the democratic coun-
ries on all questions of foreign policy. These countries, and in
he first place the new democracies—Yugoslavia, Poland, Czecho-
lovakia and Albania, which played a big part in the war of liber-
tion from fascism, as well as Bulgaria, Rumania, Hungary and to
ome extent Finland, which have joined the anti-fascist front—
ave proved themselves in the post-war period staunch defenders of
eace, democracy and their own liberty and independence against
ll attempts on the part of the United States and Great Britain to
urn them back in their course and to bring them again under the
mperialist yoke.

The successes and the growing international prestige of the
emocratic camp were not to the liking of the imperialists. Even
hile World War II was still on, reactionary forces in Great Brit-
in and the United States became increasingly active, striving to
revent concerted action by the Allied powers, to protract the war,
o bleed the U.S.S.R. and to save the fascist aggressors from ut-
er defeat. The sabotage of the second front by the Anglo-Saxon
mperialists, headed by Churchill, was a clear reflection of this
endency, which was in point of fact a continuation of the Munich
olicy in the new and changed conditions. But while the war was
till in progress, British and American reactionary circles did
ot venture to come out openly against the Soviet Union and the
emocratic countries, realizing that they had the undivided sym-
athy of the masses all over the world. But in the concluding
onths of the war the situation began to change. The British
nd American imperialists already manifested their unwillingness
o respect the legitimate interests of the Soviet Union and the

democratic countries at the Potsdam tripartite conference, in Jul
1945.

The foreign policy of the Soviet Union and the democratic
countries in these two past years has been a policy of consistently working for the observance of democratic principles in the post
war settlement. The countries of the anti-imperialist camp have
loyally and consistently striven for the implementation of these
principles, without deviating from them one iota. Consequently,
the major objective of the post-war foreign policy of the democratic states has been a democratic peace, the eradication of the
vestiges of fascism and the prevention of a resurgence of fascist
imperialist aggression, the recognition of the principle of the
equality of nations and respect for their sovereignty, and a general reduction of all armaments and the outlawing of the most destructive weapons, those designed for the mass slaughter of the
civilian population. In their effort to secure these objectives,
Soviet diplomacy and the diplomacy of the democratic countries met
with the resistance of Anglo-American diplomacy, which since the
war has persistently and unswervingly striven for the rejection of
the general principles of the post-war settlement proclaimed by
the Allies during the war, and to replace the policy of peace and
consolidation of democracy by a new policy, a policy aiming at vio
lating general peace, protecting fascist elements, and persecuting
democracy in all countries.

Of immense importance are the joint efforts of the diplomacy
of the U.S.S.R. and the other democratic countries to secure a reduction of armaments and the outlawing of the most destructive of
them—the atomic bomb.

On the initiative of the Soviet Union, a resolution was moved
in the United Nations calling for a general reduction of armaments
and the recognition, as a primary task, of the necessity to pro-
hibit the production and use of atomic energy for warlike purposes
This motion of the Soviet government was fiercely resisted by the
United States and Great Britain. All the efforts of the imperialist elements were concentrated on sabotaging this decision by
erecting endless and fruitless obstacles and barriers, with the
object of preventing the adoption of any effective practical measures. The activities of the delegates of the U.S.S.R. and the
other democratic countries in the agencies of the United Nations
bear the character of a systematic, stubborn, day-to-day struggle
for democratic principles of international co-operation, for the
exposure of the intrigues of the imperialist plotters against the
peace and security of the nations.

This was very graphically demonstrated, for example, in the
discussion of the situation on Greece's northern frontiers. The
Soviet Union and Poland vigorously objected to the Security Council being used as a means of discrediting Yugoslavia, Bulgaria and
Albania, who are falsely accused by the imperialists of aggressive
acts against Greece.

Soviet foreign policy proceeds from the premise that the two systems—capitalism and Socialism—will exist side by side for a long time. From this it follows that co-operation between the U.S.S.R. and countries with other systems is possible, provided that the principle of reciprocity is observed and that obligations once assumed are honoured. Everyone knows that the U.S.S.R. has always honoured the obligations it has assumed. The Soviet Union has demonstrated its will and desire for co-operation.

Britain and America are pursuing the very opposite policy in the United Nations. They are doing everything they can to renounce their commitments and to secure a free hand for the prosecution of a new policy, a policy which envisages not co-operation among the nations, but the hounding of one against the other, violation of the rights and interests of democratic nations, and the isolation of the U.S.S.R.

Soviet policy follows the line of maintaining loyal, good-neighbour relations with all states that display the desire for co-operation. As to the countries that are its genuine friends and allies, the Soviet Union has always behaved, and will always behave, as their true friend and ally. Soviet foreign policy envisages a further extension of friendly aid by the Soviet Union to these countries.

Soviet foreign policy, defending the cause of peace, discountenances a policy of vengeance towards the vanquished countries.

We know that the U.S.S.R. is in favour of a united, peace-loving, demilitarized and democratic Germany. Comrade Stalin formulated the Soviet policy towards Germany when he said: "In short, the policy of the Soviet Union on the German question reduces itself to the demilitarization and democratization of Germany. . . . The demilitarization and democratization of Germany form one of the most important guarantees for the establishment of a stable and lasting peace." However, this policy of the Soviet Union towards Germany is encountering frantic opposition from the imperialist circles in the United States and Great Britain.

The meeting of the Council of Foreign Ministers in Moscow in March and April 1947 demonstrated that the United States, Great Britain and France are prepared not only to prevent the democratic reconstruction and demilitarization of Germany, but even to liquidate her as an integral state, to dismember her, and to settle the question of peace separately.

Today this policy is being conducted under new conditions, now that America has abandoned the old course of Roosevelt and is passing to a new policy, a policy of preparing for new military adventures.

III.   The American Plan for the Enthrallment of Europe

The aggressive and frankly expansionist course to which Ameri
can imperialism has committed itself since the end of World War II
finds expression in both the foreign and the home policy of the
United States. The active support rendered to the reactionary,
anti-democratic forces all over the world, the sabotage of the
Potsdam decisions which call for the democratic reconstruction and
demilitarization of Germany, the protection given to Japanese reactionaries, the extensive war preparations and the accumulation
of atomic bombs—all this goes hand in hand with an offensive
against the elementary democratic rights of the working people in
the United States itself.

Although the U.S.A. suffered comparatively little from the
war, the vast majority of the Americans do not want another war,
with its accompanying sacrifices and limitations. This has induced monopoly capital and its servitors among the ruling circles
in the United States to resort to extraordinary means in order to
crush the opposition at home to the aggressive expansionist course
and to secure a free hand for the further prosecution of this dangerous policy.

But the campaign against Communism proclaimed by America's
ruling circles with the backing of the capitalist monopolies leads
as a logical consequence to attacks on the fundamental rights and
interests of the American working people, to the fascization of
America's political life, and to the dissemination of the most
savage and misanthropic "theories" and views. Obsessed with the
idea of preparing for a new, a third world war, American expansion
ist circles are vitally interested in stifling all possible resist
ance within the country to adventures abroad, in poisoning the
minds of the politically backward and unenlightened American masses with the virus of chauvinism and militarism, and in stultifying
the average American with the help of all the diverse means of
anti-Soviet and anti-Communist propaganda—the cinema, the radio,
the church and the press. The expansionist foreign policy inspired and conducted by the American reactionaries envisages simul
taneous action along all lines:

1.   Strategical military measures.
2.   Economic expansion.
3.   Ideological struggle.

The strategical plans for future aggression are connected
with the desire to utilize to the maximum the war production facilities of the United States, which had grown to enormous proportions by the end of World War II. American imperialism is

persistently pursuing a policy of militarizing the country. Expenditure on the U.S. army and navy exceeds 11,000,000,000 dollars per annum. In 1947-48, 35 per cent of America's budget was appropriated for the armed forces, or eleven times more than in 1937-38.

On the outbreak of World War II the American army was the seventeenth largest in the capitalist world; today it is the largest. The United States is not only accumulating stocks of atomic bombs; American strategists say quite openly that it is preparing bacteriological weapons.

The strategical plans of the United States envisage the creation in peacetime of numerous bases and vantage grounds situated at great distances from the American continent and designed to be used for aggressive purposes against the U.S.S.R. and the new democracies. America has, or is building, air and naval bases in Alaska, Japan, Italy, South Korea, China, Egypt, Iran, Turkey, Greece, Austria and Western Germany. There are American military missions in Afghanistan and even in Nepal. Feverish preparations are being made to use the Arctic for purposes of military agression.

Although the war has long since ended, the military alliance between Britain and the United States and even a combined Anglo-American military staff continue to exist. Under the guise of agreements for the standardization of weapons, the United States has established its control over the armed forces and military plans of other countries, notably of Great Britain and Canada. Under the guise of joint defence of the Western Hemisphere, the countries of Latin America are being brought into the orbit of America's plans of military expansion. The American government has officially declared that it has committed itself to assist in the modernization of the Turkish army. The army of the reactionary Kuomintang is being trained by American instructors and armed with American material. The military are becoming an active political force in the United States, supplying large numbers of government officials and diplomats who are directing the whole policy of the country into an aggressive military course.

Economic expansion is an important supplement to the realization of America's strategical plan. American imperialism is endeavouring, like a usurer, to take advantage of the post-war difficulties of the European countries, in particular of the shortage of raw materials, fuel and food in the Allied countries that suffered most from the war, to dictate to them extortionate terms for any assistance rendered. With an eye to the impending economic crisis, the United States is in a hurry to find new monopoly spheres of capital investment and markets for its goods. American economic "assistance" pursues the broad aim of bringing Europe into bondage to American capital. The more drastic the economic situation of a country is, the harsher are the terms which the American monopolies endeavour to dictate to it.

But economic control logically leads to political subjugation
to American imperialism. Thus, the United States combines the extension of monopoly markets for its goods with the acquisition of
new bridgeheads for its fight against the new democratic forces of
Europe. In "saving" a country from starvation and collapse, the
American monopolies at the same time seek to rob it of all vestiges of independence. American "assistance" almost automatically in
volves a change in the political line of the country to which it
is rendered: parties and individuals come to power that are prepared, on directions from Washington, to carry out a program of
home and foreign policy suitable to the United States (France,
Italy and so on).

Lastly, the aspiration to world supremacy and the anti-democratic policy of the United States involve an ideological struggle
The principal purpose of the ideological part of the American stra
tegical plan is to deceive public opinion by slanderously accusing
the Soviet Union and the new democracies of aggressive intentions,
and thus representing the Anglo-Saxon bloc in a defensive role and
absolving it of responsibility for preparing a new war. During
the Second World War the popularity of the Soviet Union in foreign
countries was enormously enhanced. Its devoted and heroic struggle against imperialism earned it the affection and respect of
working people in all countries. The military and economic might
of the Socialist State, the invincible strength of the moral and
political unity of Soviet society were graphically demonstrated to
the whole world. The reactionary circles in the United States and
Great Britain are anxious to erase the deep impression made by the
Socialist system on the working people of the world. The warmon-
gers fully realize that long ideological preparation is necessary
before they can get their soldiers to fight the Soviet Union.

In their ideological struggle against the U.S.S.R., the Ameri
can imperialists, who have no great insight into political questions, demonstrate their ignorance by laying primary stress on the
allegation that the Soviet Union is undemocratic and totalitarian,
while the United States and Great Britain and the whole capitalist
world are democratic. On this platform of ideological struggle—
on this defence of bourgeois pseudo-democracy and condemnation of
Communism as totalitarian—are united all the enemies of the working class without exception, from the capitalist magnates to the
Right Socialist leaders, who seize with the greatest eagerness on
any slanderous imputations against the U.S.S.R. suggested to them
by their imperialist masters. The pith and substance of this
fraudulent propaganda is the claim that the earmark of true democracy is the existence of a plurality of parties and of an organized opposition minority. On these grounds the British Labourite
who spare no effort in their fight against Communism, would like
to discover antagonistic classes and a corresponding struggle of
parties in the U.S.S.R. Political ignoramuses that they are, the

cannot understand that capitalists and landlords, antagonistic classes, and hence a plurality of parties, have long ceased to exist in the U.S.S.R. They would like to have in the U.S.S.R. the bourgeois parties which are so dear to their hearts, including pseudo-socialistic parties, as an agency of imperialism. But to their bitter regret, these parties of the exploiting bourgeoisie have been doomed by history to disappear from the scene.

The Labourites and other advocates of bourgeois democracy will go to any length to slander the Soviet regime, but at the same time they regard the bloody dictatorship of the fascist minority over the people in Greece and Turkey as perfectly normal, they close their eyes to many crying violations even of formal democracy in the bourgeois countries, and say nothing about the national and racial oppression, the corruption and the unceremonious abrogation of democratic rights in the United States of America.

One of the lines taken by the ideological campaign that goes hand in hand with the plans for the enslavement of Europe is an attack on the principle of national sovereignty, an appeal for the renouncement of the sovereign rights of nations, to which is opposed the idea of a "world government." The purpose of this campaign is to mask the unbridled expansion of American imperialism, which is ruthlessly violating the sovereign rights of nations, to represent the United States as a champion of universal laws, and those who resist American penetration as believers in an obsolete and "selfish" nationalism. The idea of a "world government" has been taken up by bourgeois intellectual cranks and pacifists, and is being exploited not only as a means of pressure, with the purpose of ideologically disarming the nations that defend their independence against the encroachments of American imperialism, but also as a slogan specially directed against the Soviet Union, which indefatigably and consistently upholds the principle of real equality and protection of the sovereign rights of all nations, big and small. Under present conditions imperialist countries like the U.S.A., Great Britain and the states closely associated with them become dangerous enemies of national independence and the self-determination of nations, while the Soviet Union and the new democracies are a reliable bulwark against encroachments on the equality and self-determination of nations.

It is a noteworthy fact that American military-political intelligence agents of the Bullitt breed, yellow trade union leaders of the Green brand, the French Socialists headed by that inveterate apologian of capitalism, Blum, the German Social-Democrat Schumacher and Labour leaders of the Bevin type are all united in close fellowship in carrying out the ideological plan of American imperialism.

At this present juncture the expansionist ambitions of the United States find concrete expression in the "Truman doctrine" and the "Marshall plan." Although they differ in form of presentation, both are an expression of a single policy, they are both an embodiment of the American design to enslave Europe.

The main features of the "Truman doctrine" as applied to Europe are as follows:

1. Creation of American bases in the Eastern Mediterranean with the purpose of establishing American supremacy in that area.
2. Demonstrative support of the reactionary regimes in Greece and Turkey as bastions of American imperialism against the new democracies in the Balkans (military and technical assistance to Greece and Turkey, the granting of loans).
3. Unintermitting pressure on the new democracies, as expressed in false accusations of totalitarianism and expansionist ambitions, in attacks on the foundations of the democratic regime, in constant interference in their domestic affairs, in support of all anti-national, anti-democratic elements within these countries and in the demonstrative breaking off of economic relations with these countries with the idea of creating economic difficulties, retarding their economic development, preventing their industrialization and so on.

The "Truman doctrine," which provides for the rendering of American assistance to all reactionary regimes which actively oppose the democratic peoples, bears a frankly aggressive character. Its announcement caused some dismay even among circles of American capitalists that are accustomed to everything. Progressive public elements in the U.S.A. and other countries vigorously protested against the provocative and frankly imperialistic character of Truman's announcement.

The unfavourable reception which the "Truman doctrine" met with accounts for the necessity of the appearance of the "Marshall plan," which is a more carefully veiled attempt to carry through the same expansionist policy.

The vague and deliberately guarded formulations of the "Marshall plan" amount in essence to a scheme to create a bloc of states bound by obligations to the United States, and to grant American credits to European countries as a recompense for their renunciation of economic, and then of political, independence. Moreover, the cornerstone of the "Marshall plan" is the restoration of the industrial areas of Western Germany controlled by the American monopolies.

It is the design of the "Marshall plan," as transpired from the subsequent talks and the statements of American leaders, to

render aid in the first place, not to impoverished victor countries, America's allies in the fight against Germany, but to the
German capitalists, with the idea of bringing under American sway
the major sources of coal and iron needed by Europe and by Germany,
and of making the countries which are in need of coal and iron dependent on the restored economic might of Germany.

In spite of the fact that the "Marshall plan" envisages the
ultimate reduction of Britain and France to the status of second-
rate powers, the Attlee Labour Government in Britain and the Ramadier Socialist Government in France clutched at the "Marshall
plan" as at an anchor of salvation. Britain, as we know, has already practically used up the American loan of 3,750,000,000 dollars granted to her in 1946. We also know that the terms of this
loan were so onerous as to bind Britain hand and foot. Even when
already caught in the noose of financial dependence on the U.S.A.
the British Labour Government could conceive of no other alternative than the receipt of new loans. It therefore hailed the
"Marshall plan" as a way out of the economic impasse, as a chance
of securing fresh credits. The British politicians, moreover,
hoped to take advantage of the creation of a bloc of Western European debtor countries of the United States to play within this
bloc the role of America's chief agent, who might perhaps profit
at the expense of weaker countries. The British bourgeoisie hoped,
by using the "Marshall plan," by rendering service to the American
monopolies and submitting to their control, to recover its lost
positions in a number of countries, in particular in the countries
of the Balkan-Danubian area.

In order to lend the American proposals a specious gloss of
"impartiality," it was decided to enlist as one of the sponsors
of the implementation of the "Marshall plan" France as well, which
had already half sacrificed her sovereignty to the United States,
inasmuch as the credit she obtained from America in May 1947 was
granted on the stipulation that the Communists would be eliminated
from the French government.

Acting on instructions from Washington, the British and
French governments invited the Soviet Union to take part in a discussion of the Marshall proposals. This step was taken in order
to mask the hostile nature of the proposals with respect to the
U.S.S.R. The calculation was that, since it was well known beforehand that the U.S.S.R. would refuse American assistance on the
terms proposed by Marshall, it might be possible to shift the responsibility on it for "declining to assist the economic restoration of Europe," and thus incite against the U.S.S.R. the European
countries that are in need of real assistance. If, on the other
hand, the Soviet Union should consent to take part in the talks,
it would be easier to lure the countries of East and Southeast
Europe into the trap of the "economic restoration of Europe with
American assistance." Whereas the Truman plan was designed to

terrorize and intimidate these countries, the "Marshall plan" was
designed to test their economic staunchness, to lure them into a
trap and then shackle them in the fetters of dollar "assistance."

In that case, the "Marshall plan" would facilitate one of the
most important objectives of the general American program, namely,
to restore the power of imperialism in the new democracies and to
compel them to renounce close economic and political co-operation
with the Soviet Union.

The representatives of the U.S.S.R., having agreed to discuss
the Marshall proposals in Paris with the governments of Great Brit
ain and France, exposed at the Paris talks the unsoundness of attempting to work out an economic program for the whole of Europe,
and showed that the attempt to create a new European organization
under the aegis of France and Britain was a threat to interfere in
the internal affairs of the European countries and to violate
their sovereignty. They showed that the "Marshall plan" was in
contradiction to the normal principles of international co-operation, that it harboured the danger of splitting Europe and the
threat of subjugating a number of European countries to American
capitalist interests, that it was designed to give priority of assistance to the monopolistic concerns of Germany over the allies,
and that the restoration of these concerns was obviously desig-
nated in the "Marshall plan" to play a special role in Europe.

The clear position of the Soviet Union stripped the mask from
the plan of the American imperialists and their British and French
coadjutors.

The all-European conference was a resounding failure. Nine
European states refused to take part in it. But even in the countries that consented to participate in the discussion of the "Marshall plan" and in working out concrete measures for its realization, it was not greeted with any especial enthusiasm, all the
more so since it was soon discovered that the U.S.S.R. was fully
justified in its supposition that what the plan envisaged was far
from real assistance. It transpired that, in general, the U.S.
government was in no hurry to carry out Marshall's promises. U.S.
Congress leaders admitted that Congress would not examine the ques
tion of granting new credits to European countries before 1948.

It thus became evident that in accepting the Paris scheme for
the implementation of the "Marshall plan," Britain, France and
other Western European states themselves fell dupes to American
chicanery.

Nevertheless, the efforts to build up a Western bloc under
the aegis of America are being continued.

It should be noted that the American variant of the Western
bloc is bound to encounter serious resistance even in countries
already so dependent on the United States as Britain and France.
The prospect of the restoration of German imperialism, as an effec
tive force capable of opposing democracy and Communism in Europe,
cannot be very alluring either to Britain or to France. Here we

have one of the major contradictions within the Anglo-American-French bloc. Evidently the American monopolies, and the international reactionaries generally, do not regard Franco and the Greek fascists as a very reliable bulwark of the United States against the U.S.S.R. and the new democracies in Europe. They are therefore staking their main hopes on the restoration of capitalist Germany, which they consider would be a major guarantee of the success of the fight against the democratic forces of Europe. They trust neither the British Labourites nor the French Socialists, whom, in spite of their manifest desire to please, they regard as "semi-Communists," insufficiently worthy of confidence.

It is for this reason that the question of Germany and, in particular, of the Ruhr, as a potential war-industrial base of a bloc hostile to the U.S.S.R., is playing such an important part in international politics and is an apple of discord between the U.S.A. and Britain and France.

The appetites of the American imperialists cannot but cause serious uneasiness in Britain and France. The United States has unambiguously given it to be understood that it wants to take the Ruhr out of the hands of the British. The American imperialists are also demanding that the three occupation zones be merged, and that the political separation of Western Germany under American control be openly implemented. The United States insists that the level of steel output in the Ruhr must be increased, with the capitalist firms under American aegis. Marshall's promise of credits for European rehabilitation is interpreted in Washington as a promise of priority assistance to the German capitalists.

We thus see that America is endeavouring to build a "Western bloc" not on the pattern of Churchill's plan for a United States of Europe, which was conceived as an instrument of British policy, but as an American protectorate, in which sovereign European states, not excluding Britain itself, are to be assigned a role not very far removed from that of a "49th state of America." American imperialism is becoming more and more arrogant and unceremonious in its treatment of Britain and France. The bilateral, and trilateral, talks regarding the level of industrial production in Western Germany (Great Britain-U.S.A., U.S.A.-France), apart from constituting an arbitrary violation of the Potsdam decisions, are a demonstration of the complete indifference of the United States to the vital interests of its partners in the negotiations. Britain, and especially France, are compelled to listen to America's dictates and to obey them without a murmur. The behaviour of American diplomats in London and Paris has come to be highly reminiscent of their behaviour in Greece, where American representatives already consider it quite unnecessary to observe the elementary decencies, appoint and dismiss Greek ministers at will and conduct themselves as conquerors. Thus, the new plan for the Dawesization of Europe essentially strikes at the vital interests

of the peoples of Europe, and represents a plan for the enthrallment and enslavement of Europe by the United States.

The "Marshall plan" strikes at the industrialization of the
democratic countries of Europe, and hence at the foundations of
their integrity and independence. And if the plan for the Dawesization of Europe was doomed to failure, at a time when the forces
of resistance to the Dawes plan were much weaker than they are now
today, in post-war Europe, there are quite sufficient forces, even
leaving aside the Soviet Union, and if they display the will and
determination they can foil this plan of enslavement. All that is
needed is the determination and readiness of the peoples of Europe
to resist. As to the U.S.S.R., it will bend every effort in order
that this plan be doomed to failure.

The assessment of the "Marshall plan" given by the countries
of the anti-imperialist camp has been completely confirmed by the
whole course of developments. In relation to the "Marshall plan,"
the camp of democratic countries have proved that they are a
mighty force standing guard over the independence and sovereignty
of all European nations, that they refuse to yield to browbeating
and intimidation, just as they refuse to be deceived by the hypo-
critical maneuvers of dollar diplomacy.

The Soviet government has never objected to using foreign,
and in particular American, credits as a means capable of expedit-
ing the process of economic rehabilitation. However, the Soviet
Union has always taken the stand that the terms of credits must
not be extortionate, and must not result in the economic and political subjugation of the debtor country to the creditor country.
From this political stand, the Soviet Union has always held that
foreign credits must not be the principal means of restoring a
country's economy. The chief and paramount conditions of a country's economic rehabilitation must be the utilization of its own
internal forces and resources and the creation of its own industry
Only in this way can its independence be guaranteed against encroachments on the part of foreign capital, which constantly dis-
plays a tendency to utilize credits as an instrument of political
and economic enthrallment. Such precisely is the "Marshall plan,"
which would strike at the industrialization of the European countries and is consequently designed to undermine their independence

The Soviet Union unswervingly holds the position that political and economic relations between states must be built exclusively on the basis of equality of the parties and mutual respect for
their sovereign rights. Soviet foreign policy and, in particular,
Soviet economic relations with foreign countries, are based on the
principle of equality, on the principle that agreements must be of
advantage to both parties. Treaties with the U.S.S.R. are agreements that are of mutual advantage to both parties, and never contain anything that encroaches on the national independence and
sovereignty of the contracting parties. This fundamental feature

of the agreements of the U.S.S.R. with other states stands out
particularly vividly just now, in the light of the unfair and unequal treaties being concluded or planned by the United States.
Unequal agreements are alien to Soviet foreign trade policy. More,
the development of the Soviet Union's economic relations with all
countries interested in such relations demonstrates on what principles normal relations between states should be built. Suffice
it to recall the treaties recently concluded by the U.S.S.R. with
Poland, Yugoslavia, Czechoslovakia, Hungary, Bulgaria and Finland.
By this way the U.S.S.R. has clearly shown along what lines Europe
may find the way out of its present economic plight. Britain
might have had a similar treaty, if the Labour Government had not,
under outside pressure, disrupted the agreement with the U.S.S.R.
which was already on its way to achievement.

The exposure of the American plan for the economic enslavement of the European countries is an indisputable service rendered
by the foreign policy of the U.S.S.R. and the new democracies.

It should be borne in mind that America herself is threatened
with an economic crisis. There are weighty reasons for Marshall's
official generosity. If the European countries do not receive
American credits, their demand for American goods will diminish,
and this will tend to accelerate and intensify the approaching economic crisis in the United States. Accordingly, if the European
countries display the necessary fortitude and readiness to resist
the enthralling American credit terms, America may find herself
compelled to beat a retreat. . . .

SUGGESTED ADDITIONAL DOCUMENTATION AND READINGS

Byrnes, James F. *Speaking Frankly*. New York, 1947. By the former Secretary of State. See esp. Ch. 14, pp. 277-297, "What
Are the Russians After?"

Marshall, George C. "Problems of European Revival and German and
Austrian Peace Settlements," *Vital Speeches of the Day*, XIV
(December 1, 1947), 98-101. Marshall's preview of the London
conference of foreign ministers, 1947, and its relation to
the Marshall Plan.

Molotov, V. M. *Problems of Foreign Policy: Speeches and Statements, April 1945-November 1948*. Moscow, 1949, esp. pp. 465-
470, for statement of Soviet nonparticipation in the Marshall
Plan, given in Paris on July 2, 1947, and pp. 471-499, for
speech on the thirtieth anniversary of the Russian Revolution,
November 6, 1947.

Steel, Ronald. *Pax Americana*. New York, 1967. A highly critical
    survey of U.S. foreign policies since World War II.

Ulam, Adam B. *Expansion and Coexistence: The History of Soviet
    Foreign Policy, 1917-1967*. New York, 1968. A general survey,
    esp. pp. 432-455.

PART 4

COMMENTARIES ON COLD WAR LITERATURE

    Two of the three articles in this section review the more prominent and influential interpretations of cold war origins. The other selection, by Hughes, while equally concerned with the literature on the subject, also emphasizes American-Russian relations as viewed by participants in 1946-1947. He finds that revisionists and cold warriors alike have tended to see the issues in sharper focus than was possible in the immediate postwar years. The essays by Lasch and Maier are historiographical treatments. Lasch surveys and differentiates among the orthodox, realist, revisionist, and radical interpreters. The concluding article, by Maier, concentrates on the revisionists and examines the conceptual bases of their approach to historical research.

THE SECOND YEAR OF THE COLD WAR:
A MEMOIR AND AN ANTICIPATION*

H. Stuart Hughes

H. Stuart Hughes is Gurney Professor of History and Political Science at Harvard University. His wartime experience in the Office of Strategic Services, Research and Analysis Branch, 1942-1946, and his postwar service as chief of the Division of Research for Europe, Department of State, 1946-1948, provide the basis for the selection that follows. Hughes is the author of several books on modern European history, including Consciousness and Society *(1958) and* Contemporary Europe: A History *(1961).*

In this very personal and reflective essay on the cold war, Hughes reproaches the revisionists for being intolerant of untidy realities. He does not deal with their works title by title, or issue by issue. He is more concerned with their failure to appreciate "the feel and taste of the late 1940's," an omission that often leads them to place cold war events "in a sharper and simpler outline than they had at the time."

On the other hand, Hughes is equally critical of the self-righteous moralism characteristic of State Department professionals in the immediate postwar years. Indicating a passionate conviction that Communist revolution and subversion threatened a crisis of monumental proportions in Europe and lacking a sense of history, their rhetoric and actions contributed significantly to closing off channels for constructive negotiations with the Soviet Union.

Looking back to 1946 and 1947, Hughes observes that Soviet domination of all of east-central Europe was a fact of life, and antagonisms between East and West were certain to arise as a consequence. The situation could have been managed by a spheres-of-influence agreement, but accumulated mistakes and misunderstandings on both sides tragically eroded the idea. Hughes rejects the revisionist claim that American policy and actions had closed out the possibilities of an agreement as early as 1945, just as in 1946 and 1947 he challenged those cold warriors who refused to accept the fact of a Russian presence in east-central Europe. He concludes that "In 1946 and 1947, as before and after, hostility to Communism made sense in certain contexts and was blind and self-defeating in others."

To someone who has been out of government service, as I have, for more than twenty years, the present spate of revisionist history on the origins of the cold war makes curious reading. One's first reaction is pleasure: it seems that those of us who originally opposed the cold-war mentality have now been rehabilitated; a stand that once was branded as mistaken, quixotic, or possibly even "subversive," in the light of today's ideological temper (at least among intellectuals), looks very good indeed. The second reaction is more perplexed: the current accounts, many of them by younger historians who did not experience the events in question at first hand, strike us as just barely out of focus. The lapse of two decades, joined to the new perspective our country's colossal mistakes in Vietnam have suggested, has etched the opening stages of the cold war in a sharper and simpler outline than they had at the time. In ceasing to be current events and becoming "history," they have acquired an unsuspected firmness of contour; today's young historians know crucial details that at the time were the closely-guarded secrets of the top policy-makers. Yet there has been a corresponding loss along the way: something of the feel and taste of the late 1940's has slipped into oblivion.

Thus much of the present polemic goes far beyond the arguments characteristic of the era itself: the reasoning of the handful of civil servants in positions of middle-range responsibility who were trying to persuade their colleagues to damp down the mounting hostility to the Soviet Union was more ambiguous and nuanced than the judgments we are offered today. It was also less moralistic: what offended a number of us at the time was the self-righteous tone both of our country's public rhetoric and of the private talk of the conventional Foreign Service types. Now, twenty years later, we are faced with moralism from the other direction: it is the United States rather than Russia that currently stands accused. Still more, from the present historical vantage point the decisive American acts of hostility seem to have come very early in the game—in the months immediately following the death of President Roosevelt in April 1945. The events of the succeeding period receive lesser attention. Yet to contemporaries it did not appear that way: when I myself got into the act, in the winter of 1946, I did not have the impression that I was arriving on the spot too late; although I found the ideological atmosphere in Washington quite different from what it had been when I had reported briefly back from Europe a year earlier, I did not think that the future had been foreclosed. The range of choice might be narrowing, but alternative paths still lay open. The year and quarter from March 1946 to July 1947 is the period of the incipient cold war that I know the best—indeed, the only one on which I can testify with any confidence. It is also the one

during which our country and the Soviet Union together reached the
point of no return.[1]
   My own involvement in these events was somewhat accidental.
As a former intelligence officer in the OSS, I had found my part
of that organization—the scholarly, non-secret part—reassigned
to the Department of State while I was still in Germany and in
uniform. Coming home, unlike most of my friends, who quickly returned to academic life, I decided to tarry on in Washington. A
few months later I found myself in charge of a large, sprawling,
demoralized staff of experts known as the Division of Research for
Europe. I had only just turned thirty: to all outward appear-
ances, I had fallen into a prestigious job, with responsibilities
unusual for one so young. The reality was rather different: my
new division floated in limbo, distrusted by the State Department
professionals and seldom listened to. After two years of bureaucratic frustration, I departed in early 1948, impelled by a mixture of ideological disappointment and the lure of university
teaching.
   But at least I had had a ringside seat on the cold war's
shift from tentative to definitive shape and, in the slow-paced
life of pre-air-conditioned Washington, a chance to reflect on
what was going on. These reflections were not all of a piece:
they oscillated between weary resignation and occasional explosions of wrath at the obtuseness of the conventional judgments—
explosions that in moments of particular annoyance at official
complacency might sound pro-Communist. My area of expertise, of
course, was Europe. In the second year of the cold war, European
concerns still dominated the international scene. China had not
yet been "lost," and besides, my counterparts in the research division for the Far East were accepted by the Foreign Service people far more as equals than was true on the European side. The
purge of "old China hands" which was to sweep up diplomats and
professors indiscriminately was as yet only a distant menace.
   My main point of opposition to the wisdom of the State Department professionals had to do with their apocalyptic outlook on Europe. In the West, where they emphasized the threat of Communist
subversion and revolution, I drew attention to the conservative recovery that was already taking place and to the possibility that
the United States might eventually find itself aligned with author-
itarian regimes of the Right. Where they saw crisis and collapse,
I detected elements of continuity with the past and viewed the danger to society less in terms of what militant Communists might do

----

[1]The emphasis it puts on this period is one of the many merits of
Walter LaFeber's judicious study, *America, Russia, and the Cold
War, 1945-1966*, Wiley, 1967.

than as the result of what routine-minded governments might fail
to do in alleviating the misery of populations just emerging from
the trials of war. In the East, I similarly found reasons for
taking Soviet domination more calmly than was considered good form
at the time. In short, I discovered the outlines of a new and unfamiliar kind of stabilization on both sides of what Winston
Churchill had just baptized the "iron curtain."

Churchill's address at Fulton, Missouri, delivered in Truman's presence in March 1946, marked the opening of the cold-war
phase in question. Matters that the statesmen of the West had previously spoken of in diplomatic euphemisms—however blistering
their language in private—had now been laid bluntly on the line.
The iron-curtain speech was followed almost immediately by a series of Soviet moves which suggested that Stalin in his own fashion agreed with Churchill's gloomy estimate—more particularly a
strengthening of ideological curbs at home associated with the
rise of Andrei Zhdanov and a shift of economic policy in Germany
presaging the partition of the country. Such were the actions and
the responses that sent the Soviet-American antagonism into high
gear. A year later a similar cluster of events gave the cold war
in Europe its permanent configuration: in March, the enunciation
of the Truman Doctrine and the launching of a "Security Loyalty
Program" in the United States; in May, the departure of the Communist ministers from the governments of France and Italy, and the
Soviet-inspired elimination of the democratic leader Ferenc Nagy
as prime minister of Hungary; finally, on the second of July, the
Russian refusal to cooperate in the Marshall Plan and the veto on
Polish and Czech participation that was its inevitable sequel.
The assumptions from which I—and a small group of friends
and associates—judged this series of events differed both from
the conventional cold-war stance that was then emerging and from
the revisionist view that has recently become so widespread. Perhaps our standpoint was eccentric; certainly it seems forgotten
today. Recalling it may help to restore to the year 1946-1947 the
quality of bewilderment and moral untidiness it had at the time.
Our first assumption was that the cold war, however distasteful we might find it, was something more than the product of in-
flamed American imaginations; it was based on the irrefutable
realities of an unprecedented situation—the Soviet domination of
the whole of East Central Europe. I remember looking at a map in
the autumn of 1944—when the Red Army, having chased the Germans
from the Balkans, stood at the gates of Warsaw and Budapest—and
concluding that a severe political reaction would set in at home
when my countrymen awoke to what had happened. It never occurred
to me that the American government could do anything to induce the
Russians to "behave"; hence the subsequent controversy about Yalta
struck me as largely beside the point. The cold war, or something

resembling it, I took as a fact of life, the dominant fact in the
lives of the unusual breed of civil servants among whom I worked:
it could be reduced or attenuated—that was the purpose of our
labors—but it could not be completely avoided, as some of the revisionist historians seem to imagine.

At just about the time in late 1944 when I was taking my look
at the map, Churchill went to see Stalin in Moscow. The result
was the celebrated spheres-of-influence agreement which assigned
to the Russians a predominant role in the Balkans, while leaving
Greece under Western supervision. The United States never accepted this arrangement, and its exact status remained unclear. Nor
did those at my level in the State Department know of its existence. I first learned about it a half decade later when Churchill
published the concluding volume of his wartime memoirs. I also
learned later still that a minority of highly-placed figures in
the American government, including Henry L. Stimson, Henry A. Wallace, and George F. Kennan, at various times and with varying emphases, had pushed the spheres-of-influence line.[2] In the second
year of the cold war, my friends and I were quite in the dark on
these matters: we reached the notion of spheres of influence on
our own. This became our second assumption—that the readiest way
to mitigate the ravages of the incipient cold war was for our country to keep to its side of the iron curtain in the hope that the
Soviet Union would oblige us by doing the same.

Thus in our minds the real drama—and tragedy—of the cold
war was the progressive erosion or degradation of the spheres-of-
influence idea. It was not within our style of thought to assign
exclusive or even predominant blame for this state of affairs to
one side or the other. We saw it rather as the result of a cumu-
lative, mutually reinforcing series of mistakes and misunderstandings—an elaborate counterpoint in which our government and that
of the Soviet Union seemed almost to be working hand in hand to
simplify the ideological map at the expense of minor political
forces, intermediate groups, and nuances of opinion. Our contention had been that if each side would stay out of the other's
sphere, then each could tolerate substantial dissent within that
sphere. Our prize exhibits were, in the East, the quasi-democrat-
ic functioning of the governments of Hungary and Czechoslovakia
and, in the West, the presence of Communists in the French and
Italian ministries. But as the year 1946-1947 wore on, it became
increasingly apparent that all such "bridges" or way stations were
doomed. Their mere existence offered an excuse for one side to
accuse its adversary of maintaining a fifth column in its midst.

----

[2]Arthur M. Schlesinger, Jr., "Origins of the Cold War," *Foreign
Affairs*, XLVI (October 1967), pp. 28-29.

Virtually every move of either one—however neutral its intent—bred suspicion in the other. As Russians and Americans alike tried to shore up the governments of the countries dependent on them, each act of ideological buttressing was bound to produce a corresponding reaction in the opposing camp.

It may sound paradoxical to have believed that a de facto partitioning of Europe would have facilitated rather than hindered the building of bridges from one side to the other. But that was what eventually proved true. In the crucial year 1946-1947 the Russians were treating this partitioning as the legitimate consequence of their military victories and the indispensable guarantee of their national security: the Americans were speaking of it as abnormal and immoral. Such at least was their public rhetoric; in actuality our government was to accept piece by piece over the years a situation it had originally rejected in toto. The proof came a decade later, in the autumn of 1956, when the United States failed to go to the aid of the anti-Communist insurrection in Hungary. And the result was what my friends and I had predicted: once the Russians knew that the Americans would not step over the line into what they had always considered their own sphere of influence, a thaw in the cold war, the beginnings of liberalization in Eastern Europe, and the inauguration of East-West cultural contacts finally became possible.

But that is to get ahead of our story. In the context of the cold war's second year, what was of prime importance was that the spheres-of-influence concept survived in the State Department's bureaucratic underground. Moreover, those of us who thought in such terms acted on the conviction, which we seldom, if ever, explicitly expressed, that our chiefs did not mean quite what they said. This was our third assumption—that neither our own country nor the Soviet Union had any serious intention of resorting to force in its dealings with the other; neither would attempt a real power play at the other's expense. Perhaps there was wishful thinking in our attitude; certainly we needed to grasp at some shred of comfort to get us through the rigors of an inordinately depressing year. Yet we were less far afield than the revisionist historians who have defined "the object of American policy" in the immediate postwar era as "not to defend Western or even Central Europe but to force the Soviet Union out of Eastern Europe."[3] In my own experience in Washington I never found any solid evidence of such a plan. There were warlike noises aplenty —everyone from President Truman down talked tough when the occasion (ordinarily incarnate as Congress) seemed to demand it. But

----

[3]Christopher Lasch, "The Cold War, Revisited and Re-visioned," *New York Times Magazine*, January 14, 1968, p. 54.

these pronouncements were exceedingly vague; they were far less sinister than they have appeared in retrospect. Before the Korean War the American capability in conventional arms was patently inadequate for the task of "liberating" Eastern Europe, and while atomic blackmail may always have been lurking in the wings, Stalin and Molotov, who prided themselves on their nerves of steel, were not allowing themselves to be frightened.

If a military showdown was tacitly ruled out, what remained? Was it simply a choice between preserving the close Soviet-American relationship of the period 1942-1944, and the institutionalized hostility in the form of the cold war, as revisionist historiography seems to argue? At the time, my friends and I thought otherwise—and this was our fourth and final assumption. We believed that one could find an intermediate course between armed antagonism and a cordial *modus vivendi*. Such a course, we recognized, was inordinately difficult to chart, and I am far from sure today what its outlines might have been. The best I can think of is some formula like wary, cautious, mutually suspicious relations handled with the "correctness" and consummate diplomatic tact that Europe's precarious situation required.

With the options thus narrowed, what was there that a middle-level official with my convictions could do? Naturally it was very little: in my division at least, we felt most of the time as though we were firing our memoranda off into a void. The atmosphere was that of Kafka's *Castle*, in which one never knew who would answer the telephone or even whether it would be answered at all. Two tasks, however, seemed possible: one was to try to explain that Soviet actions which our superiors thought outrageous would look rather less so if viewed in a spheres-of-influence context; the second was the notion of using America's economic power to build bridges between East and West.

While a whole succession of Soviet moves in the autumn and winter of 1946-1947 aroused official ire in Washington, the key event occurred in Hungary the following May. Hungary, we subsequently learned, had been treated in the original spheres-of-influence agreement in a peculiar fashion: as opposed to Bulgaria and Rumania, in which Soviet influence was to predominate, it had been assigned fifty-fifty to the Russians and to those oddly referred to as "the others." Parenthetically, it is also worth noting that Czechoslovakia and Poland were not covered by this agreement at all—hence the ramifying post-Yalta difficulties, particularly with regard to the latter. Such fine distinctions were lost on my friends and me: not knowing that any accord existed (even if unrecognized by our country), we simply assumed that the Soviet sphere should be considered coterminous with the area in which the presence or vicinity of the Red Army was the primary fact of life. Thus it seemed natural to us to lump with the two Balkan countries,

where Soviet influence was already entrenched, the three nations
to the west of them, two of which had held relatively free elections and were struggling to maintain the basic minimum of democratic procedures.

The overthrow of democracy in the second of these, Czechoslovakia, in early 1948 has so caught the attention of historians
as to dim the importance of the similar series of events that occurred in Hungary a year earlier. Yet viewed in retrospect, the
destruction of Ferenc Nagy's Smallholders' party may be the more
important of the two, as offering the first sign of what the Russians would and would not tolerate in the part of Europe they regarded as theirs. I am not sure today that I was right in saying
as flatly as I did—I quote from a memorandum I wrote at the time
—that "it was not the democratic character of the Hungarian government that brought down upon it the wrath of the Soviet Union.
It was its foreign policy of cultivating the favor of the Western
democracies, particularly the United States." The subsequent fate
of Czechoslovakia was to suggest that with the cold war in high
gear, internal policies alone might be sufficient to arouse Russian suspicion. Yet I think I was correct in arguing that the
action in Hungary was a "routine and anticipated move on the part
of the USSR to plug an obvious gap in its security system." Although "whittling down the Smallholder majority . . . had been
going on for months, . . . the enunciation of the Truman doctrine
accelerated the process," as did "the removal of the Communist
ministers from the governments of France and Italy. . . . Once the
United States had served notice that it was beginning to organize
a counter-bloc," the Soviet Union was bound to tighten its grip on
its own client states. And I concluded: "The coup in Hungary has
really altered nothing: it has only destroyed a few illusions."

Some of the illusions, of course, were my own. On rereading
after more than twenty years my note on Hungary, I find in it the
tone of a rear-guard action and of slightly desperate special
pleading. The time was fast running out in which an effort to explain Soviet actions in East Central Europe could find a hearing
in Washington. My second self-imposed task was more promising.
Fortunately enough, my division was awarded the job of preparing
preliminary studies for what later became the Marshall Plan. Besides reviving the flagging spirits of my associates, this technically challenging and ideologically congenial assignment gave me a
chance to put on paper my thoughts as to the form an economic recovery program for Europe should take.

A month before Secretary Marshall gave his celebrated com-
mencement address at Harvard, I had noted down the following:

  1. The aid program should be administered by an international body. . . .

   2. Aid should be granted solely on objective economic rather than political grounds.
      a. No discrimination against Soviet satellites.
      b. No effort to give overt or tacit support to
any particular political groups or parties.
      c. Reliance solely on the indirect political
effect of improved standard of living, etc.

   In a very general sense, the offer which Marshall made to the
Europeans conformed to these criteria. I believed at the time and
still believe that the plan which went by his name was the most
statesmanlike action the United States took in the opening years
of the cold war—indeed the only one that held out a real chance
of bridging the widening chasm in Europe. And its rejection by
the Soviet Union came as the last and bitterest of the succession
of disappointments that my friends and I had experienced over the
previous year. There is no need to retrace here the process of
gradual reinterpretation by which the Marshall Plan eventually
came to be viewed by both sides in a cold-war context. What is
more relevant is to recall that such had been from the start the
view of a large and influential body of State Department professionals; in their eyes the extension of the offer of economic aid
to Eastern Europe was always rather perfunctory. Hence the sharp,
dogmatic tone of my own memorandum on the subject. I felt that I
was in the minority and that I had to argue hard. I also sensed
that even small changes in the manner in which the offer was made
might be crucial to its acceptance or rejection—that the Russians
might oblige the hard-liners in my own country by confirming their
predictions. My memorandum ended on a note of warning: "Any program stated in terms of 'either the Soviet Union cooperates or . .
.' would almost certainly eventuate in the latter alternative being adopted; those already skeptical of the merits of a Europe-
wide, undiscriminatory program would be proved right, and an outright anti-Soviet program would be the result."

   Thus the curtain came down on a cruel year, during the course
of which the mutually reinforcing squeeze from East and West final
ly left my friends and me without a standing-ground. I spent my
last six months in Washington in a state of mild depression, punc-
tuated by gloomy (and exaggerated) predictions of the fate that
was about to overtake the democratic Left. Nor was my conscience
as clear as in retrospect might be supposed of one who had fought
and lost the good fight for Soviet-American reconciliation. In
the summer of 1947 I had the trial and execution of Nikola Petkov
to reckon with and that I found extremely hard to bear.
   If Ferenc Nagy is almost forgotten today—as opposed to Imre
Nagy, of 1956 fame—his agrarian counterpart in Bulgaria, Nikola

Petkov, is probably even less remembered. Yet at the time these two, along with Stanislaw Mikolajczyk, the Polish peasant spokesman, and like Nagy a fugitive abroad, were celebrated as offering a democratic middle course between Communist domination and the rightist-authoritarian, anti-Soviet type of government that had ruled most of East Central Europe before the Second World War. It was hard not to feel sympathy for agrarian leaders who, after the briefest of respites, were finding themselves once more in the state of political persecution that had been their usual lot before the "liberation" of their countries. And among them the case of Petkov was the most compelling. As opposed to Mikolajczyk and Nagy, the Bulgarian chose the more perilous course of staying on in his own country and fighting what he must have known was a hopeless battle. Tried on trumped-up charges of collusion with the United States, he was condemned to death in August 1947 and hanged the following month.

My associates followed with anguished interest Petkov's stubborn struggle for survival. I recall a friend's showing me a report of a scene in the Bulgarian parliament and of the taunt "You are trembling, Nikola Petkov" hurled at him by a political enemy. The words struck me like a body blow—as though I were in some sense guilty of Petkov's approaching death. And, as emotional truth, my reaction was not exaggerated. In our spheres-of-influence reasoning, in our anxiety to preserve good relations with the Soviet Union, my friends and I had hardened our hearts and in effect condemned Petkov and his like, just as we had consigned the populations of East Central Europe to Communist tyranny. We had done this with regret; we had sought to make a stand at every halting place along the way; but in the end we had bowed our shoulders and given up as lost the agrarian leaders and the electoral majorities that either had voted for them or would have voted for them if they could.

This emotional actuality is above all what gets lost in revisionist historiography on the origins of the cold war—the doubts by which we of the bureaucratic opposition were shaken and which gave our policy recommendations so fumbling and tentative a character. The State Department professionals, the fledgling cold warriors, were troubled by no such scruples; they saw the moral issues in simple terms; their consciences were clear. Not ours—our efforts to adopt the coolly detached stance of junior statesmen were constantly undercut by a half conscious recognition that we might be mistaken and that the policy we advocated carried with it an enormous price in human misery.

It was to be more than a decade before I recovered my equilibrium, before I was able to see clearly in what sense I had been right and in what sense the majority of American intellectuals had been wrong. Until the late 1950's the view prevailed that sympathy for the people of East Central Europe dictated a moral anti-Communism and that this sense of outrage in turn required an endorsement of the cold war. I simplify, of course—but such I think was the tacit assumption of most of the intellectual community: hence their reluctance to engage in any far-reaching critique of the official wisdom. Nor did the events of 1956 change many people's minds: the lesson of their country's total inability to react to the Soviet occupation of Budapest was lost on most of them. Not until the 1960's, and more particularly with the replay of Budapest that occurred in Prague twelve years later, did it finally sink in that in this case armed hostility was an inappropriate and counterproductive form in which to manifest the moral indignation with which it had so long been justified.

Throughout the first eight months of 1968 I was haunted by a sense that I was back where I had come in, at first joyous as the Czech idyll took a course which was too good to be fully believed, then profoundly depressed. The familiar litany—1938, 1948, 1968—had a special personal immediacy for one who had been in State Department service two decades earlier. And this was as true of the spring of expectation as it was of the autumn of bitterness. Just as the 1948 coup in Prague had snuffed out the last flickers of the political "openness" in which my friends and I had vested our hopes, so in 1968 Alexander Dubcek suddenly materialized as the reincarnation of those hopes, as the living embodiment of the ideological synthesis—left Socialist in the West, liberal Communist in the East—that our moments of optimism had sketched out. The promised land we had glimpsed had never been very substantial. Yet this non-dogmatic, neutralist, Popular-Front type of government had been precisely what a large and distinguished part of the Resistance to Hitler had longed for. Events had seemed to doom it utterly. And then quite unexpectedly, in the early months of 1968, Dubcek and his colleagues were on their way to making it a reality.

This time the subsequent disappointment banished any thought of a cold-war solution. Those in the West who twenty years earlier had been profoundly divided on Czechoslovakia now saw eye to eye. Nearly everyone dismissed a military response as inappropriate: even the calls for a reinvigoration of NATO sounded perfunctory. It was as though it had taken two decades to realize that the cold war and the fate of the populations under Soviet control were separable issues and that an emphasis on the one was of little help to the other. The armed standoff between the two superpowers could contribute nothing to improving the lot of the peoples of East Central Europe—rather the contrary; a question that was at bottom one of civil liberties, or of the quality of life, could not be dealt with by military means. In this respect, the Second World War had been the great exception to the more usual human experience: in 1944 and 1945 it had in fact proved possible

—at least in the West—to liberate whole populations from tyranny at a price that the liberated were willing to pay. With the cold war and the thermonuclear nightmare which accompanied it, such surgery became too dangerous to be attempted. But the memory and example of the "crusade" that had succeeded confused men's minds— and especially those of intellectuals—for a half-generation.

It was in this sense that my friends and I had been right two decades earlier. In the late 1940's I had been as incapable as the cold warriors of separating out the military from the civil-liberties aspect of events—hence my qualms of conscience. Today, in the light of what happened in Czechoslovakia in 1968, I am happier than I was at the time about the stand I took in the year and a half preceding the first seizure of power in Prague. Yet I am by no means satisfied with how revisionist historiography treats the events of twenty years ago. I refuse to accept the notion that my countrymen's anti-Communism was evil or misguided all along the line. In 1946 and 1947, as before and after, hostility to Communism made sense in certain contexts and was blind and self-defeating in others. More particularly it was not until a few Communist regimes or parties began to give a minimum respect to the human decencies that liberal-minded Americans could entertain much sympathy for them. And it is perhaps well that those too young to remember the immediate postwar era should hear such a simple truth from someone who twenty years ago labored under the suspicion of being "soft on Communism."

SUGGESTED ADDITIONAL READINGS

Bohlen, Charles E. *The Transformation of American Foreign Policy*. New York, 1969. A former State Department official reviews the policies he helped to create.

Halle, Louis J. *The Cold War as History*. New York, 1967. By a former State Department official. The cold war is a crisis in the balance of power, similar to the crises caused by Napoleon, Kaiser William II, and Hitler. Many useful insights and observations on the nature of the cold war.

Harriman, W. Averell. *America and Russia in a Changing World: A Half Century of Personal Observation*. New York, 1971. A leading participant's memoirs. See esp. pp. 13-44.

Kolko, Gabriel. *The Roots of American Foreign Policy: An Analysis of Power and Purpose*. Boston, 1969. Revisionist and critical, in the tradition of William A. Williams.

Neal, Fred Warner. "The Cold War in Europe, 1945-1967," *Struggle against History: U.S. Foreign Policy in an Age of Revolution*, ed. Neal D. Houghton. New York, 1968, pp. 20-39. A general survey.

"Origins of the Post-War Crisis: A Discussion," *The Journal of Contemporary History*, III, No. 2 (April 1968), 217-252. A summary report of a conference of leading scholars on the origins of the cold war, sponsored by the Institute of Contemporary History, Wiener Library, London.

Schlesinger, Arthur M., Jr. "Origins of the Cold War," *Foreign Affairs*, 46 (October 1967), 22-52. A response to the revisionists and a defense of Truman's policies after 1945.

Shulman, Marshall D. *Beyond the Cold War*. New Haven, Conn., 1966, esp. pp. 1-17. Discussion of origins, with emphasis on the Soviet and American misconceptions of each other's policies. Good on the emotional climate that produced the Truman Doctrine.

THE COLD WAR,
REVISITED AND RE-VISIONED*

Christopher Lasch

Christopher Lasch is a professor of history at Northwestern University. His special interest is recent American history, and he has been recognized as one of the leading writers of the New Left. He has published The American Liberals and the Russian Revolution *(1962),* The New Radicalism in America, 1889-1963 *(1965), and* The Agony of the American Left *(1969).*

In the following selection, Lasch categorizes the various interpretations of cold war origins as orthodox (liberal), realist, revisionist, and radical. The orthodox interpretation appeared in response to charges by the political right that Communist successes in 1948 and 1949 were made possible by Roosevelt's misguided practice of trusting the Russians. George F. Kennan, the most influential of the orthodox school, argued that Russian strength had been vastly increased by the war, and in 1945 the United States was in no position to dislodge Soviet armies from the areas they occupied. Stalin, by breaking the agreements he entered into at Yalta, was the villain in the piece, not Roosevelt. Thus, wrote Kennan, the United States should contain the Soviet Union until its power broke up or until it mellowed.

With Herbert Feis as their leading representative, the realists shared Kennan's opinion that the cold war was essentially an American response to Soviet expansionism. Realists also maintained that the United States should have been more willing to accept balance-of-power arrangements.

Unlike the orthodox and realist interpreters, revisionists assert that Russia was extremely weak at the end of the war, at least compared with the United States. This dictated that Russia pursue a policy of cooperation with the West, but her efforts to do so were rebuffed by an American leadership unalterably opposed to Communism and confident of its military superiority.

William A. Williams, currently at Oregon State University, had an extraordinary influence in promoting the revisionist interpretation of the cold war. In The Tragedy of American Diplomacy *(1959), Williams advanced the argument that the United States has adhered to a policy of the "open door" on a global scale throughout*

----

this century, a policy required by capitalism's need for ever ex-
panding markets.   The cold war, then, was the inevitable conse-
quence of an American effort to make the world safe for capitalism
*   Using the Williams thesis as a point of departure, but with-*
out his blessings, radicals maintain that American foreign poli-
cies "cannot be changed unless American society itself undergoes
a revolutionary change."

More than a year has passed since Arthur Schlesinger, Jr.
announced that the time had come "to blow the whistle before the
current outburst of revisionism regarding the origins of the cold
war goes much further." Yet the outburst of revisionism shows no
signs of subsiding. On the contrary, a growing number of historians and political critics, judging from such recent books as Ronald Steel's *Pax Americana* and Carl Oglesby's and Richard Shaull's
Containment and Change, are challenging the view, once so widely
accepted, that the cold war was an American response to Soviet expansionism, a distasteful burden reluctantly shouldered in the
face of a ruthless enemy bent on our destruction, and that Russia,
not the United States, must therefore bear the blame for shatter-
ing the world's hope that two world wars in the 20th century would
finally give way to an era of peace.
     "Revisionist" historians are arguing instead that the United
States did as much as the Soviet Union to bring about the collapse
of the wartime coalition. Without attempting to shift the blame
exclusively to the United States, they are trying to show, as Gar
Alperovitz puts it, that "the cold war cannot be understood simply
as an American response to a Soviet challenge, but rather as the
insidious interaction of mutual suspicions, blame for which must
be shared by all."
     Not only have historians continued to re-examine the immedi-
ate origins of the cold war—in spite of attempts to "blow the
whistle" on their efforts—but the scope of revisionism has been
steadily widening. Some scholars are beginning to argue that the
whole course of American diplomacy since 1898 shows that the United States has become a counterrevolutionary power committed to the
defense of a global status quo. Arno Mayer's monumental study of
the Conference of Versailles, *Politics and Diplomacy of Peacemaking,* which has recently been published by Knopf and which promises
to become the definitive work on the subject, announces in its
subtitle what a growing number of historians have come to see as
the main theme of American diplomacy: *Containment and Counterrevo
lution.*
     Even Schlesinger has now admitted, in a recent article in
Foreign Affairs, that he was "somewhat intemperate," a year ago,
in deploring the rise of cold-war revisionism. Even though

revisionist interpretations of earlier wars "have failed to stick," he says, "revisionism is an essential part of the process by which history . . . enlarges its perspectives and enriches its insights." Since he goes on to argue that "postwar collaboration between Russia and America [was] . . . inherently impossible" and that "the most rational of American policies could hardly have averted the cold war," it is not clear what Schlesinger thinks revisionism has done to enlarge our perspective and enrich our insights; but it is good to know, nevertheless, that revisionists may now presumably continue their work (inconsequential as it may eventually prove to be) without fear of being whistled to a stop by the referee.

The orthodox interpretation of the cold war, as it has come to be regarded, grew up in the late forties and early fifties— years of acute international tension, during which the rivalry between the United States and the Soviet Union repeatedly threatened to erupt in a renewal of global war. Soviet-American relations had deteriorated with alarming speed following the defeat of Hitler. At Yalta, in February, 1945, Winston Churchill had expressed the hope that world peace was nearer the grasp of the assembled statesmen of the great powers "than at any time in history." It would be "a great tragedy," he said, "if they, through inertia or carelessness, let it slip from their grasp. History would never forgive them if they did."

Yet the Yalta agreements themselves, which seemed at the time to lay the basis of postwar cooperation, shortly provided the focus of bitter dissension, in which each side accused the other of having broken its solemn promises. In Western eyes, Yalta meant free elections and parliamentary democracies in Eastern Europe, while the Russians construed the agreements as recognition of their demand for governments friendly to the Soviet Union.

The resulting dispute led to mutual mistrust and to a hardening of positions on both sides. By the spring of 1946 Churchill himself, declaring that "an iron curtain has descended" across Europe, admitted, in effect, that the "tragedy" he had feared had come to pass. Europe split into hostile fragments, the eastern half dominated by the Soviet Union, the western part sheltering nervously under the protection of American arms. NATO, founded in 1949 and countered by the Russian-sponsored Warsaw Pact, merely ratified the existing division of Europe.

From 1946 on, every threat to the stability of this uneasy balance produced an immediate political crisis—Greece in 1947, Czechoslovakia and the Berlin blockade in 1948—each of which, added to existing tensions, deepened hostility on both sides and increased the chance of war. When Bernard Baruch announced in April, 1947, that "we are in the midst of a cold war," no one felt inclined to contradict him. The phrase stuck, as an accurate description of postwar political realities.

Many Americans concluded, moreover, that the United States was losing the cold war. Two events in particular contributed to this sense of alarm—the collapse of Nationalist China in 1949, followed by Chiang Kai-shek's flight to Taiwan, and the explosion of an atomic bomb by the Russians in the same year. These events led to the charge that American leaders had deliberately or unwittingly betrayed the country's interests. The Alger Hiss case was taken by some people as proof that the Roosevelt Administration had been riddled by subversion.

Looking back to the wartime alliance with the Soviet Union, the American Right began to argue that Roosevelt, by trusting the Russians, had sold out the cause of freedom. Thus Nixon and McCarthy, aided by historians like Stefan J. Possony, C. C. Tansill and others, accused Roosevelt of handing Eastern Europe to the Russians and of giving them a preponderant interest in China which later enabled the Communists to absorb the entire country.

The liberal interpretation of the cold war—what I have called the orthodox interpretation—developed partly as a response to these charges. In liberal eyes, the right-wingers made the crucial mistake of assuming that American actions had been decisive in shaping the postwar world. Attempting to rebut this devil theory of postwar politics, liberals relied heavily on the argument that the shape of postwar politics had already been dictated by the war itself, in which the Western democracies had been obliged to call on Soviet help in defeating Hitler. These events, they maintained, had left the Soviet Union militarily dominant in Eastern Europe and generally occupying a position of much greater power, relative to the West, than the position she had enjoyed before the war.

In the face of these facts, the United States had very little leeway to influence events in what were destined to become Soviet spheres of influences, particularly since Stalin was apparently determined to expand even if it meant ruthlessly breaking his agreements—and after all it was Stalin, the liberals emphasized, and not Roosevelt or Truman, who broke the Yalta agreement on Poland, thereby precipitating the cold war.

These were the arguments presented with enormous charm, wit, logic and power in George F. Kennan's *American Diplomacy* (1951), which more than any other book set the tone of cold war historiography. For innumerable historians, but especially for those who were beginning their studies in the fifties, Kennan served as the model of what a scholar should be—committed yet detached—and it was through the perspective of his works that a whole generation of scholars came to see not only the origins of the cold war, but the entire history of 20th century diplomacy.

It is important to recognize that Kennan's was by no means an uncritical perspective—indeed, for those unacquainted with Marxism, it seemed the only critical perspective that was available in the fifties. While Kennan insisted that the Russians were primarily to blame for the cold war, he seldom missed an opportunity to criticize the excessive moralism, the messianic vision of a world made safe for democracy, which he argued ran "like a red skein" through American diplomacy.

As late as 1960, a radical like Staughton Lynd could still accept the general framework of Kennan's critique of American idealism while noting merely that Kennan had failed to apply it to the specific events of the cold war and to the policy of containment which he had helped to articulate. "Whereas in general he counseled America to 'admit the validity and legitimacy of power realities and aspirations . . . and to seek their point of maximum equilibrium rather than their reform or their repression'— 'reform or repression' of the Soviet system were the very goals which Kennan's influential writings of those years urged."

Even in 1960, however, a few writers had begun to attack not the specific applications of the principles of *Realpolitik* but the principles themselves, on the ground that on many occasions they served simply as rationalizations for American (not Soviet) expansionism. And whereas Lynd in 1960 could still write that the American demand for freedom in Eastern Europe, however misguided, "expressed a sincere and idealistic concern," some historians had already begun to take a decidedly more sinister view of the matter— asking, for instance, whether a country which demanded concessions in Eastern Europe that it was not prepared to grant to the Russians in Western Europe could really be accused, as the "realist" writers had maintained, of an excess of good-natured but occasionally incompetent altruism.

Meanwhile the "realist" interpretation of the cold war inspired a whole series of books—most notably, Herbert Feis's series (*Churchill-Roosevelt-Stalin; Between War and Peace; The Atomic Bomb and the End of World War II*); William McNeill's *America, Britain and Russia: Their Cooperation and Conflict*; Norman Graebner's *Cold War Diplomacy*; Louis J. Halle's *Dream and Reality* and *The Cold War as History*; and M. F. Herz's *Beginnings of the Cold War*.

Like Kennan, all of these writers saw containment as a necessary response to Soviet expansionism and to the deterioration of Western power in Eastern Europe. At the same time, they were critical, in varying degrees of the legalistic-moralistic tradition which kept American statesmen from looking at foreign relations in the light of balance-of-power considerations.

Some of them tended to play off Churchillian realism against the idealism of Roosevelt and Cordell Hull, arguing for instance, that the Americans should have accepted the bargain made between Churchill and Stalin in 1944, whereby Greece was assigned to the Western sphere of influence and Rumania, Bulgaria and Hungary to the Soviet sphere, with both liberal and Communist parties sharing in the control of Yugoslavia.

These criticisms of American policy, however, did not challenge the basic premise of American policy, that the Soviet Union was a ruthlessly aggressive power bent on world domination. They assumed, moreover, that the Russians were in a position to realize large parts of this program, and that only counterpressure exerted by the West, in the form of containment and the Marshall Plan, prevented the Communists from absorbing all of Europe and much of the rest of the world as well.

It is their criticism of these assumptions that defines the revisionist historians and distinguishes them from the "realists." What impresses revisionists is not Russia's strength but her military weakness following the devastating war with Hitler, in which the Russians suffered much heavier losses than any other member of the alliance.

Beginning with Carl Marzani's *We Can Be Friends: Origins of the Cold War* (1952), revisionists have argued that Russia's weakness dictated, for the moment at least, a policy of postwar cooperation with the West. Western leaders' implacable hostility to Communism, they contend, prevented them from seeing this fact, a proper understanding of which might have prevented the cold war. This argument is spelled out in D. F. Fleming's two-volume study, *The Cold War and Its Origins* (1961); in David Horowitz's *The Free World Colossus* (1965), which summarizes and synthesizes a great deal of revisionist writing; in Gar Alperovitz's *Atomic Diplomacy: Hiroshima and Potsdam* (1965); and in the previously mentioned *Containment and Change*.

But the historian who has done most to promote a revisionist interpretation of the cold war, and of American diplomacy in general is William Appleman Williams of the University of Wisconsin, to whom most of the writers just mentioned owe a considerable debt. William's works, particularly *The Tragedy of American Diplomacy* (1959), not only challenge the orthodox interpretation of the cold war, they set against it an elaborate counterinterpretation which, if valid, forces one to see American policy in the early years of the cold war as part of a larger pattern of American globalism reaching as far back as 1898.

According to Williams, American diplomacy has consistently adhered to the policy of the "open door"—that is, to a policy of commercial, political and cultural expansion which seeks to extend American influence into every corner of the earth. This policy was consciously and deliberately embarked upon, Williams argues, because American statesmen believed that American capitalism needed ever-expanding foreign markets in order to survive, the closing of the frontier having put an end to its expansion on the continent of North America. Throughout the 20th century, the makers of American foreign policy, he says, have interpreted the national interest in this light.

The cold war, in Williams' view, therefore has to be seen as the latest phase of a continuing effort to make the world safe for democracy—read liberal capitalism, American-style—in which the United States finds itself increasingly cast as the leader of a world-wide counterrevolution.

After World War II, Williams maintains, the United States had "a vast proportion of actual as well as potential power vis-à-vis the Soviet Union." The United States "cannot with any real warrant or meaning claim that it has been *forced* to follow a certain approach or policy." (Compare this with a statement by Arthur Schlesinger: "The cold war could have been avoided only if the Soviet Union had not been possessed by convictions both of the infallibility of the Communist word and of the inevitability of a Communist world.")

The Russians, by contrast, Williams writes, "viewed their position in the nineteen-forties as one of weakness, not offensive strength." One measure of Stalin's sense of weakness, as he faced the enormous task of rebuilding the shattered Soviet economy, was his eagerness to get a large loan from the United States. Failing to get such a loan—instead, the United States drastically cut back lend-lease payments to Russia in May, 1945—Stalin was faced with three choices, according to Williams:

He could give way and accept the American peace program at every point—which meant, among other things, accepting governments in Eastern Europe hostile to the Soviet Union.

He could follow the advice of the doctrinaire revolutionaries in his own country who argued that Russia's best hope lay in fomenting world-wide revolution.

Or he could exact large-scale economic reparations from Germany while attempting to reach an understanding with Churchill and Roosevelt on the need for governments in Eastern Europe not necessarily Communist but friendly to the Soviet Union.

His negotiations with Churchill in 1944 according to Williams, showed that Stalin had already committed himself, by the end of the war, to the third of these policies—a policy, incidentally, which required him to withdraw support from Communist revolutions in Greece and in other countries which under the terms of the Churchill-Stalin agreement had been conceded to the Western sphere of influence.

But American statesmen, the argument continues, unlike the British, were in no mood to compromise. They were confident of America's strength and Russia's weakness (although later they and their apologists found it convenient to argue that the contrary had been the case). Furthermore, they believed that "we cannot have full employment and prosperity in the United States without the foreign markets," as Dean Acheson told a special Congressional committee on postwar economic policy and planning in November, 1944. These considerations led to the conclusion, as President

Truman put it in April, 1945, that the United States should "take
the lead in running the world in the way that the world ought to
be run"; or more specifically, in the words of Foreign Economic
Administrator Leo Crowley, that "if you create good governments in
foreign countries, automatically you will have better markets for
ourselves." Accordingly, the United States pressed for the "open
door" in Eastern Europe and elsewhere.

In addition to these considerations, there was the further
matter of the atomic bomb, which first became a calculation in
American diplomacy in July, 1945. The successful explosion of an
atomic bomb in the New Mexican desert, Williams argues, added to
the American sense of omnipotence and led the United States "to
overplay its hand"—for in spite of American efforts to keep the
Russians out of Eastern Europe, the Russians refused to back down.

Nor did American pressure have the effect, as George Kennan
hoped, of promoting tendencies in the Soviet Union "which must
eventually find their outlet in either the break-up or the gradual mellowing of Soviet power." Far from causing Soviet policy to
mellow, American actions, according to Williams, stiffened the Russians in their resistance to Western pressure and strengthened the
hand of those groups in the Soviet Union which had been arguing
all along that capitalist powers could not be trusted.

Not only did the Russians successfully resist American demands in Eastern Europe, they launched a vigorous counterattack in
the form of the Czechoslovakian coup of 1948 and the Berlin blockade. Both East and West thus found themselves committed to the
policy of cold war, and for the next 15 years, until the Cuban missile crises led to a partial detente, Soviet-American hostility
was the determining fact of international politics.

Quite apart from his obvious influence on other revisionist
historians of the cold war and on his own students in other areas
of diplomatic history, Williams has had a measurable influence on
the political radicals of the sixties, most of whom now consider
it axiomatic that American diplomacy has been counterrevolutionary and that this fact reflects, not a series of blunders and mistakes as some critics have argued, but the basically reactionary
character of American capitalism.

Some radicals now construe these facts to mean that American
foreign policy therefore cannot be changed unless American society
itself undergoes a revolutionary change. Carl Oglesby, for instance, argues along these lines in *Containment and Change*. From
Oglesby's point of view, appeals to conscience or even to enlightened self-interest are useless; the cold war cannot end until the
"system" is destroyed.

Williams thought otherwise. At the end of the 1962 edition
of *The Tragedy of American Diplomacy*, he noted that "there is at
the present time no radicalism in the United States strong enough
to win power, or even a very significant influence, through the

processes of representative government"—and he took it for granted that genuinely democratic change could come about only through
representative processes. This meant, he thought, that "the well-
being of the United States depends—*in the short-run but only in
the short-run*—upon the extent to which calm and confident and enlightened conservatives can see and bring themselves to act upon
the validity of a radical analysis."

In an essay in *Ramparts* last March, he makes substantially
the same point in commenting on the new radicals' impatience with
conservative critics of American diplomacy like Senator Fulbright.
Fulbright, Williams says, attracted more support for the position
of more radical critics than these critics had attracted through
their own efforts. "He hangs tough over the long haul, and that
is precisely what American radicalism has never done in the 20th
century."

As the New Left becomes more and more beguiled by the illusion of its own revolutionary potential, and more and more intolerant of radicals who refuse to postulate a revolution as the only
feasible means of social change, men like Williams will probably
become increasingly uncomfortable in the presence of a movement
they helped to create. At the same time, Williams' radicalism,
articulated in the fifties before radicalism came back into fashion, has alienated the academic establishment and prevented his
works from winning the widespread recognition and respect they deserve. In scholarly journals, many reviews of Williams' work—
notably a review by Oscar Handlin of *The Contours of American History* in the *Mississippi Valley Historical Review* a few years ago—
have been contemptuous and abusive in the extreme. The result is
that Williams' books on diplomatic history are only beginning to
pass into the mainstream of scholarly discourse, years after their
initial publication.

Next to Williams' *Tragedy of American Diplomacy*, the most important attack on the orthodox interpretation of the cold war is
Alperovitz's *Atomic Diplomacy*. A young historian trained at Wisconsin, Berkeley and King's College, Cambridge, and currently a
research fellow at Harvard, Alperovitz adds very little to the interpretation formulated by Williams, but he provides Williams' insights with a mass of additional documentation. By doing so, he
has made it difficult for conscientious scholars any longer to
avoid the challenge of revisionist interpretations. Unconvention-
al in its conclusions, *Atomic Diplomacy* is thoroughly conventional
in its methods. That adds to the book's persuasiveness. Using
the traditional sources of diplomatic history—official records,
memoirs of participants, and all the unpublished material to which
scholars have access—Alperovitz painstakingly reconstructs the
evolution of American policy during the six-month period March
to August, 1945. He proceeds with a thoroughness and caution
which, in the case of a less controversial work, would command the

unanimous respect of the scholarly profession. His book is no
polemic. It is a work in the best—and most conservative—traditions of historical scholarship. Yet the evidence which Alperovitz has gathered together challenges the official explanation
of the beginnings of the cold war at every point.

What the evidence seems to show is that as early as April,
1945, American officials from President Truman on down had decided to force a "symbolic showdown" with the Soviet Union over the
future of Eastern Europe. Truman believed that a unified Europe
was the key to European recovery and economic stability, since the
agricultural southeast and the industrial northwest depended on
each other. Soviet designs on Eastern Europe, Truman reasoned,
threatened to disrupt the economic unity of Europe and therefore
had to be resisted. The only question was whether the showdown
should take place immediately or whether it should be delayed
until the bargaining position of the United States had improved.

At first it appeared to practically everybody that delay
would only weaken the position of the United States. Both of its
major bargaining counters, its armies in Europe and its lend-lease
credits to Russia, could be more effectively employed at once, it
seemed, than at any future time. Accordingly, Truman tried to
"lay it on the line" with the Russians. He demanded that they
"carry out their [Yalta] agreements" by giving the pro-Western elements in Poland an equal voice in the Polish Government (although
Roosevelt, who made the Yalta agreements, believed that "we placed
as clearly shown in the agreement, somewhat more emphasis" on the
Warsaw [pro-Communist] Government than on the pro-Western leaders)
When Stalin objected that Poland was "a country in which the
U.S.S.R. is interested first of all and most of all," the United
States tried to force him to give in by cutting back lend-lease
payments to Russia.

At this point, however—in April, 1945—Secretary of War
Henry L. Stimson convinced Truman that "we shall probably hold
more cards in our hands later than now." He referred to the atomic bomb, and if Truman decided to postpone the showdown with Russia, it was because Stimson and other advisers persuaded him that
the new weapon would "put us in a position," as Secretary of State
James F. Byrnes argued, "to dictate our own terms at the end of
the war."

To the amazement of those not privy to the secret, Truman proceeded to take a more conciliatory attitude toward Russia, an attitude symbolized by Harry Hopkins's mission to Moscow in June, 1945
Meanwhile, Truman twice postponed the meeting with Churchill and
Stalin at Potsdam. Churchill complained, "Anyone can see that in
a very short space of time our armed power on the Continent will
have vanished."

But when Truman told Churchill that an atomic bomb had been
successfully exploded at Alamogordo, exceeding all expectations,

Churchill immediately understood and endorsed the strategy of delay. "We were in the presence of a new factor in human affairs,"
he said, "and possessed of powers which were irresistible." Not
only Germany but even the Balkans, which Churchill and Roosevelt
had formerly conceded to the Russian sphere, now seemed amenable
to Western influence. That assumption, of course, had guided
American policy (though not British policy) since April, but it
could not be acted upon until the bombing of Japan provided the
world with an unmistakable demonstration of American military
supremacy.

Early in September, the foreign ministers of the Big Three
met in London. Byrnes—armed, as Stimson noted, with "the presence of the bomb in his pocket, so to speak, as a great weapon to
get through" the conference—tried to press the American advantage.
He demanded that the Governments of Bulgaria and Rumania reorganize themselves along lines favorable to the West. In Bulgaria,
firmness won a few concessions; in Rumania, the Russians stood
firm. The American strategy had achieved no noteworthy success.
Instead—as Stimson, one of the architects of that strategy, rather belatedly observed—it had "irretrievably embittered" Soviet-
American relations.

The revisionist view of the origins of the cold war, as it
emerges from the works of Williams, Alperovitz, Marzani, Fleming,
Horowitz, and others, can be summarized as follows. The object of
American policy at the end of World War II was not to defend Western or even Central Europe but to force the Soviet Union out of
Eastern Europe. The Soviet menace to the "free world," so often
cited as the justification of the containment policy, simply did
not exist in the minds of American planners. They believed themselves to be negotiating not from weakness but from almost unas-
sailable superiority.

Nor can it be said that the cold war began because the Russians "broke their agreements." The general sense of the Yalta
agreements—which were in any case very vague—was to assign to
the Soviet Union a controlling influence in Eastern Europe. Armed
with the atomic bomb, American diplomats tried to take back what
they had implicitly conceded at Yalta.

The assumption of American moral superiority, in short, does
not stand up under analysis.

The opponents of this view have yet to make a very convincing
reply. Schlesinger's recent article in *Foreign Affairs*, referred
to at the outset of this article, can serve as an example of the
kind of arguments which historians are likely to develop in opposition to the revisionist interpretation. Schlesinger argues that
the cold war came about through a combination of Soviet intransigence and misunderstanding. There were certain "problems of communication" with the Soviet Union, as a result of which "the Russians might conceivably have misread our signals." Thus the

American demand for self-determination in Poland and other East
European countries "very probably" appeared to the Russians "as a
systematic and deliberate pressure on Russia's western frontiers."
Similarly, the Russians "could well have interpreted" the
American refusal of a loan to the Soviet Union, combined with cancellation of lend-lease, "as deliberate sabotage" of Russia's post
war reconstruction or as "blackmail." In both cases, of course,
there would have been no basis for these suspicions; but "we have
thought a great deal more in recent years," Schlesinger says,
". . . about the problems of communication in diplomacy," and we
know how easy it is for one side to misinterpret what the other
is saying.
This argument about difficulties of "communications" at no
point engages the evidence uncovered by Alperovitz and others—
evidence which seems to show that Soviet officials had good reason
to interpret American actions exactly as they did: as attempts to
dictate American terms.
In reply to the assertion that the refusal of a reconstruction loan was part of such an attempt, Schlesinger can only argue
weakly that the Soviet request for a loan was "inexplicably mis-
laid" by Washington during the transfer of records from the Foreign Economic Administration to the State Department! "Of course,
he adds, "this was impossible for the Russians to believe." It is
impossible for some Americans to believe. As William Appleman Wil
liams notes, Schlesinger's explanation of the "inexplicable" loss
of the Soviet request "does not speak to the point of how the lead
ers could forget the request even if they lost the document."
When pressed on the matter of "communications," Schlesinger
retreats to a second line of argument, namely that none of these
misunderstandings "made much essential difference," because Stalin
suffered from "paranoia" and was "possessed by convictions both of
the infallibility of the Communist word and of the inevitability
of a Communist world."
The trouble is that there is very little evidence which con-
nects either Stalin's paranoia or Marxist-Leninist ideology or
what Schlesinger calls "the sinister dynamics of a totalitarian
society" with the actual course of Soviet diplomacy during the
formative months of the cold war. The only piece of evidence that
Schlesinger has been able to find is an article by the Communist
theoretician Jacques Duclos in the April, 1945, issue of *Cahiers
du communisme*, the journal of the French Communist party, which
proves, he argues, that Stalin had already abandoned the wartime
policy of collaboration with the West and had returned to the traditional Communist policy of world revolution.
Even this evidence, however, can be turned to the advantage
of the revisionists. Alperovitz points out that Duclos did not at
tack electoral politics or even collaboration with bourgeois governments. What he denounced was precisely the American Communists

decision, in 1944, to withdraw from electoral politics. Thus the
article, far from being a call to world revolution, "was one of
many confirmations that European Communists had decided to abandon
violent revolutionary struggle in favor of the more modest aim of
electoral success." And while this decision did not guarantee
world peace, neither did it guarantee 20 years of cold war.

Schlesinger first used the Duclos article as a trump card in
a letter to the *New York Review of Books*, Oct. 20, 1966, which
called forth Alperovitz's rejoinder. It is symptomatic of the general failure of orthodox historiography to engage the revisionist
argument that Duclos's article crops up again in Schlesinger's
more recent essay in *Foreign Affairs*, where it is once again cited
as evidence of a "new Moscow line," without any reference to the
intervening objections raised by Alperovitz.

Sooner or later, however, historians will have to come to
grips with the revisionist interpretation of the cold war. They
cannot ignore it indefinitely. When serious debate begins, many
historians, hitherto disposed to accept without much question the
conventional account of the cold war, will find themselves compelled to admit its many inadequacies. On the other hand, some
of the ambiguities of the revisionist view, presently submerged in
the revionists' common quarrel with official explanations, will begin to force themselves to the surface. Is the revisionist history of the cold war essentially an attack on "the doctrine of historical inevitability," as Alperovitz contends? Or does it contain an implicit determinism of its own?

Two quite different conclusions can be drawn from the body of
revisionist scholarship. One is that American policy-makers had
it in their power to choose different policies from the ones they
chose. That is, they could have adopted a more conciliatory attitude toward the Soviet Union, just as they now have the choice of
adopting a more conciliatory attitude toward Communist China and
toward nationalist revolutions elsewhere in the Third World.

The other is that they have no such choice, because the inner
requirements of American capitalism force them to pursue a consistent policy of economic and political expansion. "For matters to
stand otherwise," writes Carl Oglesby, "the Yankee free-enterpris-
er would . . . have to . . . take sides against himself. . . . He
would have to change entirely his style of thought and action. In
a word, he would have to become a revolutionary Socialist whose
aim was the destruction of the present American hegemony."

Pushed to what some writers clearly regard as its logical
conclusion, the revisionist critique of American foreign policy
thus becomes the obverse of the cold-war liberals' defense of that
policy, which assumes that nothing could have modified the character of Soviet policy short of the transformation of the Soviet
Union into a liberal democracy—which is exactly the goal the containment policy sought to promote. According to a certain type of

revisionism, American policy has all the rigidity the orthodox historians attribute to the U.S.S.R., and this inflexibility made the cold war inevitable.

Moreover, Communism really did threaten American interests, in this view. Oglesby argues that, in spite of its obvious excesses, the "theory of the International Communist Conspiracy is not the hysterical old maid that many leftists seem to think it is." If there is no conspiracy, there is a world revolution and it "does aim itself at America"—the America of expansive corporate capitalism.

Revisionism, carried to these conclusions, curiously restores cold-war anti-Communism to a kind of intellectual respectability, even while insisting on its immorality. After all, it concludes, the cold warriors were following the American national interest. The national interest may have been itself corrupt, but the policymakers were more rational than their critics may have supposed.

In my view, this concedes far too much good sense to Truman, Dulles and the rest. Even Oglesby concedes that the war in Vietnam has now become irrational in its own terms. I submit that much of the cold war has been irrational in its own terms—as witness the failure, the enormously costly failure, of American efforts to dominate Eastern Europe at the end of World War II. This is not to deny the fact of American imperialism, only to suggest that imperialism itself, as J. A. Hobson and Joseph Schumpeter argued in another context long ago, is irrational—that even in its liberal form it may represent an archaic social phenomenon having little relation to the realities of the modern world.

At the present stage of historical scholarship, it is of course impossible to speak with certainty about such matters. That very lack of certainty serves to indicate the direction which future study of American foreign policy might profitably take.

The question to which historians must now address themselves is whether American capitalism really depends, for its continuing growth and survival, on the foreign policy its leaders have been following throughout most of the 20th century. To what extent are its interests really threatened by Communist revolutions in the Third World? To what extent can it accommodate itself to a greatly diminished role in the rest of the world, without undergoing a fundamental reformation—that is, without giving way (after a tremendous upheaval) to some form of Socialism?

Needless to say, these are not questions for scholars alone. The political positions one takes depend on the way one answers them. It is terribly important, therefore, that we begin to answer them with greater care and precision than we can answer them today.

SUGGESTED ADDITIONAL READINGS

Alperovitz, Gar. "How Did the Cold War Begin?" *New York Review of Books*, VIII (March 23, 1967), 6-12. All the ammunition in the revisionist arsenal is brought to bear on the United States.

Divine, Robert A. *Roosevelt and World War II*. Baltimore, © 1969. A series of lectures dealing with F.D.R. the isolationist, the internationalist, the realist, and the pragmatist. The book indirectly lends weight to the revisionist argument that the advent of Truman represented a change in policy toward Russia.

Druks, Herbert. *Harry S. Truman and the Russians, 1945-1953.* New York, 1968. A favorable treatment of U.S. diplomacy, particularly of Harry S. Truman's leadership.

Kolko, Gabriel. *The Politics of War: The World and United States Foreign Policy, 1943-1945.* New York, 1968. Massive study of U.S. wartime foreign policy, essentially from Teheran to Potsdam. Strongly revisionist and highly critical of the United States. Marred by its ponderous style, its loose constructions, its generalizations from scant research (see German policy), and its speculations disguised as conclusions.

Lynd, Staughton. "How the Cold War Began," *Commentary*, November 30, 1960, pp. 379-389. An early revisionist interpretation of the cold war as a struggle between capitalist nations and the newly strengthened Socialist nations.

Warner, Geoffrey. "The United States and the Origins of the Cold War," *International Affairs* (London), 46 (July 1970), 529-544. A review article of the Yalta papers, the Potsdam papers, and the nine volumes of *Foreign Relations of the United States, 1945.* Relates the documentation to the current literature on cold war origins and provides a good summary of U.S. policy in 1945.

Williams, William A. "The Cold-War Revisionists," *The Nation*, 205 (November 13, 1967), 492-495. A critique of A. M. Schlesinger, Kennan, and the traditional view in general, by the "dean" of the cold war revisionists.

REVISIONISM AND THE
INTERPRETATION OF COLD WAR ORIGINS*

Charles S. Maier

Charles S. Maier is a professor of history and a research associate of the Institute of Politics of the John F. Kennedy School of Government at Harvard University. He specializes in twentieth century European history. His interest in the cold war derives, in part, from an oral history project with W. Averell Harriman that he directed for the Institute of Politics.

The first part of Maier's article discusses the entire range of revisionist disagreements with traditionalist interpretations of cold war origins. Maier agrees that had the United States handled the Lend-Lease question and the Russian request for an American credit generously and effectively, mounting Russian suspicions might well have been offset. As for the Alperovitz thesis that America used the atomic bomb against Japan to intimidate Russia, Maier finds the case circumstantial and points out that "one-sided possession of the bomb was bound to evoke mistrust." There was, he adds, "no way for its influence to be exorcized from international relations."

In the second half of the essay, when he turns to a critique of the more radical revisionism of William A. Williams and Gabriel Kolko, Maier is particularly trenchant. For revisionists, most of the decisions and events producing international conflict are explained in terms of American domestic affairs and conditions. Revisionists do not accept a view of the decision-making process as being extensively decentralized and shaped "by imperceptible commitments and bureaucratic momentum," whether in America or abroad. Instead, they place an excessive emphasis on personal factors and, from a neo-Marxist frame of reference, see inequality and class as being at the heart of the cold war.

If international harmony were the normal state of affairs, there would be greater cogency in the revisionist argument. But, asks Maier, is harmony a normal state? The conceptual basis of revisionism leaves no room for the impulses to conflict, resulting from a broad division of sovereignty among the nations of the world. Indeed, the a priori values revisionists bring to their analyses of specific issues exclude the possibility of dialogue;

----

*Reprinted, without footnotes, from Perspectives in American History, IV (1970), 313-347, by permission of the author.

history either fits the mold they have fashioned for it, or history will be made to conform.

Few historical reappraisals have achieved such sudden popularity as the current revisionist critique of American foreign policy and the origins of the Cold War. Much of this impact is clearly due to Vietnam. Although the work of revision began before the United States became deeply involved in that country, the war has eroded so many national self-conceptions that many assumptions behind traditional Cold War history have been cast into doubt. For twenty years the Soviet-American conflict was attributed to Stalin's effort to expand Soviet control through revolutionary subversion, or, as in a more recent formulation, to "the logic of his position as the ruler of a totalitarian society and as the supreme head of a movement that seeks security through constant expansion." Revisionist assailants of this view have now found readers receptive to the contrary idea that the United States must bear the blame for the Cold War. The preoccupation with America's historical guilt distinguishes the new authors not only from anti-communist historians but from earlier writers who felt the question of blame was inappropriate. William McNeill, for example, in an outstanding account written at the height of the Cold War, stressed a nearly inevitable falling out among allies who had never been united save to fight a common enemy. This viewpoint has been preserved in some recent accounts; but since Denna Fleming's massive Cold War history of 1961, the revisionists have gone on to indict the United States for long-term antipathy to communism, insensitivity to legitimate Soviet security needs, and generally belligerent behavior after World War II.

The revisionist version of Cold War history includes three major elements: an interpretation of Eastern European developments; an allegation of anti-Soviet motives in the Americans' use of the atomic bomb; and a general Marxian critique of the alleged American search for a world capitalist hegemony. Since these three elements comprise a detailed reassessment of the role of the United States in world politics they deserve to be discussed and evaluated in turn; but in the end one must consider the more fundamental question of the conceptual bases of revisionist history.

The revisionists are divided among themselves about the turning points and the causes of American aggressiveness, but all agree that the traditional description of the crucial events in Eastern Europe must be radically altered. The old version of the roots of the Cold War charged Soviet Russia with progressively tightening totalitarian control from mid-1944. In effect the earlier historians only confirmed the diagnosis of Ambassador Averell Harriman in Moscow, whose cables between late 1943 and eary 1945

changed from emphasizing the needs of a functioning wartime alli-
ance to stressing the difficulties of prolonging cooperation in
the face of Soviet ambitions. In this evolution of views, the
Russian refusal to facilitate Anglo-American supply flights to the
Warsaw uprising of August 1944 and Moscow's backing for its own
Polish government later in that year provoked major Western disil-
lusionment. It was agreed after 1945 that the germs of the Cold
War lay in Stalin's intransigence on the Polish issue.

In contrast to this interpretation, the revisionists charge
that the United States forced Stalin into his stubborn Polish policy by backing the excessive aspirations of the exile Polish government in London. Revisionist accounts emphasize how antagonistic the State Department's refusal to sanction any territorial
changes during the war must have appeared in Moscow. They point
out that the territory that the Soviets had annexed in 1939, and
which the Poles were contesting, had restored the 1919 Curzon line
of mediation and merely reversed Poland's own acquisitions by war
in 1920-1921. At the Teheran Conference in December 1943, Churchill and Roosevelt had loosely consented to Poland's borders being
shifted westward. Even Harriman backed the British in counseling
the London Poles to accept the terms the Soviets were offering in
October 1944. Only when the Russians produced their own so-called
Lublin Committee and thereafter Polish government—allegedly out
of frustration and bitterness at the unyielding stance of the London Poles—did the focus switch from the question of territory to
that of regimes. At the Yalta Conference, Stalin agreed to add
some Western Poles to the communist-based government and to move
toward free elections; and if the United States had continued to
accept the Yalta provisions in a generous spirit, the revisionists
maintain, the earlier disputes might have been overcome. Gar Alperovitz argues in detail that after Yalta Roosevelt sought to
persuade Churchill to move toward the Soviet position on the key
question of who would determine which Western Polish leaders might
be invited to join the expanded Warsaw government. But Roosevelt's successors, notably President Truman and Secretary of State
James Byrnes, put up a harsh fight to reverse this supposed acquiescence in the creation of a basically communist-dominated gov-
vernment.

This American attitude toward Polish issues, the revisionists
claim, was typical of a wide range of Eastern European questions
where the United States appeared to be set upon frustrating Russia's international security. From the summer of 1945 Truman and
Byrnes, it is charged, sought to reverse the pro-Soviet governments in Rumania and Bulgaria by blustering with atomic weapons.
The American opposition to Soviet demands for territorial security
and friendly neighboring states allegedly forced the Russians away
from their minimal aims of 1943-1945, which envisaged United Front

coalition regimes, to the ruthless communization they imposed by 1947-1948. Had the United States not demanded total openness to Western influence, the revisionists imply, Poland, Bulgaria, and Rumania might have survived as Hungary and Czechoslovakia did until 1947-1948 and Finland thereafter. But in fact, they argue, the parties and social groups that Washington desired to entrench could only intensify Stalin's mistrust. In revisionist eyes these groups were either unworthy or unviable: unworthy because they regrouped pre-war reactionary elements who had often been pro-German, unviable because even when democratic they were doomed to fall between the more intransigent right and the Russian-backed left.

Even more fundamental from the revisionist point of view, there was no legitimacy for any American concern with affairs in that distant region. However ugly the results in Eastern Europe, they should not really have worried Washington. Russia should have been willingly accorded unchallenged primacy because of her massive wartime sacrifices, her need for territorial security, and the long history of the area's reactionary politics and bitter anti-bolshevism. Only when Moscow's deserved primacy was contested did Stalin embark upon a search for exclusive control.

These revisionist assessments of the United States' political choices in Eastern Europe are valid in some respects, simplistic in others. It is true that American policy makers sought to establish agrarian democracies and based their hopes upon peasant proprietors and populist-like parties whose adherents had oscillated between left and right before the war. As revisionist accounts suggest, these occupied a precarious middle ground in Polish politics and an even narrower one in the former Axis satellites, Rumania and Bulgaria, where the Russians may have felt entitled to complete hegemony. Churchill for one felt that his "percentages" agreement of October 1944 had sanctioned Soviet control over these countries as a *quid pro quo* for the Russians' acceptance of British dominance in Greece. And whatever the effective status of that arrangement, Stalin might well have considered his domination of Rumania no more than the counterpart of Allied exclusion of the Soviets from any effective voice in Italy.

But despite revisionist implications to the contrary, the major offense of the middle- and pro-Western groups in Soviet eyes was not really their collusion with rightists. The Russians themselves, after all, supported the far more fascist-tainted Marshall Badoglio as Italian premier. The major crime in the pro-Western elements seems really to have been the desire to stay independent of Soviet influence in a situation of Soviet-American polarization that made independence seem enmity. Perhaps the pro-Westerners acted imprudently by looking to Washington: Benes won three years of Czech democracy by collaboration with Moscow—but one might argue from his example that either the collaboration prolonged the

Czech respite or that it helped contribute to the final undermining of Prague's independence. In any case the outcome throughout
the area was communist dictatorship. Between 1945 and 1947 the
peasant party and social democratic leaders were harassed in their
assemblies and organizations, tried for treason by communist interior ministries, driven abroad or into silence, and finally, as
with the case of Nikola Petkov, the Bulgarian agrarian party leader, executed.

This bleak result naturally undercut those who advocated voluntarily relinquishing United States influence in the area. Opposing the official American rejection of spheres of influence,
Henry Wallace on one side, and Henry Stimson and George Kennan on
the other, counseled restraint and acceptance of the new status
quo; but few contemporary advocates could wholeheartedly celebrate
a policy of spheres of influence. It was justified from expedi-
ence and a second-best alternative. As a former advocate recalls,
it had always to be advanced as a melancholy necessity, especially
as the men for whom Western liberals felt most sympathy were liquidated. To follow a policy of abnegation might indeed have allowed
more openness in Eastern Europe; on the other hand, the Stalinist
tendencies toward repression might well have followed their own
Moscow-determined momentum.

If as a group the revisionists condemn the American role in
Eastern Europe, they diverge beyond that point of criticism. One
major area of debate among them concerns the use of the atomic
bomb, which while it must be weighed as an important issue in its
own right also signals a basic methodological division. Although
the revisionist writing that often seems most hostile to received
opinion is that of Gar Alperovitz he is not the most radical of
the dissenting historians. His writings involve a less thorough-
going critique of United States institutions than the contributions of either William Appleman Williams or Gabriel Kolko. What
has elevated Alperovitz to the role of the revisionist *enfant terrible* is his thesis that the United States used nuclear weapons
against the Japanese largely to overawe the Soviets. Still, his
version of events hinges less on structural elements in American
life than on the contingent roles of personality and technological
opportunity.

There are two aspects of Alperovitz's thesis: first, that
before Hiroshima, expectation of the bomb's availability caused
decisive tactical changes in American diplomacy; second, that the
weapon was used wantonly when it became available, in part to
limit Soviet penetration into the Far East, and more generally because only a combat demonstration would create a sufficient impression to prevent absolute Soviet control over Eastern Europe. Only
the desire to have the atomic bomb in hand, Alperovitz argues, led
Truman to reverse his harsh diplomatic approach of late April 1945,
to dispatch Harry Hopkins to Moscow, and to delay the Potsdam conference despite Churchill's misgivings.

More disturbing than this charge is Alperovitz's subsequent argument that Americans did not merely wish to possess the bomb but actually used it to enhance the country's position vis-à-vis the Soviets. Alperovitz repeats the charge that by the spring of 1945 most Washington officials believed neither the bomb nor an invasion was necessary to end the war. Either continued blockade or a Russian declaration of war could achieve victory. The bomb, however, would obviate the need for Soviet participation in the Pacific war, and, allegedly, the United States wanted desperately to keep Russia out. Along with hastening the technical preparations for Hiroshima, the United States supposedly had the Chinese Nationalists prolong their negotiations with Moscow so that the Sino-Soviet treaty would remain a stumbling block to Stalin's entry.

Interestingly enough, the historiographical factions in this debate have crossed the usual lines. Kolko offers the most cogent response to Alperovitz and the most plausible reconstruction of Potsdam. On the other hand, Herbert Feis—the major traditionalist historian of wartime diplomacy—has so tempered his conclusions that despite himself he grudgingly gives the Alperovitz view considerable credence. Alperovitz has indeed documented a reversal in May 1945 of some initial efforts at confrontation and then a renewed American toughness after Potsdam. But whether calculations about the bomb were decisive remains unproven. The evidence adduced must remain circumstantial: the increased hostility to Russia that was thrust upon the new President; Stimson's and Byrnes' awareness that possession of nuclear weapons might bestow significant diplomatic leverage; and the pushing back of a Big Three parley. In light of this conjunction of events a calculated strategy of delay, such as Alperovitz develops, does remain a possible component of Truman's motivation. But the initial months of the new administration formed a period of contradictory needs and approaches. For a while Truman may have been thinking in terms of disengaging from the disquieting Soviet repression in Bulgaria and Rumania by withdrawing from the Allied Control Commission rather than attempting to reverse the course of events by exerting pressure within it. The Hopkins mission was well suited to many purposes: perhaps an effort to appease Stalin until nuclear weapons were at hand, but more immediately an attempt to secure agreements in their own right and to halt further deterioration of relations as a worthy goal in itself. For Truman, as even Alperovitz realizes, the Hopkins trip was probably viewed not as a reversal of his earlier harsh language to Molotov on April 23, but as a complementary démarche, another approach to a dramatic unjamming of issues.

What also makes the Alperovitz view so difficult to evaluate is the fact, as the author himself admits, that the debate has been largely a retrospective one. Actors at the time hardly saw the significance of the alternatives as later historians have. The place that the idea of using the bomb might have been thrashed out was in the so-called Interim Committee dominated by Stimson and Byrnes, both of whom were committed to dropping the weapon. In this forum it was easy to dismiss any alternative to the incineration of a real city as beset with one fatal obstacle or another. And beyond the Interim Committee, except for a group of scientific dissenters at Chicago who felt they had been turned into sorcerers' apprentices, there was no fundamental challenge to using the weapon. Moreover, if the bomb represented a threshold in terms of weapons technology, it no longer represented one in terms of casualties: the Tokyo incendiary raids in March of 1945 produced about 84,000 deaths; Dresden, between 60,000 and 130,000; Hiroshima, about 70,000. The significant ethical question was that of area versus precision bombing, and the Allies had long since steeled their conscience on that issue. If the Navy and Air Force, moreover, were confident that they could starve the Japanese into submission, the Joint Chiefs never gave their collective imprimatur to such a view because the Army would not endorse it. Many thought the collapse of Japan was likely; official plans were drawn up to deal with a sudden surrender; but no one in authority felt he could assume official responsibility for advocating restraint so long as some prolonged Japanese resistance was remotely possible. If Byrnes, Harriman, and Admiral Leahy would have preferred to complete the Pacific war without obligations to Moscow, Truman still felt it his duty to cling to the contingency plans of the Joint Chiefs of Staff and seek Soviet help at Potsdam. Even at Potsdam, when Japanese capitulation seemed near, a host of factors militated against reappraisal: the ambivalence of the Tokyo response to the Potsdam ultimatum (itself only the vaguest of warnings); concern that die-hard Japanese militarists would seek to "protect" their monarch against those who counseled surrender; the debate in Washington over retention of the Emperor, which delayed a surrender formula both sides might accept; the belief that the nation responsible for the Pearl Harbor attack could be requited from the air hundreds of times over without any injustice; and no doubt the vested interests in making the bomb contribute to the war effort. If in addition to these pressures Byrnes also entertained an ulterior anti-Soviet motive, it probably represented a marginal, additional payoff of a policy long established on other grounds.

Alperovitz seems to feel it wrong that the atomic bomb became a major factor in American policy calculations. Certainly, however, it was natural to give deep consideration to the new weapon's diplomatic implications. And despite Alperovitz's linkage, there is insufficient evidence that possession of nuclear weapons was decisive in motivating a hard line on Bulgaria and Rumania in the latter half of 1945. This approach followed naturally from the administration's view of Eastern European developments since Yalta and would have been pursued without an atomic monopoly. It is questionable, too, whether the United States could have utilized a veiled atomic threat except in regard to the distant future, for Washington was not prepared to threaten the use of nuclear weapons over Russian targets in 1945. Despite the revisionist view that the United States enjoyed a preponderance of power and therefore must be charged with the greater responsibility in the generation of the Cold War, the Soviet Union still exerted effective control over the area that was central to the dispute. This is not to deny that outside its borders the United States seemed to be flaunting its nuclear capacity. Harriman reported from Moscow in November that the Soviets felt America was trying to intimidate them with the atomic bomb, while to observers in Washington Truman and Byrnes often seemed bolstered by an inner assurance of American invincibility.

Indeed it may have appeared by late 1945 and early 1946 as if the United States were wrapping iron fist in iron glove; but even had there been a far more sophisticated and reserved approach, the simple fact of one-sided possession of the bomb was bound to evoke mistrust. There was no way for its influence to be exorcized from international relations.

Alperovitz's charges are, of course, profoundly disquieting. But at least he suggests that things might have been different. Had Roosevelt lived he might have smoothed out differences with Moscow. Had Stimson been heeded, the United States might have bargained by offering to share atomic secrets and not by seeking, as it is alleged to have done, to intimidate with the weapon itself. Gabriel Kolko, in contrast, can dismiss Alperovitz's arguments about atomic diplomacy because they are unnecessary for what he considers the more important indictment, namely, that the United States, in order to serve its economic needs and ambitions, opposed any threat to its world-wide military and political power.

This view produces a more radical interpretation of both American foreign relations and the country's internal history. William Appleman Williams, for instance, argues that the long-term American quest for universal market and investment arenas, even into Eastern Europe, naturally collided with quite moderate Soviet wartime aspirations and thereby helped the Kremlin's own hardliners and ideologues to prevail. For both Williams and Kolko, moreover, a critique of United States foreign policy forms only a part of a wider reassessment of American liberal institutions. The anti-communist effort is depicted as the natural product of an industrial society in which even major reform efforts have been intended only to rationalize corporate capitalism.

The more the revisionists stress the continuity of American capitalist goals and de-emphasize the importance of the Roosevelt-Truman transition, the more they tend to condemn all of America's

earlier policies as contributing to the Cold War. The revisionists in general have stressed the direct pre-1945 clashes with the
Soviets. They emphasize the significance of the Allies' delay in
opening a Second Front in Europe; and while anti-Soviet historians
duly cite Russia's non-aggression pact with Germany, the revisionists usually argue that the Soviets were forced into this arrangement by the Western powers' appeasement policies and their exclusion of Moscow from any common defense plans. Finally, revisionists like Fleming recall the United States' original hostility to
bolshevism and the interventions of 1918-1920. In short, all revisionists are mindful of the Western treatment of the Soviets as
a pariah regime.

The more radical revisionists, however, go on to depict all
of twentieth-century foreign policy as woven into a large counter-
revolutionary fabric of which the Cold War itself is only one portion. Their logic links a hesitant and ineffective anti-Nazi
foreign policy with a zealous anti-communism and thus finds that
the issues of the 1930's adumbrate Cold War attitudes. Similarly,
revisionists who discuss pre-war diplomacy have attacked the usual
image of American isolationism by stressing the country's persistent economic stakes abroad. All this vaguely serves to hint that
the lateness of United States enlistment against Nazism is no
longer explainable in terms of deep internal divisions about involvement in European quarrels: the United States responded only
as it perceived threats to foreign economic interests. Receding
even further, the revisionists view Woodrow Wilson as a major
architect of liberal but counter-revolutionary interventionism.
And even before Wilson the roots of the Cold War can be discerned,
they feel, in the economic lobbying that backed the Open Door policy and the capitalist expansion of the late nineteenth century.
Finally, under the stresses of a market economy, even the otherwise virtuous farmers felt it necessary to seek world markets and
back imperialist expansionism. The private economy, for Williams
and others, taints with acquisitiveness the Jeffersonian Eden that
America might have been.

There is a further aspect of this radical revisionism. Since
it concentrates on American expansionism in general, its focus
shifts from the Soviet-American conflict to the alleged American
imperialist drive against all forces of radicalism, or what Kolko
loosely calls the New Order. Not an insouciant blundering, and
not the arrogance of power, but only capitalist megalomania suf-
fices to explain American efforts to prop up an international Old
Order of discredited and outworn parties and elites. Within this
perspective, Kolko's explanation of the events of 1943-1945 becomes most clear. He offers three major areas of evidence: United States policy in respect to its future enemy, that is, the
effort to reduce Russia to dependency; United States policy
against its own ally, that is, the insistence on the economic

multilateralism designed to reduce Great Britain to dependency; and United States policy in respect to the "Third World" and the Resistance, the effort to smash all truly independent challenges to American hegemony.

Under Kolko's scrutiny the policies once adjudged to be among the most enlightened emerge as the most imperialistic. Where, for example, previous critics attacked the abandonment of Morgenthau's intended ten-billion-dollar loan to Russia, Kolko sees the proposal itself as devious. Coupled with the destruction of German industry, the contemplated loan was allegedly designed to prevent Russia from refurbishing her industrial base from German factories and thus to force her into a dependency on United States capital for which she could return raw materials. Ironically enough, the plans of Harry Dexter White—abused as a communist in the 1950's—represented a massive effort to place the U.S.S.R. in a state of semi-colonial subservience.

American aid to England emanates from analogous motives, according to Kolko and Lloyd Gardner, who have concentrated most closely on this issue. Kolko asserts that American policy aimed at keeping Britain in a viable second-rank position: rescuing her from utter collapse for reasons of world economic stability yet profiting from her distress. State Department officials, congressmen, and businessmen supporting assistance to Britain intended to penetrate the sterling bloc and the Commonwealth markets protected by tariffs since the 1930's. The celebrated Article Seven of the Mutual Aid Agreement of February 1942, the revisionists emphasize, demanded that Britain consider reduction of Commonwealth trade barriers in return for Lend-Lease, a stipulation repeated with each renewal of Lend-Lease. Finally, all the projects for post-war financial credits and arrangements, as they took form at Bretton Woods and in the 3.75-billion-dollar loan negotiated in December 1945, envisaged a sterling-dollar convertibility that would also open the Commonwealth to American goods and severely test the pound.

As the revisionists see it, the interest in convertibility and multilateralism represented the answer of post-Depression America to the chronic domestic under-consumption of a capitalist economy. In the final analysis American efforts amounted to a subtle neo-colonialism. While classical economic theorists helped to justify the international division of labor by comparative-advantage doctrine no matter how unequal the partners, the revisionists evidently feel that the costs to the less powerful or industrial nation outweigh the benefits. They emphasize that specialization can act to perpetuate relations of dependency, and they view American policy as dedicated throughout the twentieth century to fostering the bonds of economic subordination. In this interpretative framework the Cold War, in its European aspects, arose because Soviet Russia refused to allow herself or Eastern Europe to be integrated into the American neo-colonial network.

This analysis is often illuminating but sometimes exaggerated
and tendentious. One can certainly differentiate between the values of the arguments about the Soviet Union and Britain. To see
de-bolshevizing Russia as Morgenthau's underlying concern in 1944-
1945 is simply to ignore the central quest of his public life,
which was to deny Germany any future as a world industrial power.
In the policy alternatives shaping up in Washington, a bitterly
anti-German policy could, moreover, only mean a desire to collabo-
rate with the Soviet Union and not to dominate it. And by late
1944 Morgenthau viewed those opposing his projects as themselves
motivated primarily by anti-communism. The major purpose of the
loan to Russia was, in fact, to make it easier for the Soviets to
accede to the dismantling of German industry. The economic destruction of the Reich was not designed to make the Russians dependent upon America: if the Soviets would receive no reparation
from future German exports they would get many factories that
would have produced the exports.

Revisionist analysis of American economic relations with
Great Britain is more convincing. Kolko's discussion of Anglo-
American financial relations in the framework of overall United
States goals probably forms the most innovative and substantive
contribution of his study. Americans did push against British
trade barriers and mentally relegated the country to a secondary
role in a Western economic system. The pressure upon the belea-
guered Ally could be harsh: "What do you want me to do," Churchill asked about Lend-Lease renewal at Quebec in the fall of 1944,
"stand up and beg like Fala?" Nevertheless, revisionist judgments
tend to neglect the powerful ties of sentiment that motivated
Roosevelt's policy, and they minimize the critical fact that British financial commitments were over-extended in terms of her own
resources. Moreover, the focus by the revisionists on the free-
trade rapacity of an Eastern banking establishment is inappropriate. Insofar as banking representatives formed a coherent interest it was often the friendliest to London's needs. Pressures
came as much from a conservative Congress as from Wall Street.

Still, as the revisionists stress, economic self-interest was
woven into American policy even when it was most generous. The
hard fact is that until they both felt mortally threatened by Soviet power London and Washington had conflicting economic interests. There was a desire for currency convertibility on the part
of the United States Treasury which Britain naturally felt was potentially disastrous. For Britain to meet the American wishes for
sterling convertibility at a moment when she had liquidated four
billion pounds of overseas assets in order to fight the war meant
subjecting her economy to great deflationary pressure. During the
war Keynes had already asked priority for full employment and
strong domestic demands over considerations of exports and stable
exchanges. After the war the Labour government even more ferventl

stressed easy money to banish the specter of unemployment. They did not want planning, investment, and new social-service transfers to be impeded by worries about sterling outflow. The American enthusiasm for currency convertibility threatened havoc to all the delicate equilibriums in London; and it was only dire necessity that led the English to pledge an effort at convertibility as a condition for the massive credits the United States extended in late 1945. When finally the dissenting historians reach the story of 1947-1950, they will no doubt be able to depict in their terms a further effort at world economic supremacy. For similar Treasury pressures for convertibility were to continue into the America-sponsored negotiations for intra-European payments agreements in 1949 and the European Payments Union of 1950. Once again, Britain feared a flanking attack on the sterling area, and once again many of her Labour leaders worried about a deflationary thrust against schemes of economic planning.

One can agree that American objectives clashed with British economic policy without accepting the larger revisionist accusation of a pervasive neo-colonialism. As of 1945, American thinking on foreign trade and investment (as well as more general questions of colonialism) was often marked by reformist ideas. American spokesmen such as Eric Johnston of the Chamber of Commerce or Donald Nelson of the War Production Board certainly emphasized the need for sustained American exports as a safeguard against renewed depression, but a sense of the need for exports assumed that countries rich and industrialized enough to offer extensive markets were more helpful to the United States than economies kept in perpetual underdevelopment or one-sided dependency.

Underlying much revisionist criticism of United States foreign economic relations is a desire for socialist self-sufficiency: a virtuous autarchy inflicts the least damage on the rest of the world. Indeed, in theory, there might have been one alternative for the American economy that did not require either unemployment or international trade: a great program of domestic investment to remedy urban blight, improve transportation, build new TVA's—in short an expansion of the New Deal into a semi-socialized economy. But after the domestic emphasis upon small business and competition in the "Second New Deal," and after the massive infusion of business leaders into the government to run the war economy, such a public-sector commitment was not likely. In the absence of such a program the stress on international trade was probably the most reasonable United States response. Finally, one must note that a United States public-sector solution for full employment would not necessarily have benefited foreign countries. Their problems were not entirely owing to outsiders' exploitation; they needed investments, and socialist governments, whether British or Soviet, were no less likely to draw profits from abroad where they could.

The revisionists' reasoning on this point fits in analytically with one of their major current preoccupations: the role of the United States in the third world of peasant movements. The same revisionist argument that sees foreign trade as a means to subordination and control also suggests that the United States had to be hostile to movements seeking genuine self-determination and local independence. Thus American hostility to popular resistance movements, including those of World War II, forms one more logical extension of the country's counter-revolutionary and imperialist drive in the wake of World War II. Kolko makes much of the British suppression of the Greek resistance movement in December 1944, of the American preference for continued dealings with Vichy, of the dislike of Tito's partisans, and of the joint Anglo-American efforts to restrain the left-wing forces in the Italian resistance. When it is remembered that the United States is still fighting the heirs of the Vietnamese resistance to the Japanese and later the French, or that the Haiphong incidents between French and Vietminh occurred within two years after the British put down the Greek resistance cadres in Athens, the emotional thrust of the revisionist argument becomes more understandable.

This concern with the continuities of counter-revolution arises in part from the natural fact that revisionists want to explain the origins of the Cold War against the background of Vietnam. Ironically enough, the result is to downgrade the importance of the Soviet-American antagonism that originally preoccupied revisionist authors. What in fact increasingly distinguishes the more radical historians is their emphasis upon a Soviet "conservatism" that sought to discourage revolutionary action for the sake of acquiring territorial buffers. Stalin's treaty with Chiang at the expense of Mao, his distrust of Tito, and his abandonment of the Greek communists complement American objectives. In view of this supposed convergence of Moscow and Washington, the Cold War becomes little more than a mistaken enmity deriving from the United States' panicky identification of Soviet policies with indigenous Marxist or merely democratic movements. This finding confirms a "third world" viewpoint which can indict both major world powers and supply a "usable past" for those morally overwhelmed by an updated Holy Alliance between Moscow and Washington. Through the mid 1960's, in short, the revisionists could still be fixed upon explaining the origins of conflict with Moscow; by the end of the decade they were concerned with the antagonism with Havana, Hanoi, and Peking.

Attractive though it may be in light of current events, this third-world perspective has serious analytical deficiencies. First of all, its Marxian basis imposes an overly schematic view of motivation; it precludes any possibility that American policymakers might have acted from genuine emancipatory impulses or even in uncertainty. The war had united the country around democratic ideas that were genuinely held, even if too abstract for implementation in the areas they were aimed at. It can be argued that the economic aspirations that State Department draftsmen grafted onto the policy statements the revisionists cite were just as ritualistic as the political formulas, and that there was still cause for a genuine dismay at the developments in Eastern Europe. The revisionist presentation conveys no sense of America's anti-totalitarian commitment and thus little understanding of the seeds of the post-1945 disillusionment.

Furthermore, the new revisionist writings composed under the impact of Vietnam attribute too consistently ideological an opposition to the resistance movements in Western Europe. For anyone with sympathy for the "vision" of the Resistance, vague as it was, American policy often does appear as misguided or willful. At times tactical considerations were influential; at times the wartime authority that devolved upon conservative proconsuls such as Robert Murphy was critical; at times United States policy acquiesced in a joint Allied position more rightist than Washington alone would have preferred, as when the exigencies of coalition warfare led Roosevelt to accede to Churchill's reactionary policies in Italy and Greece. Yet most basically what militated against the Resistance was a big-power paternalism and the wartime habit of viewing military success as an end in itself. United States spokesmen accused Resistance leaders of seeking their own political advantage above the destruction of the Germans, though what Americans saw as narrow partisanship was to Resistance leaders a battle against collaborators and a fascist or semi-fascist right—a struggle for regeneration within to match the fight against the occupying power. The British and Americans preferred to think of the Resistance as a vanguard of saboteurs who might soften up the Germans and pin down their troops but not as an army or regime in embryo. Centralization and control, the distrust of independent authority and pretensions, characterized all three great powers. But unless decentralization itself is made synonymous with radicalism while centralization is defined as reactionary *per se*, it is misleading to condemn American behavior toward the Resistance movements as consistently conservative.

Finally, what is perhaps most misleading about the neo-Marxian point of view is its suggestion that Europe in 1945 was as socially malleable as underdeveloped societies today. By projecting a third-world image upon the West the revisionists overestimate the power of the radical forces and the structural possibilities for change. The United States did help to brake fundamental change especially after V-E Day, but the major limits on reconstruction were set by the internal divisions within the Resistance and the conservative attitude of the communist parties and the other two Allies.

No more in institutional than in political terms did America
alone abort a New Order. Kolko's New Order represents a normative
image of revolution borrowed from predominantly peasant countries
or Yugoslavia and applied to industrial Europe. But not even 1945
Europe was so shaky: the Germans, not the Russians, had occupied
the area and left most elites intact. Even where nominally socialist remedies such as nationalization were to be tried, they rarely
incorporated any revolutionary tendencies. Pre-war economies had
already evolved toward pluralist balances among labor, heavy industry, and small producers and merchandisers. The communists
were concerned primarily with retaining their share of the trade-
union component in this equilibrium of forces. They sought a social and economic buffer as Stalin sought territorial buffers. A
renovation of society on new principles would have required smash-
ing the corporate pluralism in which left-wing as well as conservative leaders found comfort. America did not really have to rescue
Europe from radical change because no significant mass-based elements advocated a radical transformation. The so-called New Order
—an amalgam in the revisionist mind of Yugoslavian factory coun-
cils and Algerian, Vietnamese, or Greek national resistance movements—had no solid peacetime constituency in the West.
    What in fact was new in the West was precisely the conglomera-
tion of business, labor, and government that the revisionists lament. In America the New Deal and the wartime economic effort
worked to dissolve many of the old lines between public and private spheres. In Fascist Italy, Vichy France, and Nazi Germany a
similar interweaving occurred, as it did in a democratic Britain
that submitted to extensive planning and welfare measures. Revisionists such as Kolko would accept this description of trends—
in fact, Kolko examined the precursor of this private-public inter-
penetration in his critique of Progressivism—but the revisionists
regard these developments as clearly elitist and conservative.
Ultimately their general interpretation conceives of the issues behind the Cold War in terms of inequality and class: the Cold War
represents to them a continuation of an international civil war in
which Russian and later peasant revolutionary forces have succes-
sively championed the cause of the oppressed in all countries,
while the United States has become the leader of the world's
elites.
    But no matter what importance this conceptualization may have
for today's world, it obscures the historical development. If
there has been a growth in international class conflict over the
past generation, so too in Western societies there has been an increase of bureaucratic and administrative solutions for social conflict—solutions to which labor contributed, solutions that were
conservative in leaving intact private control and ownership, yet
still social compromises that commanded wide assent. The forces
for compromise sprang from the bureaucratic trends of modern

industrial society as they existed in Europe as well as in the
United States. The revisionist view splits the world into an
industrial half that America supposedly stabilized on behalf of
a bureaucratic capitalism and a peasant world where the United
States has since met its match. But if peasant society has proved
hard to manipulate, Western industrial society has also proved re-
fractory; the neo-Marxians overestimate the fragility of its capitalist order, and overvalue the American contribution to counterrevolution as well as the will to impose it. There is still no
well-modulated portrayal of what the United States sought in the
world, even less of the real possibilities of institutional change.

No full evaluation of revisionist history, however, can be
content with weighing particular interpretations against available evidence. For beneath the details of specific revisionist
arguments are more fundamental historiographical problems—implicit conceptual models and underlying assumptions about the decisive factors in American foreign relations.

The revisionists' approach to international conflict and foreign policy formation is a narrow one. They are interested in certain specific modes of explanation and no others. Rejecting any
model of international society that sees crucial impulses to conflict as inherent in the international system itself, they seek
explanations in American domestic conditions. But for them all
domestic conditions are not equally valid. They are unwilling to
accept any description that tends to stress the decentralized nature of decision-making or that envisages the possibility of expansionist policy taking shape by imperceptible commitments and
bureaucratic momentum. Above all, they approach history with a
value system and a vocabulary that appear to make meaningful historical dialogue with those who do not share their framework impossible.

The revisionists presuppose international harmony as a normal
state and have a deep sense of grievance against whatever factors
disturb it. This common assumption shapes their work from the outset in terms of both analysis and tone. But is international harmony a normal state? The division of sovereignty among nation-
states makes it difficult to eliminate friction and tension, as
theorists from the time of Machiavelli and Hobbes have pointed out.
The disputes of 1944-1945 especially were not easy to avoid. With
a power vacuum in Central Europe created by the defeat of Germany
and with the expansion of American and Soviet influence into new,
overlapping regions, some underlying level of dispute was likely.
Angered by the scope that the Cold War finally assumed, the revisionists do not really ask whether conflict might have been totally avoided or what level of residual disagreement was likely to
emerge even with the best intentions on both sides.

Once mutual mistrust was unchained—and much already existed—
all disputes were burdened by it. The initiatives that would have

been required to assuage incipient conflict appeared too risky to
venture in terms either of domestic public opinion or of international security. By late 1945 the United States and Russia each
felt itself to be at a competitive disadvantage in key disputes.
Each felt that the other, being ahead, could best afford to make
initial concessions, while gestures on its part would entail dis-
proportionate or unilateral sacrifice. Perhaps more far-sighted
leaders could have sought different outcomes, but there were pressures on all policy-makers to make decisions that would harden conflict rather than alleviate it. Some details on this point are
particularly worth considering.

In retrospect there appear to have been several areas of negotiation where compromise might at least have been possible,
where accommodation demanded relatively little cost, and where the
continued absence of greater concession probably deepened suspicion. Some additional flexibility on the issues of both atomic
control and financial assistance might have helped to alleviate
the growing estrangement. Innovative and generous as our plans
for atomic energy control appeared to Americans at the time, the
provisions for holding all United States weapons until controls
were complete, as well as the demand that the Russians renounce
their United Nations veto on all atomic-energy matters, probably
doomed the proposal. With such an imbalance of obligations the
Soviet advocates of their own country's atomic arsenal were likely
to prevail over those willing to acquiesce in nuclear inferiority
for a decade or so. As so often after 1946, the reluctance to
give up an advantage that at best could only be transitory led to
a further spiral in the arms race.

With far less objective risk than was presented by the nuclear issue, liberality with aid might also have offered United
States policy-makers a chance to dissipate quarrels. Unfortunate-
ly, Lend-Lease was brusquely cut off in a way that could not help
but offend the Russians, although it was slated to end with the
close of the war in any case. Had transitional aid or a significant post-war loan been available, the termination of Lend-Lease
might not have proved so abrasive. But the loan proposal was always keyed to the extraction of political concessions, and the Russians had no need to become a suppliant. As it turned out a postwar credit was less crucial to the Soviets than to the British,
who faced a mammoth balance of payments crisis that Russia did not
have to cope with. Washington could not really use the loan to
wrest concessions; instead, her failure to provide funds precluded
any chance for post-war credits to help improve the general international atmosphere and re-establish some minimal trust.

Disagreement at the start over Eastern Europe had undermined
the chances of those peripheral initiatives that might in turn
have helped to alleviate overall tension. By becoming trapped in
a position where apparently unilateral démarches were needed to

break a growing deadlock, policy was far more likely to be vetoed
by the State Department, Congress, or the President's immediate
advisers. It was far harder to justify financial assistance or
atomic renunciation when Russia was already felt to be uncoopera-
tive. Domestic constraints and the suspicions fed by international rivalry interacted to intensify a serious deadlock.

Although the revisionists do not readily soften their judgments about American policy-makers in light of these pressures,
they do use them to make Soviet responses appear more acceptable.
They explain that the Russians had to reckon with the death of an
exceptionally friendly President and the replacement of his key
policy-makers by tougher spokesmen; with a tooth-and-nail resistance to the German reparations that Russia felt she clearly deserved; and with the curt United States dismissal of a Soviet
voice in the occupation of Japan, an influence over the Dardanel-
les, and a base in the Mediterranean. Neither side was likely to
see in the opposing moves anything but a calculated effort to expand power, or, with a little more subtlety, the upshot of a con-
test between the other power's doves and hawks with the doves increasingly impotent. Such interpretations tended to produce a
response in kind. In the absence of any overriding commitment to
conciliation, the Cold War thus contained its own momentum toward
polarization and deadlock.

It would, however, also be inappropriate to fix too much
blame for the origins of the Cold War upon the Hobbesian nature of
the international system, though it is a major element the revisionists ignore. As revisionists insist, domestic factors are
clearly required to explain the timing and trajectory of the Soviet-American antagonism. But significantly absent from revisionist
writing is any sense of the bureaucratic determinants of policy—
an element of increasing interest to historians and social scientists seeking to respond to the revisionist indictment. In the
view of these writers, decisions are seen as the outcome of organizational disputes within an overall government structure. Policy emerges not so much as a way of maximizing a well-defined national "interest" as the outcome of struggles among bureaucratic
forces, each seeking to perpetuate its own *raison d'etre* and to
expand its corporate influence. Recent studies have shown, for
instance, that much of the impulse toward a cold-war defense posture after 1945 came from the fact that both the Air Force and the
Navy sought out new strategic conceptions and justifications to
preserve their wartime size and status.

Study of the German and reparations issues also reveals how
American foreign policy emerged from interdepartmental contention,
in this case between Henry Morgenthau and the Treasury on the one
hand, and on the other a more conservative State Department desir-
ous of recreating economic stability in Central Europe. After V-E
Day the Army military government agencies also demanded that their

American occupation zone be as economically self-sufficient as possible. The result of these pressures, and of Morgenthau's loss of
influence under Truman, was that the United States quarreled bitterly with the Soviets to limit reparations. The American insistence at Potsdam that each power largely confine its reparations to
its own zone helped lead to the very division of Germany that the
United States officially deplored. The intent was not to build
Germany up at the expense of Russia: Byrnes after all offered the
Soviets a 25 or 40-year treaty against German aggression in late
1945 and the spring of 1946. But each agency's struggle for the
priorities it set in terms of its own organizational interest
helped shape a narrow policy that was not subordinated to a clear
sense of our more general relations with the Soviet Union.

     This approach to policy analysis, which opens up a new range
of motivation and offers an alternative to an undue emphasis on
personal factors, contrasts with the explanatory model suggested
by the neo-Marxist revisionists. For the latter group, what ultimately explains policy is a "system" arising out of the property
and power relations within a society, a system causative in its
own right and within which institutions and organizations do not
lead independent lives but relate to each other dialectically.
For these revisionists the explanation of events in terms of
intragovernmental structure and struggles is simply formalistic,
oriented to the procedural aspects of policy formation and begging
the substantive questions. For them, the processes of government
might as well be a black box: if one understands the distribution of wealth and influence then policy follows by an almost de-
ductive logic. To attribute decisive influence to bureaucratic
pressures seems additionally frivolous to the revisionists since
allegedly only certain elites ever rise to the top of those bureaucracies. For those, on the other hand, who stress the political infighting among bureaucracies what is important about history
tends to be the successive modifications of action—in short, political process, not social structure.

     Both of these approaches are deceptive and limiting if taken
to extremes. For those who stress history as bureaucratic process
all questions of historical responsibility can appear ambiguous
and even irrelevant. Foreign policy emerges as the result of a
competition for fiefs within governmental empires. Bureaucratic
emphases can produce a neo-Rankean acquiescence in the use of power that is no less deterministic than the revisionist tendency to
make all policies exploitative in a liberal capitalist order.
But what is perhaps most significant about these alternative caus-
al models is that they are addressed to different questions. The
non-revisionists are asking how policies are formed and assume
that this also covers the question why. The revisionists see the
two questions as different and are interested in the why. And by
"Why?" revisionists are asking what the meaning of policies is in

terms of values imposed from outside the historical narrative.
The revisionists charge that the historian must pose this question
of meaning consciously or he will pose it unconsciously and accept
the values that help to uphold a given social system. History,
they suggest, must serve the oppressors or the oppressed, if not
by intent then by default. The historian who wishes to avoid this
iron polarity can reply that social systems rarely divide their
members into clear-cut oppressors and oppressed. He can also insist that even when one despairs of absolute objectivity there are
criteria for minimizing subjectivity. On the other hand, he must
also take care that the history of policy-making not become so
focused on organizational processes that the idea of social choice
and responsibility is precluded.

In the end it is this attempt by the revisionists to analyze
specific historical issues on the basis of *a priori* values about
the political system that most strongly affects the controversies
their writings have touched off. For their values cannot be derived from the mere amassment of historical data, nor do they follow from strictly historical judgments, but rather underlie such
judgments. This is true in some sense, no doubt, of history in
general, but the whole of Cold War historiography seems particularly dependent upon defined value systems.

For the revisionists, on the one hand, the key issues hinge
not upon facts or evidence but upon assessments as to how repres-
sive or non-repressive contemporary liberal institutions are.
These judgments in turn must be made within ground rules that allow only polar alternatives for evaluating political action. What
is non-revolutionary must be condemned as counter-revolutionary,
and reformist political aspirations are dismissed in advance. Similarly, the foreign policies of Western powers cannot escape the
stigma of imperialism, for imperialism and exploitation are defined by the revisionists as virtually inherent in any economic
intercourse between industrialized and less developed states, or
just between unequals. But how can one decide whether the economic reconstruction that America financed was beneficial or "exploitative" for countries brought into a cooperative if not subordinate relationship to the United States? How does one judge
the value of multilateral or bilateral trading relations that
benefit each side differentially? Judgments must rest upon definitions of exploitation or fairness that logically precede the
historical narrative and cannot be derived from it.

The non-revisionist, on the other hand, can refuse to accept the ground rules that presuppose exploitation, dependency, or
automatic neo-colonialism; he can refuse to accept the definitions
that allow no choice between revolution and reaction. But traditional Cold War historians no less than the revisionists have been
involved in tautologies. Historical explanations are normally
tested by efforts to find and weigh contradictory evidence, but
Cold War analyses on both sides have relied upon propositions that

cannot be disproven. Sometimes disproof is precluded by prior assumptions, and while revisionists may believe America's capitalist
economy necessitates a voracious expansionism, Cold War theorists
have similarly argued that any commitment to communism is *ipso
facto* destructive of a "moderate" or "legitimate" international
order. Often disproof is impossible because the explanations are
totalistic enough to accommodate all contradictory phenomena into
one all-embracing explanatory structure. So writers who condemned
the Soviets cited Marxist ideology as evidence of real intention
when it preached revolution and as evidence of deviousness when it
envisaged United-Front coalitions. Conversely, according to the
revisionists, when the United States withdrew foreign assistance
it was seeking to bring nations to heel; when it was generous, it
sought to suborn. When the United States bowed to British desires
to delay the Second Front it justified Soviet suspicions; when it
opposed Churchill's imperial designs it did so in order to erect
a new economic hegemony over what England (and likewise France or
the Netherlands) controlled by direct dominion. Spokesmen for
each side present the reader with a total explanatory system that
accounts for all phenomena, eliminates the possibility of disproof
and thus transcends the usual processes of historical reasoning.
More than in most historical controversies, the questions about
what happened are transformed into concealed debate about the nature of freedom and duress, exploitation and hegemony. As a result much Cold War historiography has become a confrontation
manqué—debatable philosophy taught by dismaying example.

SUGGESTED ADDITIONAL READINGS

Graebner, Norman A. "Cold War Origins and the Continuing Debate:
    A Review of Recent Literature," *The Journal of Conflict Reso-
    lution*, XIII (March 1969), 123-132. Survey of recent liter-
    ature, an attempt to classify the writers, and a prediction
    of a more pronounced revisionist attack on established views.

Harrington, Michael. "Dividing the World," *The New Republic*, 158
    (March 30, 1968), 25-26. A review of Fontaine's history of
    the cold war, and a commentary on the revisionists and tradi-
    tionalists. Discussion of early critics of containment.

Lichtheim, George. "The Cold War in Perspective," *Commentary*, 37
    (June 1964), 21-26. A British writer predicts the gradual
    end to the cold war. Contains interesting summaries of
    European interpretations of the cold war, especially British
    and French.

Morgenthau, Hans J. "Arguing about the Cold War: A Balance Sheet," *Encounter*, 28 (May 1967), 37-41. A brief review of cold war origins, comments on writers, and an attempt to classify writers into schools of thought.

Seabury, Paul. "Cold War Origins, I," *The Journal of Contemporary History*, III, No. 1 (January 1968), 168-182. A discussion of revisionism and revisionists, especially Fleming, Horowitz, Alperovitz, and Deutscher.

Thomas, Brian. "Cold War Origins, II," *The Journal of Contemporary History*, III, No. 1 (January 1968), 183-198. Discussion of revisionist contributions to recent history, especially on the Nazi-Soviet Pact, Greece and Rumania, Russian actions in 1947, and so on. Deals with Blackett, Fleming, Alperovitz, Horowitz, and Zilliacus.

Thomas, Brian. "What's Left of the Cold War," *Political Quarterly*, 40 (April-June, 1969), 173-186. British view that the cold war is over, but that neither of the two major powers admits it publicly. Privately they do, as the Cuban and Czechoslovakian crises seem to show.

Williams, Geoffrey, and Joseph Frankel. "A Political Scientist's Look at the Cold War as History," *Political Studies*, 16 (June 1968), 285-292. Brief notes and comments on books dealing with the cold war. An attempt to identify periods, phases, and turning points.